GLOBALIZATION, DEMOCRATIZATION AND MULTILATERALISM

MULTILATERALISM AND THE UN SYSTEM

Programme Coordinator for the United Nations University
Robert W. Cox, Professor Emeritus of Political Science, York University,
Ontario

Titles in the subseries include:

Robert W. Cox (*editor*)
THE NEW REALISM: Perspectives on Multilateralism and World Order

Stephen Gill (*editor*)
GLOBALIZATION, DEMOCRATIZATION AND MULTILATERALISM

Published within the International Political Economy Series. General
Editor: Timothy M. Shaw, Professor of Political Science and International
Development Studies, and Director of the Centre for Foreign Policy
Studies, Dalhousie University, Nova Scotia

Globalization, Democratization and Multilateralism

Edited by

Stephen Gill

St. Martin's Press
New York

GLOBALIZATION, DEMOCRATIZATION AND MULTILATERALISM
Copyright © 1997 by The United Nations University
The United Nations University
53–70, Jingumae 5–chome,
Shibuya-ku, Tokyo 150, Japan

St. Martin's Press, Scholarly and Reference Division,
175 Fifth Avenue, New York, N.Y. 10010

First published in the United States of America in 1997

This book is printed on paper suitable for recycling and
made from fully managed and sustained forest sources.

Printed in Great Britain

ISBN 0–312–17283–4

Library of Congress Cataloging-in-Publication Data
Globalization, democratization, and multilateralism / edited by
Stephen Gill.
p.   cm.
Includes bibliographical references and index.
ISBN 0–312–17283–4 (cloth)
1. International economic relations.   2. Competition,
International.   3. Democracy.   I. Gill, Stephen, 1950–
HF1359.G585 1997
337—dc21
                                                          96–52292
                                                               CIP

In memory of
Takehiko Kamo
(1942–96)
who worked tirelessly for a more
democratic, equitable, peaceful and multilateral world order

Contents

List of Tables and Figures

Tables

Figure

List of Abbreviations

ANC   African National Congress (South Afric)
ARDL   Asian Regional Division of Labour
ASEAN   Association of Southeast Asian Nations
CEA   Chinese Economic Area
EBRD   European Bank for Reconstruction and Development
ERT   European Round Table of Industrialists
EU   European Union
FAO   Food and Agriculture Organization (UN)
G–7   Group of Seven
GATT   General Agreement on Tariffs and Trade
GDP   Gross Domestic Product
GEF   Global Environmental Facility (World Bank)
HDI   Human Development Index (UNDP)
IDL   International Division of Labour
IMF   International Monetary Fund
ILO   International Labour Organization
LO   Trade Union Federation (Sweden)
MUNS   Multilateralism and the UN System
NAFTA   North American Free Trade Agreement
NATO   North Atlantic Treaty Organization
NGOs   Non-Governmental Organizations
NIDL   New International Division of Labour
NIEs   Newly Industrialising Economies
OECD   Organization for Economic Cooperation and Development
OPEC   Organization of Petroleum Exporting Countries
PRC   People's Republic of China
PTA   Preferential Trade Area for Eastern and Southern Africa
RDP   Reconstruction and Development Plan (South Africa)
SADC   Southern African Development Community
SAP   Social Democratic Party (Sweden)
SAPs   Structural Adjustment Policies/Programmes
SDC   Commission on Sustainable Development (UN)
TC   Trilateral Commission
UK   United Kingdom
UN   United Nations
UNDP   UN Development Programme
UNEP   UN Environmental Programme

USA	United States of America
USSR	Union of Soviet Socialist Republics
WHO	World Health Organization (UN)
WID	Women in Development
WTO	World Trade Organization

Acknowledgements

The work of many people went into the preparation of this book and not all of them can be mentioned here. However the work here owes a special debt of gratitude to Dr Takeo Uchida for initiating the research programme that led to this book, and for his gracious and careful stewardship of the administrative aspects of the project whilst he was at the United Nations University.

The book stemmed from papers delivered at a symposium held in Norway in 1993. On behalf of the authors, I would like to express appreciation to Elizabeth Abiri and Björn Hettne for organizing the excellent local Scandinavian conference facilities and arrangements in Vikersund. I would also like to express my appreciation to the Nordic International Studies Association (NISA) for inviting a number of the symposium's participants to present lectures to help launch NISA. These lectures were delivered at the University of Oslo in August 1993 and were also part of the process that led to the production of this volume.

With regard to this project, I am also grateful for intellectual and personal support from Robert and Jessie Cox, Fantu Cheru, David Law, James H. Mittelman, Kees van der Pijl, Yoshikazu Sakamoto, Magnus Ryner, James Rosenau, Helge Hveem and Taivo Taivainen, as well as to the authors who have contributed to this collection.

I would also like to thank both the Canadian Social Sciences and Humanities Research Council and the Department of Political Science and the Faculty of Arts of York University for providing valuable research support and time release to facilitate the completion of this work.

In the final stages I was given assistance with proofing by Greg Chin. Martin Henson compiled the index. My thanks are due to each of them.

Finally, this work would not have been possible without the support of Astrid Eberhart. To her I give my heartfelt thanks for her love and generosity.

STEPHEN GILL

Notes on the Contributors

Isabella Bakker is Associate Professor of Political Science, York University, Canada, and specializes in the political economy of spending and taxation, the welfare state and gender dimensions of labour market and macroeconomic policies. She is conducting a joint project with the North–South Institute, of which she is an associate, and the Centre for Women's Development Studies (New Delhi) on the impact of structural adjustment and change on women in India and Canada. Her publications include *The Strategic Silence: Gender and Economic Policy* (editor, 1994) and *Rethinking Restructuring: Gender and Change in Canada* (editor, 1996).

Fantu Cheru is Associate Professor of African and Development Studies at the School of International Service, The American University, Washington, DC, specializing in political economy of development and the international relations of Southern Africa. His publications include *Dependence, Underdevelopment and Unemployment in Kenya* (1987), *The Silent Revolution in Africa: Debt, Development and Democracy* (1989), and (as co-editor) *Ethiopia: Options for Rural Development* (1990).

Robert W. Cox is Professor Emeritus of Political Science, York University, Canada. He is the founder and director of the MUNS programme. He specializes in international relations, international political economy and social and political thought. His publications include *Production, Power and World Order: Social Forces in the Making of History* (1987) and a collection of essays, *Approaches to World Order*, with Timothy J. Sinclair (1995).

Stephen Gill is Professor of Political Science at York University, Toronto, Canada, and he specializes in international relations and political economy. His publications include *Atlantic Relations: Beyond the Reagan Era* (editor, 1989); *American Hegemony and the Trilateral Commission* (1990); *Gramsci, Historical Materialism and International Relations* (editor, 1993) and *Restructuring Global Politics* (1996, in Japanese, translated by Seiji Endo).

David Law is Senior Lecturer in Economics, University of Wolverhampton, UK, and specializes in international economics,

international political economy and Third World development. He is
the co-author, with Stephen Gill, of *The Global Political Economy:
Perspectives, Problems and Policies* (1988).

James H. Mittelman is Professor of International Relations at the
School of International Service, The American University, Washington, DC, specializing in international political economy and development issues. He is the author of *Ideology and Politics in Uganda*
(1975); *Underdevelopment and the Transition to Socialism: Mozambique and Tanzania* (1981); *Out from Underdevelopment Revisited* (1996)
with Mustapha Kamal Pasha; and, as editor, *Globalisation: Critical
Reflections* (1996).

Hélène Pellerin is Assistant Professor of International Relations
at Glendon College, York University, Canada, and was formerly a
Postdoctoral Research Fellow at the University of Amsterdam. She
specializes in international political economy and issues of international migration and has published a number of articles on these
topics.

Kees van der Pijl is Professor of International Relations and International Law at the University of Amsterdam, specializing in international relations and political economy. He is the author of *The
Making of an Atlantic Ruling Class* (1984) and *World Order and Power
Politics: a History of International Relations from Dante to Fukuyama*
(1992, in Dutch and German; English translation in preparation).

Magnus Ryner is Postdoctoral Research Fellow in International
Relations and International Law at the University of Amsterdam,
specializing in comparative and international political cconomy and
European politics. An Associate of Arbetslivscentrum (Swedish
Centre for Working Life) he is the author of a number of articles
on European and Swedish political change.

1 Global Structural Change and Multilateralism

Stephen Gill

What underlies this book is a collective effort of many scholars. It forms a part of a research programme that began in 1990 to study and explain the interrelationship between structural change, multilaterialism and world order. The project of which it is a part, 'Multilateralism and the United Nations System' (MUNS), was conceived by Robert Cox in the late 1980s as a means of re-examining issues relating to changes in world order and the reform of the UN at the end of the twentieth century in ways that might go beyond mainstream scholarship. This volume is a successor and counterpart to that edited by Yoshikazu Sakamoto (1994) that built on the proceedings of a symposium in Yokohama in March 1992, in the section of the programme dealing with global structural change. This, the Oslo volume, is based upon papers initially presented and discussions at a symposium held in Vikersund, near Oslo, Norway, in August, 1993.[1] The purpose of this chapter is to outline the place of this collection in the MUNS framework, and then to sketch a brief framework for analyzing questions of globalization and multilateralism at the end of the millennium.

THE MUNS PROGRAMME: STRUCTURAL CHANGE AND DEMOCRATIZATION

Yoshikazu Sakamoto's earlier volume was wide-ranging and included discussion of aspects of the restructuring of global society; the internationalization of the state; processes of regionalization; the role of globalizing élites and ruling classes; production and migration; aspects of global finance and indebtedness, social cleavages and the formation of new identities; democratization and social movements; and the processes of change, both violent and non-violent. All of the above included reference to the gender dimensions of change. The major theme of the Yokohama volume was the dialectic between two engines

1

of fundamental social change – internationalization or globalization on the one hand, and democratization on the other – themes that are also central to this collection. In principle there is nothing necessarily contradictory between these two sets of forces: a global society could be a democratic one. However, in practice contradictions have arisen and much of the evidence of the past two decades tends to support the argument that global structural change has tended to reinforce the position of global élites and ruling classes, widened social inequality within and between nations, and exacerbated disparities in inter-state power relations.

Nevertheless, there is nothing inevitable about this re-concentration of power. One reason for this is that a process of democratization has also developed, and in some senses it is extending – although as yet this process has not involved a substantial democratization of control over economic forces. Part of the reason for democratization is resistance against unresponsive, callous or indifferent ruling classes and structures of privilege (Gill, 1996). Here the case of South Africa and the dismantling of apartheid and the emergence of liberal democracy is instructive. It shows that even when social and economic inequality is intensified and is sustained by a violent and repressive regime, the ethico-political aspects of politics are crucial for mobilization and for progressive political change. The South African case shows not only that freedom is indivisible, in the sense that no person can be free, whilst others are unfree, but also that political change requires struggle and sacrifice, and a long-term as well as a short-term perspective on human possibility. In this sense, we may be already in a new phase of a greater social transformation which goes back to the birth of the democratic idea, involving, as it were, the *longue durée* of political emancipation and struggle for recognition. In the words of the South African President, Nelson Mandela, incarcerated for most of his adult life by the Afrikaner state, and written after he had cast a vote for the first time in his life – that is in the nation's first free elections:

> I never lost hope that this great transformation would occur. Not only because of the great heroes [of the liberation struggle] I have already cited, but because of the courage of the ordinary men and women of my country. I always knew that deep down in every human heart there is mercy and generosity. No one is born hating another person because of the color of his skin, or his background, or his religion. People must learn to hate, and if they can learn to

hate, then they can be taught to love, for love comes more naturally to the human heart than its opposite. Even in the grimmest times in prison, when my comrades and I were pushed to our limits, I would see a glimmer of humanity in one of the guards, perhaps just for a second, but it was enough to reassure me and keep me going. Man's goodness is a flame that can be hidden but never extinguished. (Mandela, 1994: 542)

Nevertheless, the political economy of the South African transition away from apartheid – like those occurring in the former communist-ruled nations – is taking place in the context of internal and external pressure to adopt neo-liberal reforms. Such reforms will integrate the nation more comprehensively into the structures of the global political economy, partly at the expense of a more co-operative and mutually constructive form of regionalism (see Chapter 10). In this sense the great transformation that President Mandela speaks of is, as yet, far from complete, especially from the vantage point of the mass of the population in South Africa.

Whilst the Yokohama volume tended to emphasize the political-structural context of world order, this collection seeks to cast the problem of structural change with a focus more upon the political economy aspects, or the economic-structural aspects of change including the production of knowledge. In this sense, we take up the issues of transformation and the limits of the possible where the quote from Nelson Mandela stops. This is because the authors of this volume – albeit in varied ways – take the view that the political economy constitutes the anatomy for change in local and in global civil and political society. Such a perspective implies the transcendence of not only the traditional North–South and East–West divides of consciousness, civilization and political economy, but also of traditional methodological distinctions between 'domestic' and 'international' and 'political' and 'economic' in its form of analysis.

Any theory of knowledge production thus needs to have a power dimension. According to Robert Cox (Cox, 1981), much mainstream scholarship takes the historically constituted structures of world order as given. Its main normative orientation is towards the *status quo*: for example in the field of multilateralism it seeks to improve the operation of international organization in an incrementalist approach and to correct perceived malfunctions of the existing order, that is commensurate with the reproduction of existing structures and forms of power. The ontology that is associated with what Cox calls problem-solving theory – that is its core explanatory categories and the inter-relationship it designates between social forms – are derivative from the principles and practices of sovereignty and inter-state power politics and liberal market economics, that is an ontology of 'states and markets' (Gill, 1994b). Its epistemology is largely positivist and trans-historical in application, that is seen to be valid across time and space.

By contrast, the MUNS programme is consistent with 'critical theory'. This approach attempts to understand structural change by analyzing the interplay between ideas, institutions and material capacities in different dimensions of political life (local/global), and in regard to interrelated spheres of human collective action: production broadly defined (including military capabilities), forms of state and world order. These relatively abstract conceptualisations, are, however, based on a close reading of history and realities of existing conditions at particular moments and in particular locations (Braudel, 1981). Thus the meaning of these concepts is concretised and modified in the explanation of particular problems or issues – for example migration, production and the global division of labour.

In more normative terms, conceptions of historical change can be related to the idea of the making of history as an active process involving human collective action, understood as a social movement, as a potential, and as a normative goal of human emancipation. This goal includes engagement to promote greater social equity and an enhanced diffusion of power; the standard of non-violence in dealing with conflicts; and the principle of the equality of civilizations and their perspectives on world order. By perhaps helping to form a collective political will, progressive political forces might be synergized, for example, so as to democratize the restructuring processes associated with Anglo-American style capitalism, and more broadly the trends towards neo-liberal forms of 'economic globalization'.

The globalization of capitalism presupposes significant changes, or restructuring of, prevailing forms of society, of ethics and expectations, changes which often provoke severe social conflict. These changes are especially pronounced in those urbanized areas where the processes of commodification have only recently penetrated, for example in much of the Third World (Vieille, 1988), and more recently in the former communist states of Europe. Indeed, the process of globalization as it is defined and examined in this book involves tendencies towards the spread of the power of internationally-mobile capital involving, at its vanguard, primarily an Anglo-American, neo-liberal set of theories (for instance, associated with the ideas of F.A. von Hayek and Milton Friedman) and practices, as well as ideologies that justify these trends and equate them with progress and civilization.

These tendencies, associated with the power and reach of transnational corporations and financial services firms at the vanguard of capital-intensive and high technology production, prevailing norms and patterns of consumption and what some have called the emergence of the symbolic economy, are also part of the broader nexus of cultural forms and practices that Samir Amin calls 'Eurocentrism'. By this he means the claim to social hegemony of a set of particular, culturally rooted practices and ideological/intersubjective understandings that are presented as having a universal applicability. They are equated with the path towards 'progress', although such progress is defined in a particular way. As Amin puts it, '[Eurocentrism] claims that imitation of the Western model by all peoples is the only solution to the challenges of our time' (Amin, 1989: vii).

Nevertheless, the concept of globalization is a dialectical one: as defined here it is also taken to include, by its very nature, politico-economic and socio-cultural counter-tendencies. These are both progressive and reactionary in nature, but what many of them have in common is that they seek collectively to countervail and to find alternatives to the dominant neo-liberal patterns of political economy and an associated spread of a more commodified 'market civilisation' (Gill, 1995a). This is because the neo-liberal form of globalization is in fact the universalization of a particular set of cultural forms, in ways that tend to make for greater social hierarchy and cultural homogenization on a world scale. At the same time this process contains profound social, political and ecological contradictions. The contradictions place limits on the substantial shift towards the neo-liberal form of global political economy. Put differently, neo-liberal politico-economic forms lack legitimacy and thus reflect more of a politics of dominance or a moment of supremacy, rather than one of integral hegemony in a Gramscian sense. This is notwithstanding the fact that many Third World leaders and urban élites and middle classes are attracted to neo-liberal ideas and to metropolitan lifestyles and patterns of consumption. Many of them would subscribe to the view expressed by United States' President George Bush before the World Environmental Summit in Rio in 1992, namely 'our lifestyle is not negotiable' (see Chapter 8) although globalization of US lifestyles would lead to ecological disaster.

Following Polanyi's idea of the 'double movement' of the forces of state and society that organized to control and to re-channel those associated with global *laissez-faire* in the 1930s (these encompassed not only New Deal forces in the USA but also populist authoritarianism, fascism and Nazism) we can hypothesize that part of a new global politics will involve political counter-action against socially atomizing unfettered market forces. As in nineteenth-century Britain, such market forces are associated politically with the creation of a 'market society' of planetary proportions (the commercialization of outer space and the colonization and appropriation of life forms and genetic codes are but extensions of this idea). Just as the reaction against liberal (and utilitarian) forms of capitalist development began in the nineteenth century under conservative leaders such as Bismarck and Disraeli, fusing politically with labour and reform movements and thus with other social and class forces, in the 1930s a second form of the 'double movement' reflected attempts to assert national and authoritative control over international market forces. Some of the developments of the 1930s subsequently formed prototypes for the post-Second World War welfare states. Today, perhaps, we may see the emergence of a new version of the double movement, although under very different conditions, one of which is the lack of congruence between territoriality, political authority and accountability, and economic activity. Under these new conditions, that include a resurgence of fascism and other right-wing forms of political organization, a rethinking of the constituent elements and ethics of global politics is mandatory. What is needed is a strategy, building from the bottom up but linked to the top-down developments in the state, international organization and more broadly in global politics. This volume seeks to contribute to aspects of such a new strategy.

GLOBAL RESTRUCTURING AND MULTILATERALISM: A FRAMEWORK FOR ANALYSIS

Much of the history of multilateralism has been studied from the 'top down', that is in the form of sets of institutions of global governance, such as the Concert of Europe, the League of Nations, the post-war Bretton Woods and UN agencies, and more recently the Group of Seven (G-7).[2] Each of these sets of institutions and practices has tended to define the problem of world order from the vantage point of established or predominant power, and to construct and codify sets of rules, norms and principles which would institutionalise the supremacy of prevailing elements. Much of the renewed interest in multilateralism stems from recent events, in particular the Gulf War of 1991, when the UN was perceived as a more acceptable instrument for the use of Western powers, notably by the USA (for example Ruggie, 1992; 1993). It is also reflected in the large literature on 'regimes' (for instance, for money, trade, finance) and its general concern to 'manage' inter-state co-operation so as to reproduce the existing patterns of power in the world order.

However there is no inherent or obvious meaning to the term multilateralism. In so far as its use has been associated with liberal institutionalist and neo-realist approaches to world politics, here we would suggest that, in fact the meaning of the term is 'essentially contestable'. Like that of 'sustainable development': it means very different things to different people, depending on their theoretical perspective or discourse (see Chapter 8). In this way, the process of multilateralism can be further understood as a means of promoting global co-operation as well as a site of political and ideological struggle for the forces of an emerging global political and civil society.

This study self-consciously takes critical distance from the mainstream perspectives on multilateralism. In so doing it begins with a basic ontological question: what are the key entities and constituents of the global political economy and what are their basic relationships? And how do these relationships change over time? A concern with structural change is also linked to a practical set of issues reflected in the question, 'what are the challenges and conflicts that multilateralism needs to confront as we approach the new millennium?' Thus multilateralism can be defined as a political means, partly involving international organizations, through which processes of structural change are articulated and projected on the one hand, and potentially channelled and institutionalized on the other. A critical approach to multilateralism must therefore attempt to understand the processes of globalization and how these might be mediated by international organization and different forms and levels of regulation so that democratically forged visions of social purpose can re-shape global politics. It must therefore be concerned with the transformation of the inter-state (or Westphalian) system. It must ask, for example, whether we are in a period of transition towards a more multi-level system in which microregions, city-states, as well as macro-regional political, associations are emerging to produce what in Hedley Bull's term (1977), might approximate, at least in terms of its political units, a 'new medievalism'. Yet another dimension is ecological, in so far as the logic of existing patterns of accumulation and consumption run counter to the laws of thermodynamics and generate degradation of the environment and threats to the eco-sphere (Altvater, 1993).

A central dimension of contemporary restructuring involves a constellation of political forces in governments and in the private sector that form what is called in this book the 'G-7 nexus' (Gill, 1994a). The operation of this nexus can be identified, for example, with regard to debt strategy and systemic management in international finance. In the 1980s, both the IMF and World Bank came to closely co-ordinate their structural adjustment in the context of G-7 directives, attaching policy conditionality for new loans (Feinberg, 1989). Structural adjustment programmes in the 1980s dramatically increased the status of the IMF, even more than that of the World Bank. Moreover, private credit-rating agencies such as Moody's and Standard & Poor's began to assume greater importance in the 1980s, providing financial (but highly political) assessments of the creditworthiness of governments (local to federal) as well as corporations, which could be used by investors to decide on the advisability of further loans.

None the less, when one examines the G-7 nexus' attempts to steer the transition in the former communist states – initially premised on rapid 'shock therapy', with transformation scenarios involving one to two years (as was stated in the case of Poland) – one might wonder if very much had really been learned since the Marshall Plan years, given the strategic stakes which were involved for the G-7 countries at the end of the Cold War. According to Polanyi (1957), the transition to a market society in nineteenth-century Britain took at least 70 years, where the foundation of modern capitalism had already been partly built. To expect a swift transition in the former communist-ruled states is an example of extreme market utopianism, or a plan to demobilize the enemy, or both – at least if one examines the case of Poland and Russia in the 1990s. In the Marshall Plan years the US government was in effect a kind of interim dictatorship in the defeated Axis powers and presided over both political and economic reconstruction. It had the power and the resources to implement far-reaching change, and a leadership which was willing and able to do so.

Today the situation with regard to the G-7 and the 'eastern question' is rather different. The term G-7 nexus is not meant to imply unity of perspective or purpose – rather it denotes central entities that form the dominant forces within the prevailing global economic governance structure. Whereas these forces are committed to the reproduction of the global capitalist economic order this does not mean that agreement on the most appropriate means to this end is easily forthcoming – agreement may not rest on consensus and may require coercion, for example by the USA in the Gulf War to force Japan, Germany and Saudi Arabia to pay for most of the cost of the conflict (Gill, 1991a). On many issues the members of the G-7 are divided, and a long-standing rift has existed over policies towards the former Soviet bloc (see Gill, 1990: 179–88). UK/US–German rivalry remains important (see Chapter 9), and potential and actual divisions between Japan and the USA are often in the background as the Gulf War was to demonstrate. Partly because of the divisions in the G-7 ranks, much of the burden of the reform effort has fallen onto the IMF, the World Bank, the new European Bank for Reconstruction and Development, and various European Union and OECD agencies. Even collectively, these organizations do not appear to have the resources or political power to deal politically with a nation as strategically important and complex as Russia. Indeed, conditions in post-communist Russia seem to be such that in large part the reform process has become ungovernable. The failure to deal with the situation in the former Soviet Union in ways which enhance global security may, however, prove to be an Achilles heel of G-7 global strategy – along with problems in the global financial system (see Chapter 7).

Finance, debt and the 'limits of the possible'

The process of accumulating debt which was a central characteristic of the 1980s and 1990s in much of the world has involved people worldwide: it is not just Third World debtors who are 'entrapped' by the problem of debt: so are mortgage-holders, indebted farmers and highly-leveraged corporations and the millions of consumers who are not careful with their credit cards (see Chapter 3). A growth in indebtedness reinforces the everyday and longer-term awareness of financial constraints, as market discipline acts to condition the appreciation and consideration of alternative courses of action for different individuals, groups, and governments, and binds such agents to the market system.

Marginalization from global capital markets might, in this context, be compared to excommunication from Catholicism at the apogee of the social power of the Holy Roman Empire: the equivalent of an eternity in purgatory or damnation, especially for those who equate the access to credit with membership of the holy orders of a con-

sumerist society. In so far as there is internalization of such constraints, and if governments and citizens feel there is no alternative
to the acceptance of financial discipline and structural adjustment,
this can be said to be akin to the achievement of a hegemonic moment
for global (especially financial) capital – although we submit, there is
considerable doubt as to how long this moment can last.

Regulatory and systemic weaknesses in the world's financial system
continue to be major items of concern (for example, the Japanese
Finance Minister, Mr Hata, publicly acknowledged the parlous condition of Japan's financial system after the imprudent lending of the
bubble economy period of 1987–90; worries of its collapse have continued during the 1990s). Financial disorder was manifest in the
September 1992 crisis of the European Monetary System, where financial speculators almost wrecked the system, whilst making massive
profits, prompting attempts to accelerate European Economic and
Monetary Union so as to curtail future foreign exchange speculation.

G-7 conflicts over financial matters were also visible in the IMF–US
led bail-out of their star pupil, Mexico, after the massive depreciation
of the peso that occurred in December 1994 following a bungled
devaluation and against the political backdrop of peasant revolt in
Chiapas, urban unrest and a spate of political assassinations and
accusations of murder and corruption directed at the leaders of the
previous government under President Salinas. The package involved
breaking the rules governing IMF quotas and by far the largest loan
ever made by the Fund (about $17.6 billion). The total rescue package
was about $50 billion.[3] It was put together with little consultation
with IMF or other G-7 members and against Congressional opposition and in the face of the anger from the German, French and to a
much lesser extent British authorities. Many European leaders – and
many in the United States Congress – saw the measures as a bail-out
for large Wall Street banks and bond-traders as much as it was for the
rich of Mexico. Subsequently, in the context of an IMF-designed
'shock therapy' policy Mexico has experienced its worst recession this
century, with a wave of bankruptcies, spiralling unemployment and
further vaporization of the peso's value on the exchanges. This
prompts the question, 'restructuring of what, and for whom?'

International institutionalization and new constitutionalism

One dimension of capitalist multilateralism 'from above' is designed
to help manage such contradictions from the vantage point of the

interests of transnational capital. I call this the 'new constitutional-ism', that is the provision of a quasi-constitutional framework for the reconstitution of the legal rights, prerogatives and freedom of move-ment for capital on a world scale (Gill, 1992a, 1992b). Here we have in mind frameworks such as NAFTA, GATT, the European Union's Maastricht accords, as well as other initiatives such as the introduc-tion of constitutional amendments requiring balanced budgets and autonomous central banks (with zero inflation targets) and other means whereby important areas of economic policy are taken out of the control of (elected) governments. These arrangements are intended to be politically locked in so that economic agents will be able to realize their investment plans with a longer political 'shadow of the future'. Thus the new constitutionalism involves a combination of short-term financial and micro-economic discipline, (allowing, for example, smaller loss-making firms to go bankrupt and eliminating nationalist subsidies and forms of protection) and long-term political discipline on behalf of the interests of (mobile) capital (on concepts of discipline see Gill, 1995a; 1996).

The major constituency in favour of the new constitutionalism is a grouping of institutional investors in the financial markets, and trans-national corporations, especially those contemplating foreign direct investment or acquisitions in the Third World. Of importance here for transnational corporations are the 'transition programmes' for not only the former communist-ruled countries, but also the largest Third World economies which have not, as yet, been wholehearted in their commitment to free-market neo-liberal political economy or which have the capacity to sustain policies of autarky and self-sufficiency (such as India, Brazil, China).

These quasi-constitutional initiatives involve direct restrictions on the policy autonomy and economic sovereignty of nations in order to ensure and to support the rule of global market forces. However these market forces are rarely competitive in the sense of the perfect com-petition models of neo-classical economics where there are large num-bers of sellers and buyers and where the producer is simply a price taker with no market power. More frequently, today's markets are not only more global but also they are determined by oligopolistic com-petition, involving operations and interactions of transnational cor-porations, who both collude and compete, in a series of strategic alliances, consortia, joint ventures and other arrangements, often involving local partners, so as to both minimize risks and taxation liabilities and to maximize the short and long-term returns on capital.

Thus the wider framework for interpreting and explaining the new constitutionalism is the transnationalization of capital and the growing dominance of such capital relative to labour. Such developments are serving to reconfigure some of the prevailing forms of state towards the neo-liberal pattern. This means a shift away from the socialization of risk by the state towards a more privatized and individualized risk framework (for example, private health care and pension provision; private police – see Chapter 3), with banks and other financial firms increasingly specializing in risk management.

Power and production

The 1970s and 1980s were a period in which the restructuring of production world-wide went with a substantial decline in the power of organized labour to countervail the prerogatives of capital. The 1980s saw a rise in the structural power of capital, particularly internationally mobile financial and knowledge-intensive capital. This, it would appear, creates the international economic policy problematic for all states in so far as they are substantially integrated into the capitalist world economy. It creates a force field in which previously inward-looking mercantilist states are pressured into becoming more outward looking and subjected to market discipline. It sets the context for a new and global division of labour, new patterns of migration (see Chapters 4 and 5) and more broadly for social deepening and geographical extension of the process of commodification in the political economy.

Nevertheless, there are contradictions, for example involving the different time horizons and priorities associated with, respectively, financial capital and the ideology of *laissez-faire* (primarily associated with the Anglo-Saxon economies), and with productive, manufacturing capital and the need for long-term planning (associated, for example, with the dominance of manufacturing industry in Germany and Japan and east Asia). Large scale investments in manufacturing and infrastructure require long-term time horizons, since they involve not only buildings and machines, but also the recruitment and training of workers and the development of complex supplier networks. The same is true for research and development, especially given the way that scientific research requires large teams of workers to translate breakthroughs into technological innovations.

On the other hand, finance, especially in the 1980s, became more associated with a short-term, speculative mentality, apparently inimical in many ways to production, and indeed, often to political stability (viz. the case of the ERM which virtually fell apart in 1992–93 after speculative attacks on many of its currencies – similar types of speculation allied to an unsustainably high rate of exchange caused the Mexican débâcle of 1994/95). This is not to say that finance and production have, as some claim, become delinked. For example, whilst a short-term speculative mentality came to prevail in the relatively deregulated financial markets, this mentality was transferred to new organizational arrangements in the manufacturing and services sector, encouraging economies of 'flexibility' and just-in-time supply and service systems: a new synthesis of production and finance which we might call the 'flexible casino' (Gill, 1994c). The shortening of time-cycles of innovation and production is also apparent across a number of sectors, most notably in microelectronics and computer software.

Forms of state, fiscal crisis and global finance

The restructuring of global production and power also appear to have begun to transform the basis of political authority, legitimacy and accountability away from national governments, towards the increasingly transnational and global markets, as states compete to attract and to retain foreign direct investment and portfolio flows. At the same time the internal aspects of accountability and authority are being re-configured, since these market forces and market agents are located within particular territories. This has emerged at the same time as what I have called the 'terrain of contestability' in the politics of the OECD has shifted to the right since the 1970s with the eclipse of the Keynesian-welfarist consensus.

Two key and interrelated elements which have served to drive these changes are, on the one hand, the persistent fiscal crisis of the state (local, regional and national) and on the other, changing structural pressures from global financial markets, such as the bond markets. In the 1980s and especially in the 1990s institutional investors and new right political forces have mandated significant constraints on state budgets and have tended to press increasingly for a politics of austerity and a cut back in state provision of social, welfare, health, and public educational expenditures. This is linked to the ideology of the competition state and a willingness on the part of political leaders to return to nineteenth-century concepts of workfare and a punitive regime for the poor. Thus the neo-liberal forces have tended to promote two dimensions of change, although their effects vary considerably between nations (for example in East Asia the promotion of economic liberalization has been associated with both authoritarianism and new forms of cultural chauvinism). These dimensions are: (1) the public-private shift and the 'marketisation' of the form of state, and (2) the internationalization or, as I prefer it, the 'globalization' of the state.

In its 'domestic' political dimension, this has involved a public shift away from the welfare state to the 'competition' 'workfare' state: a new, more 'marketized' form of state, reconstituted internally so that it behaves in a market-friendly and business-oriented manner (New Zealand is a clear example of this trend). The internationalization or globalization of the state refers to the way that governments are increasingly competing to provide macro- and micro-economic, regulatory and political guarantees, supplies of 'human capital' and low-tax frameworks to encourage foreign investment. Policies have been increasingly geared to induce not only long-term direct investments, but also short-term portfolio capital to finance government operations, so that the forms of political accountability are increasingly market-based and internationalized. The question is how far and in what ways this situation is sustainable politically since it goes with an intensification of social conflict.

QUESTIONS AND CONTENTS OF THIS BOOK: CIVILIZATIONS IN THE TWENTY-FIRST CENTURY

Thus in this book we ask what are the main structural changes, tensions and contradictions in the emerging global political economy? What is their significance in terms of politics and democratic social choice? What are the limits and contradictions of the dominant structures and arrangements? What are the flaws in the knowledge structures and the divisions within the ranks of the dominant arrangements and structures associated with G-7 governments, the Bretton Woods agencies (IMF and World Bank) and internationally mobile capital? Here it is important to stress the learning and adaptive capacities of dominant forces, and their ability to promote a certain form of co-operation and mediation of conflict, and their practical effects on social outcomes and possibilities in the past two decades. For example what are the implications of these developments for governance and government, participation and representation? If UN institutions and the Bretton Woods financial agencies are to be understood as a 'terrain of struggle' then what is the balance of forces within and across these institutions and how far, and to what extent, can progressive change be mobilized within them?

Such questions are important for the understanding of the nature of and the further potential for a 'new multilateralism', one which is more democratic and emancipatory. How this might relate to existing and new forms of collective mobilization? How do we assess the potential for the further development of other, potentially countervailing types of national and transnational social forces, forces which can be either progressive or regressive politically (for instance, fascism)? One way to approach this is through analysis of transnational linkages surrounding certain crucial social problems, such as the environment and social inequality, for example the focus of the Earth Summit, the World Social Summit or the Women's Summit in Beijing. Another is through the examination of the national and global role of political parties, trades unions, business associations, other non-governmental organizations (NGOs), grass-roots organizations (GROs) and other forms of agency (see Chapters 6, 7 and 8).

Seen differently, a purpose of this book is to examine the political economy context for consideration of a range of cultural and civilizational possibilities on our planet. Here, the role of the critical and 'organic intellectual' is to assess critically but realistically the structures of power as they actually are, whilst analyzing their points of tension or contradiction, and then, through linkages to networks of citizens move towards new forms of political practice that might contribute to a more democratic world, that is to the collective ability to both interpret and to channel the forces of structural change.[4]

In the rest of the book each chapter seeks to link a specific aspect of restructuring in the 1980s and 1990s to the main substantive themes of the collection: globalization, democratization and the search for a 'new' multilateralism. Of course, it has not been possible to include all regions, problems or issues in a single collection, or to treat everything that is contained with the same degree of detail. We hope, however, that this book can bring fresh perspectives with which to address some of the questions that surround the logic and contradictions of global restructuring, and that it may help to outline what limits and possibilities this might imply for global politics at the turn of a new century.

Thus the first chapter is by Magnus Ryner. Ryner combines macrostructural analysis of the changes in the post-war global political economy with an exploration of how both global and local forces have served to reconfigure the Scandinavian region. Ryner's chapter is followed by analyses of finance, production and panopticism with a focus on North America (Stephen Gill), the global division of labour with special reference to East Asia (James Mittelman), migration dynamics, including those between Western Europe and Africa (Hélène Pellerin) and gender aspects of global restructuring (Isabella Bakker). Thereafter, structural adjustment in both African and post-Soviet contexts is analyzed (Fantu Cheru and Stephen Gill), as well as the role of the World Bank in relation to environmental changes and mobilization in global civil society after the Rio Summit (David Law). The nature of transatlantic conflicts over German unification and policy towards the former Soviet Union, especially those between Anglo-American neo-liberal forces versus the more productivist class forces within German and French leaderships, is analyzed by Kees van der Pijl. Finally, Fantu Cheru explores regional and national prospects in post-apartheid South and Southern Africa, in a situation where the new governing coalition seems to have opted for neo-liberal approaches to manage the economic transition associated with majority rule. Robert Cox concludes with epistemological, ontological and strategic reflections on the debates that took place at the Oslo symposium. These comments are apposite as a conclusion to this collection.

Notes

1. At the University of Oslo, Robert Cox, Yoshikazu Sakamoto, Kees van der Pijl, and Stephen Gill presented lectures to help to launch the Nordic International Studies Association at the University of Oslo following the Vikersund symposium in August 1993. Revised versions of the lectures have been published with an additional text of a lecture by James Rosenau (Hettne (ed.) 1995).
2. The G-7 includes Canada, France, Germany, Italy, Japan, the USA, the UK. The meetings of the G-7 leaders are periodically attended by the President of the European Union and by the Managing Director of the IMF. Leaders' meetings are annual, whereas meetings at the Ministerial level and at the deputy-minister level are more frequent. The most important meetings involve the Ministers of Finance and Heads of Central banks and their deputies. These meetings began in the early 1970s and have become progressively more formalized and extensive since that time. Within the G-7, the G-3 (USA, Japan and Germany) carry the most weight, in that order. For details on the G-7 and the wider frameworks of which it is a part, see Gill, 1993b.

3. Unless stated otherwise, all values designated $ in this book are in United States dollars.
4. On the concept of the organic intellectual and the philosophy of *praxis* see Gramsci, 1971:6–20; 60; 330; 332–5; 392–8.

2 Nordic Welfare Capitalism in the Emerging Global Political Economy

Magnus Ryner

The main objective of this chapter is to define and to explore the viability of the Nordic Models of welfare capitalism, with a particular focus on Sweden. These models were expressions of an exceptionally inclusive and egalitarian state capitalism in the era of *Pax Americana*. What are the prospects for the Nordic Models in response to forces of globalization which have developed and strengthened in the past two decades? The first step in answering this question is to sketch what I call the transformation from *Pax Americana* to the global political economy. This global framework can thus be read as a theoretical–historical background to the question of the nature and limits to globalization for the book as a whole.

FROM PAX AMERICANA TO THE GLOBAL POLITICAL ECONOMY

One way to understand the post-war transformation is to see it as a shift away from the 'Atlantic corporate' or 'embedded' liberal (Ruggie, 1983; van der Pijl, 1984) socio-political alliances (power blocs) that prevailed in the Western advanced capitalist societies. These 'growth alliances' were typically forged by forces associated with industrial capital, organized labour, and technocratic reformist intellectuals. They ensured low unemployment levels and high social wages for organized labour in exchange for the acceptance of the right for management to manage, and peaceful industrial relations.

Thus, production could be organized according to 'Taylorist' principles, applying product specific machinery on a large scale. The productivity that resulted, together with Fordist wage norms, Keynesian economic policy, and sometimes Beveridge-style social policy, ensured that this intensive regime of accumulation provided non-

19

inflationary growth and increased standards of living (Lipietz, 1987: 24–32)[1]. An important precondition for this mode of regulation was the subordination of 'circulation forms' of capital (which tend to favour market clearing and a stable money supply), to 'productive capital' (which tend to favour returns to scale), facilitated by the 1929 Wall Street crash, the New Deal, and wartime economic planning.

The world order emanated from, and was largely sustained by, the USA, which created multilateral institutions where peaceful bargaining could ensue. These institutions were consistent with the interests of the power blocs of other Western states. Consent was based upon socio-political convergence and American political and ideological intervention, which purged unacceptable radical elements from the other power blocs. Cold War discourse was crucial in ensuring cohesion. This is not to say that there were no important variations between the Western power blocs. They ranged from the relatively market oriented, 'residual' welfare states of the Anglo-Saxon world, to the *dirigiste* models of state capitalism of France and Japan, the meso-corporatist organised-capitalist German Model, and to the labour inclusive 'institutional', Social Democratic, welfare capitalism of Scandinavia. But *Pax Americana* did set definite limits to possible variations.

The Bretton Woods system (based upon US capability to provide international liquidity) ensured a fixed exchange rate regime and norms governing capital flows. It created a 'double screen' which provided a guarantee for a balance of international and domestic economic activity at close to full employment.[2] As a result, North–North trade could flourish and ensure validation of the intensive accumulation regimes in the capitalist core. The South was maintained in a peripheral role, supplying primary commodities to the core.

In the late sixties, this hegemonic order was disintegrating. First, accumulation reached production-technological frontiers, and productivity gains declined (Lipietz, 1987: 32–40). Second, the US no longer had the material capabilities to act as an international central bank, as the size of its economy, relative to the world economy, declined. Thus, it faced the choice of either restoring the domestic balance of payments equilibrium at a risk of triggering a world economic recession, or supplying dollars for the world market and exacerbating domestic inflation and the balance of payment problems. This predicament, known as the 'Triffin dilemma', undermined confidence in the American dollar and the macroeconomic aspects of the

Bretton Woods system (Block, 1977: 203–27). As a consequence, the 'double screen' was eliminated as the Bretton Woods system disintegrated. In 1971, the United States devalued the dollar and a flexible exchange rate system emerged. Third, in 1973 the OPEC cartel succeeded in massively increasing the price of oil, a strategic commodity supplied by the periphery. These factors all contributed to the 'stagflation' problems of the seventies.

The economic situation was exacerbated by an emerging legitimation crisis of welfare capitalism. This emanated from the perceived contradiction between the actual outcome of the post-war compromise and the social myth of 'the affluent society'. Movements of union militancy, civil rights, peace, environmental protection, feminism, and other 'new social movements' mobilized resistance around issues such as the intensified Taylorization of work, the continued marginalization of significant sectors of society, American imperialism (symbolized by the Vietnam War), and adverse effects of growth and bureaucratization. These political expressions of legitimation crisis did not, however, form into a coherent counter-hegemonic force. Rather, the insurrectionist forces of 1968 and the attempt by Social Democrats and left-liberals to integrate the demands of these forces, failed. Although some of the issues raised by these groups, such as sustainable development, gender equality, and racial equality have remained in the limelight, the praxis of these groups tends to be restricted to fragmented pressure politics, or they are effectively marginalised.[3]

The accumulation and legitimation crises of welfare capitalism, and failed attempts by the left to radicalize Western politics and institutions, created the space in which the neo-liberal, or (as I prefer following R. W. Cox) the 'hyper-liberal' and neo-conservative 'new right' could take the initiative. This signalled the end of the post-war 'growth coalitions'. In the context of what was considered potentially subversive effects of inflationary Keynesianism, business and economic policy élites took an antagonistic stance against unions, economic regulation, and the welfare state.[4]

Thus a new world economic order is emerging. Within the framework of an increasingly parochial or 'minimal' American hegemony, which implied that the United States used its unique structural power to pursue a narrow policy to sustain domestic growth at the expense of the world economy as a whole,[5] capitalism has taken on a more transnational form. With the rise of a new core technology (informatics and computer technology based on the 'microchip revolution') which optimises allocation decisions, and increases productivity by breaking down information bottlenecks, the process of internationalization of production has accelerated (Kaplinsky, 1984). This core technology has also radically altered the terms of the organization of the labour process. Cybernetics can now be used to create 'general purpose' machines, that facilitate competition through 'flexible specialization', rather than 'economies of scale' (Piore and Sabel, 1984: 194–280). These new terms for corporate strategy alter the relation between capital, labour and the state, and further undermine the premises of post-war welfarism.

The resurgence of global finance is equally important in this context. The failure to design new multilateral norms after the demise of Bretton Woods, the emergence of the Eurodollar market and the flexible exchange rate system, growing asymmetries between creditor and debtor nations, and mounting government debt has radically increased the velocity and volume of capital flows and the demand for credit supplied by the private sector. This has also been enhanced by the revolution in information technology. The 'quasi-public' multilateral credit system of Bretton Woods has given way to a deeply commodified, market mediated, 'private, multi-centred, global' credit system (Germain, 1992). Consequently high finance is so powerful in the allocation of resources that it has been described as the pivotal agent in the attempt to form a new, hyper-liberal global hegemony (Cox, 1987: 267). Economically, this reflects a subordination of productive forms of capital to circulation forms of capital. Rentier profit has increased in importance relative to profit from production, and increasingly, accumulation is sustained through a decrease in turnover time, rather than through productivity increases and mass consumption (van der Pijl, 1984: 265–86; Harvey, 1989).

These developments have increased the structural power of transnational capital (Gill and Law, 1989). Through transnational mobility, capital can counter attempts at regulation by states – which are in competition for scarce investment resources – and make the essence of *raison d'état* to pay court to this structural power. 'Business confidence', now more than ever, determines the direction of capital flows, the availability of finance, and future investments, upon which future production, employment, and tax revenue depends.

A relatively cohesive transnational, hyper-liberal, power bloc is in formation within these interacting ideological and material developments. Its cohesion is articulated through private-informal, as well as public-formal fora in what Gill has called the 'G-7 nexus'. This nexus encompasses and permeates key branches of state structures, such as ministries of finance and central banks. This formation has been instrumental in efforts to create a mode of international economic policy co-ordination which is intended to ensure the coherence and stability of a new transnational accumulation regime (Gill, 1993b; 1994a).

The prospects of success of such a transnational power bloc should not be underestimated. Many, notably neo-realists, have pointed to the absence of a single dominating power to provide the international public goods for global co-operation. However, in the new era, with a structurally different relationship between markets and states, a transnational power bloc may not need such a realistic 'hegemon'. Hyperliberal financial and monetary regimes (as opposed to Keynesian ones), based on private multi-centric finance, might function better without a dominant state (Helleiner, 1992).[6] Since accumulation is ensured through decreased turnover time, cost-cutting, and labour shedding, rather than through an articulation of mass consumption and mass production, the deflationary effects of neo-liberalism may not be as detrimental to capital as they would have been in the Fordist era (Harvey, 1989). Thus hyper-liberalism may be viable because the capacity of transnational capital to regulate itself has increased, whilst the capacity of the nation state to regulate the market has decreased, and the social forces which stand to benefit from authoritative regulation find it increasingly difficult to organize politically.

It should be emphasized that what is outlined above is a dominant *tendency* in a still formative stage of restructuring. A global hyperliberal order is not predestined to sustain itself. In this context, high interest rates produced by the interaction between the private multi-centric financial system and states in fiscal crisis may prove to be fatal. Also, deregulation of labour markets may not provide for the most efficient adaptation of 'post-Fordist' flexible specialization. It may hinder the acquisition of public goods such as training of skilled labour, and a fertile co-operative workplace environment where 'learning by doing' can be exploited to the fullest (Hyman and Streeck, 1988; Leborgne and Lipietz, 1988) In addition, the shortening of time horizons in investment implied by the subordination of productive capital to circulation capital may hinder a sustained, paradigmatic shift into the new technological growth trajectory altogether, unless effective demand can be boosted. Thus, it may be that the capitalist accumulation process has not freed itself from the imperative of returns to scale (Boyer, 1987a: 10–16; 1987b: 12–17).

The increased inequalities, implied in the dismantling of the welfare state, the increase in unemployment, the polarisation of the labour market, as well as the failure of the neo-liberal regime to manage environmental crises' generate antagonisms and social forces which may yet challenge the order. The Gordian knot for such social forces, however, is to mobilize and link sufficient power to challenge the structural power of capital.

There are also important antagonisms at the core of the transnational power bloc. Although the pivotal globalizing élite is in agreement on the need to exert monetarist discipline, and reduce social or public consumption, there are significant differences in outlook on how to regulate the world economy (see Gill, 1994). The principal division runs between financial consortia and states of the Anglo-Saxon heartland, and those of continental Europe ('Rhineland Capitalism') and Japan. In the latter regions there are strong state capitalist traditions, productive capital is still relatively prominent and social democracy and/or traditional conservatism are relatively strong as political movements. Here one tends to find support for 'compensatory liberalism' and public regulation based on 'new constitutionalism' (Gill 1992a, 1993b). The ideology of compensatory liberalism differs from hyper-liberalism in that it in certain instances pragmatically promotes the displacement of market mechanism in favour of public constitutionalist regulation, for the purpose of ensuring consistency and disciplining certain collective actors so they will act according to market rationality. 'New constitutionalism' implies that the state insulates certain state apparatuses, such as central banks, from discretionary political action and set norms, such as fixed exchange rates, public borrowing targets or inflation rate targets, in order to structure costs and incentives of collective actors so that they will 'act responsibly'. Compensatory liberalism may come into conflict with hyper-liberalism on a transnational level, where the former ideology may promote 'strong' transnational regimes of constitutionalist regulation, while the latter would rather abstain from such regulation and 'leave things to the market'.

A central aspect of present world order restructuring is the creation of continental–regional blocs. I would contend that the process of European integration reflects the global developments outlined above. The creation of the single market, as laid out in Lord Cockfield's *White Paper* is quite consistent with the hyper-liberal strategy on a global scale. However, behind the consensus over the single market one can discern competing accumulation strategies. Social Democratic federalists, such as the former President of the Commission, Jacques Delors, envision a 'neo-Fordist' Europe, where regimes of social and environmental standards, transnational macroeconomic policy, and a Community wide industrial policy not only sustains welfare capitalism, but also diffuses it to the periphery. Delors has advanced this agenda by pursuing a 'Russian doll' strategy. At each stage of integration, he managed to secure vague commitments from member states for further regulation, which he then vigorously pursued at timely moments (Ross, 1992). But this vision is hampered not only by the political weakness of European Social Democracy and the labour movement. It is also rendered improbable by the daunting task of creating the required new transnational institutions.

The compromises of the Maastricht Accord have had the effect of creating a European Union consistent with compensatory liberalism, reflecting the strength of continental Christian democracy, with hyper-liberal and social democratic forces 'cancelling each other out'. There is no legal clout in the social commitments of Maastricht, but there is a commitment to a transnational macroeconomic policy implied in the Monetary Union. The institutional design of the EMU reflects the monetarist objectives of the Bundesbank, not a Social Democratic neo-Fordist Europe. It is important to emphasize, though, that Maastricht does not as yet signify a stable crystallization of EU institutions.

THE POST-WAR NORDIC MODELS

The aim of the next two sections is to probe how this global transformation affects the Nordic societies and Nordic welfare capitalism. First, the specificity of the Nordic regions in relation to the norms and institutions of *Pax Americana*, will be defined. Second, the Nordic specificities of the economic crisis of the 1970s, and the transformations in the 1980s, will be explored.

Export-oriented growth structures

Nordic economies are small and export dependent. Moreover, their export sectors are composed of a narrow range of dominating industries and corporations. These developed from advantages in the production of 'staples' commodities. Fordist mass production in the Nordic countries depended upon demand in the world economy, and mass consumption depended upon imports, financed by foreign exchange earned from high value added commodities in the export sector.[7] In the Nordic context, then, one might perhaps speak of a 'disarticulated' Fordism.[8]

The composition of the export sectors of the Nordic countries varied quite considerably during the post-war era (Mjøset, 1987: 414–15). Sweden had the most diversified structure with important exports in automobiles and engineering industry inputs. Sweden also exported semi-processed forest and metal products. The corporations of the Swedish export sector were privately owned, and ownership also was, and continues to be, heavily concentrated. Characteristic of Swedish capital is the manner in which corporations are tied to a handful of banks, through cross ownership by a few family dynasties (Hermansson, 1989: 79–102).

The Norwegian export sector was composed of fishery, forestry, heavy furnace and chemical industries, and a large 'offshore' shipping enclave. Since the 1970s, the offshore sector has been dominated by an emerging oil industry, which replaced the diminishing shipping sector. In contrast to Sweden, the state has played a major role as financier and owner in the Norwegian export sector, providing investment resources in highly capital-intensive projects.

Finland was the poor neighbour of Scandinavia in the immediate post-war period, almost an 'undeveloped' country at that time. But Finland's economy has grown rapidly through the course of the post-war period. The forest industry has dominated the Finnish export sector, and as in Norway, the state has played a major role in investment and ownership. A significant manufacturing sector has emerged, particularly because of bilateral trade with the USSR. Niche production in agricultural and agricultural-related products dominated the Danish export sector well into the 1950s. Shipping also played an important role. A 'machine industrial complex', producing on a small scale for niche markets, gained prominence in the export sector in the late 1950s and the 1960s.

In contrast, the Danish economy has not been dominated by large corporations. As in Sweden, the state has played no significant role in ownership and finance. It is doubtful whether one can consider Fordist norms predominant in Danish production. With a large degree of skilled craft production, Denmark developed 'flexible specialization' already in the Fordist era (Nielsen and Pedersen, 1989: 346). However, the Danish economy suffered continuously from the *extent* of its industrialization and the size of its export sector. As mass consumption norms have developed, Denmark experienced chronic balance of payments problems.

Reformist labour organizations

A second specific feature of the Nordic region is the prominent role played by the reformist organized labour movement. Nordic countries departed from the economistic Gomperist model of organization of labour that American Fordism promoted (van der Pijl 1984: 94–100). Nordic labour movements have quite successfully pursued political power through stong organizational capacity of unions, and the ability of the Social Democratic parties to secure working class support by articulating class consciousness into a political force (Korpi, 1983; Esping-Andersen, 1985b: 223–56; Pontusson, 1988). Crucial here were red-green 'national popular' coalitions, forged between workers' and farmers' parties during the depression. They were built around the principles of liberal democracy, the welfare state, and protection of farmers and workers through state intervention in the labour and agricultural markets. As noted, these coalitions were premised upon 'growth alliance' accords with capital that acknowledged the prominent position of the red-green coalition at the 'commanding heights' of the state (Esping-Andersen, 1985a; Marklund, 1988; Therborn, 1989).

These coalitions were by no means predestined. However, 'late industrialization' in Scandinavia created a context which facilitated this. Scandinavian political 'exceptionalism' was based on a deep tradition of corporative representation, with an independent peasantry that constituted a 'Fourth Estate'. Thus the politics of modernization not only differed from that of the West where the bourgeoisie obtained a hegemonic position early, but also was distinct from the politics of 'iron and rye' in Prussia/Germany (Tilton, 1974: 561–71; Anderson 1979; Schiller, 1989: 218–34). Perhaps one might consider the Nordic countries a fourth European 'historical region', distinct from Jenö Szücs' Western, Central and Eastern Europe (Szücs, 1988).

The red-green coalitions varied. In Sweden and Norway labour movements exercised leadership in the national popular discourse. The Swedish labour movement could draw strength from their leadership in the 'popular movement' alliance that successfully struggled to obtain universal suffrage in 1917, and from their leadership during the depression and in the National Government during the Second World War. The Agrarians were the junior parliamentary coalition partner.

In Norway, the labour movement mobilized large segments of the agrarian sector, and secured majorities in Parliament up until the 1960s. Both in Norway and Sweden trade unions, politically affiliated to the parties and organized through the industry principle, effectively organized the industrial labour markets in an encompassing manner (Esping-Andersen, 1985a: 78–90, 99–111).

The labour movement was strong in Denmark. Here a liberal-agrarian political movement was also influential. Well-to-do farmers in Denmark made it difficult for Danish Social Democracy to mobilize the countryside as in Norway. And since the radical liberal farmer's party had effectively achieved political liberalization already in the nineteenth century, the Danish labour movement did not have the issue of universal suffrage available to them to articulate national leadership. Thus, in Denmark the red-green alliance tilted more in the direction of the radical-liberal farmers. A capital/labour accord had been forged already in 1899, and created state-market relations less congenial to labour mobilization than in Sweden and Norway. Moreover, the unions were divided between skilled crafts unions and unions of semi- and unskilled industrial workers (Esping-Andersen, 1985a: 73–8, 90–99).

No 'red-green' coalition or compromise between capital and labour emerged in Finland during the depression or in the immediate postwar period. Finland's civil war, fought after gaining independence in 1918, reinforced socio-political polarization. After 1945 there emerged a 'hard developmental state', headed by a 'strong presidency'. Finland nevertheless emulated some Scandinavian arrangements in the 1960s. To my knowledge, no comprehensive account exists that explains the process of this successful emulation: it seems to have hinged on a number of factors. First, there was a more 'relaxed' domestic atmosphere, that emerged during the course of the post-war period partly linked to the geo-politically exposed position of Finland (Andersson, 1989: 374–6). Secondly, there is the copying of Swedish institutional arrangements as a response to emerging policy problems (Karvonen, 1981). Deeper similarities of economic, social, and deeper cultural-historical structures (such as the nature and importance of the export sector, and labour- and farmers' communities with strong traditions of self-organization) can perhaps be considered a third set of factors.

Modes of regulation

A third specific feature of Nordic Models relates to modes of regulation. The typical Fordist mode of regulation was based on the expansion and stabilization of effective aggregate demand in the domestic economy. The Nordic modes had to fulfil this functional imperative to some extent, although demand-pull of other countries was crucial. However, Nordic countries faced two other constraints. Since the economies were disarticulated, and depended upon the export sector, the Nordic modes of regulation were particularly sensitive to balance of payments constraints. These limited the room of manoeuvre of general aggregate demand management. Modes of regulation had to be consistent with, and facilitate, the competitive advantage of the export sector as well as its flexible adjustment to world market conditions (Katzenstein, 1983; 1985). However, because of the imperatives of political legitimacy of the red-green coalitions, regulation had to be consistent with stringent demands for full employment, rising social wages, social security, and a thriving domestic agriculture. The *raison d'être* of redistribution was to 'de-commodify' the sources of income (Esping-Andersen, 1990).

Nordic regulation involved export orientation with strict controls on capital and currency markets and controls on foreign ownership. Very moderately counter-cyclical, or neutral, fiscal policy routines, with a monetary policy promoting low interest rates, were parts of this mode. Intimately connected to this general macroeconomic policy were institutions of co-ordinated wage determination, giving due regard to adequate representation of unions and employers' organizations. Moreover, selective structural policies, such as labour market policy and/or industrial policy belonged to the central policy routines. Finally, mass consumption was to a large extent public, something that manifested itself in tax-financed expansions of 'institutional' as opposed to 'marginal' or 'residual' welfare states (Korpi, 1983: 184–207).[9]

The Swedish Model reflected both a powerful labour movement and a very strong and concentrated private export sector. Financial resources were mainly allocated through the domestic credit market, dominated by a few private banks. The labour movement exerted control over the overall economic environment through a co-ordinated strategy of economic policy and bargaining within a centralised, but bipartite, negotiation structure. The government controlled money and foreign currency exchange, and promoted low interest rates, and pursued a moderately counter-cyclical fiscal policy. The Rehn–Meidner model of solidaristic wage policy and selective labour market policy ensured that a more egalitarian distribution of wages was made consistent with structural rationalization of the economy. Dynamic efficiency was ensured through high 'transformation pressure', as the Rehn–Meidner model crowded out the less profitable sectors prematurely, and provided quasi-economic rents to the more profitable sectors of the economy (Erixon, 1984: 109–10; Pekkarinen, 1989: 318–21).

The Norwegian and Swedish Models had similar policy routines concerning macroeconomic management, wage policy and welfare state expansion. Norwegian wage policy, though, was tripartite, not bipartite. However, labour market policy has not played a major role in the Norwegian Model. Rather, the Norwegian Model has been characterized by a high degree of public ownership, and by selective planning and structural industrial policy. Financial resources were selectively channelled into strategically identified sectors. In particular capital and energy intensive sectors and welfare state expansion were favoured. The Norwegian Model reflected the absence of a financially strong entrepreneurial stratum. The state had to finance large projects when there was no private venture capital available. Moreover, the state took over German property after the war (Fagerberg, Cappelen, Mjøset, and Skarstein, 1990: 65–8).

The relative weakness of Social Democracy in Denmark and Finland, and the unsynchronized relation between exports and imports in these countries, made Denmark and Finland laggards in relation to Sweden and Norway in terms of welfare state development. In Denmark, the structure of the export sector is the more important explanation for this lag, whereas a weaker labour movement is more important in explaining the Finnish case (Pekkarinen, 1989: 341). The Danish Model has been the most market-oriented of the Nordic Models since 1945. Counter-cyclical policies were weaker and more *ad hoc* than in Norway and Sweden, because of the secular balance of payments problem. The latter condition also made Denmark the only Nordic country to pursue a high interest rate policy. Labour market structure was not congenial to co-ordinated wage bargaining. Such bargaining was not institutionalized until the 1970s. Denmark was initially slow in social policy development, but during the 1960s Denmark expanded its welfare policies rapidly and caught up with Sweden and Norway (ibid.: 332–40; Nielsen and Pedersen, 1989: 349–52). However, important areas of welfare policies, such as supplemental pension and housing policy, are not based on citizen entitlement, but rather on means test and are therefore of marginal rather than institutional design (Esping-Andersen, 1985a).

Finland diverged considerably from the other models until the 1960s. The labour movement was particularly weak and the Agrarian

Party of President Kekkonen represented the export oriented forestry sector. The instability of the Finnish party system gave autonomy to the élite state managers of the 'hard developmental state', with a mercantilist outlook influenced by Friedrich List (Pekkarinen, 1989: 328–32). Finland pursued a balanced budget fiscal policy and a monetarist monetary policy, in conjunction with periodic devaluations of the Markka. The central bank enjoyed a great deal of autonomy in relation to Parliament (Uusitalo, 1984), and direct state incomes policy was used to contain wage push inflation. Economic policy was nevertheless interventionist. As in Norway, there was pervasive state ownership and an industrial policy of export promotion. Finland also gradually developed an institutional welfare state during this period, but benefit levels were considerably lower than in the other Nordic countries. Consequently Finland has had a less impressive record in terms of eradicating poverty and achieving income equality.[10] Unemployment levels fluctuated considerably and in the 1960s the levels were kept down in large part because of emigration to Sweden. The chief objective of Finnish post-war economic policy was industrial diversification through export promotion (Pekkarinen, 1989: 324, 326). Nevertheless, the Finnish economy also grew very rapidly in the post-war period, albeit with great conjunctural fluctuations. Trade with the USSR, which was not sensitive to the business cycle, had a moderating effect on these fluctuations.

CRISES AND TRANSFORMATIONS

The Nordic nations were not sheltered from the international economic situation in the 1970s. As in other Western countries, the Nordic modes of regulation were challenged by union militancy and by new social movements. This challenge provoked a response that amounted to an expansion of welfare provisions and entitlements within the framework of the existing mode of regulation. Initially, the raw materials boom in the early seventies made it seem as if this expansion of the welfare state was functional. However, as the world economic crisis reduced the demand for Nordic exports, and as the oil crisis increased the costs of imports, it became evident that these increased entitlements were hopelessly dysfunctional in relation to the mode of regulation and the economic structure. This, in turn, provoked populist hyper-liberal reactions, where tax revolt was the key articulating principle.

This reaction has not been sufficient, however, to assert a hyper-liberal mode of regulation. Rather, in the 1980s, the Nordic countries have tended to converge towards a 'compensatory liberal' model that resembles the post-war Finnish Model (Andersson and Mjøset, 1987: 237–38). The institutional welfare state is maintained, but benefit levels are cut back. International competitiveness is enhanced by devaluation, and export prices are maintained through tight monetary policy and increased state intervention in incomes policy. In recent years there has been an ambition to maintain fixed exchange rates, but without any particular success. However, in contrast to the post-war Finnish Model, and more in line with the Danish Model, the Nordic countries have followed the global trends of deregulating credit and money markets. More recently there has also been a tendency to emulate another Danish precedent: as incomes policies fail to contain high wage costs at high levels of employment, mass unemployment is accepted. Incomes policies are nevertheless maintained as a means of containing relative unit labour costs in an environment of high union density. Since Nordic unions continue to enjoy a high degree of legitimacy, 'union busting' is not on the cards.

There are also other important variations (see Mjøset, 1987: 416–45). In Norway and Sweden, Social Democratic governments, run by a new generation of technocratic Keynesians, responded to the demands of the 'new left' and the economic downturn of 1974 with deficit financed reflation and continued social reform. Norway could bridge the economic crisis of the 1970s because of the offshore oil industry. Oil reserves enabled Norway to underwrite international loans, which financed its current account and budget deficits. But uncharacteristically expansionary measures in Sweden hopelessly overextended the model. The Swedish economy was to suffer the most severe structural economic crisis of the OECD in the second half of the 1970s. Unemployment increases were prevented, though, through labour market policy, and extraordinary state support to corporations facing bankruptcy.

There was a crisis in Swedish industry. But this crisis was not *caused* by the rigidities of the institutions of the Swedish Model as neo-classical economists, such as Lindbeck (1984) would have it. Firstly, fiscal policy during the crucial 1974–5 period was much too expansionary to be considered consistent with the policy routines of the Swedish Model (Erixon, 1984: 117–18). Secondly, one should not exaggerate the role played by wages in increased production costs.[11] Thirdly, when considering the loss of Swedish market shares, it is important to note that relative prices of Swedish export commodities increased more than proportionally to the increase in total costs and relative unit labour cost. This did not occur in other Nordic countries. This phenomenon was linked to the industrial composition of the Swedish export sector. Especially important was the stage in the 'product cycle' in which the export industries found themselves.[12] Fourthly, the Rehn–Meidner model may have created barriers to entry for new firms, in favour of large export oriented corporations based on product innovations from the pre-Second World War period. However, without the Rehn–Meidner model, a dynamic Fordist trajectory would not have been achieved, and Sweden might have suffered from the Danish problem of under-industrialization (Erixon, 1984: 124–5).

The Swedish Social Democratic government of the 1980s relied upon a 20 per cent devaluation, followed by restrictive fiscal policy and interventionist wage policy, to regain macroeconomic balance without giving up the full employment commitment. The object of the policy-mix was to create a substitution effect, favouring investment over consumption and the competitive elements of the export sector (Ryner, 1993: 5–8).[13] In addition, using measures it considered supply side enhancing, the government abolished the progressivity of Swedish tax scales, and deregulated financial markets. In the early 1990s an historic shift occurred. The full employment commitment was subordinated to the fight against inflation (Bergström, 1993: 159–62).

In Norway, the Conservative-led coalition governments of the 1980s, that achieved power because of a successful co-optation of the blue wave in that country, and the long term failure of Labour to co-opt the red wave, deliberately dismantled Norwegian state capitalism (Fagerberg *et al.*, 1990: 68–76). It did so so by deregulating the capital and money markets and by large tax cuts, financed through free-riding on OPEC oil prices. The weak minority Labour governments that have succeeded the Conservative-led coalitions have not re-regulated the markets, but instead have depended upon wage policy, the only instrument left at their disposal (Fagerberg *et al.*, 1990: 75–89).

In Finland, the economic downturn of the 1970s was met with traditional pro-cyclical fiscal and monetary polices and a devaluation. The system of grand coalition governments contained and co-opted the 'red wave', since even the Communist Party was included in the government. It should be noted that Finland implemented a less statist mode of wage determination, along the lines of its Scandinavian

neighbours at this time, and there was a moderate growth and deepening of the welfare state. In part, these measures can be considered
an accommodation to the red wave. Increased bilateral trade with the
USSR mitigated external pressure and made this accommodation
possible. It had a stabilising effect on the pro-cyclical policies. More
importantly, though, the Soviet market provided an alternative outlet
for export commodities as the Western market contracted. Finland
could also substitute its imports of OPEC oil with oil from the USSR.
As a result, rapid growth resumed in Finland in the latter part of the
1970s, and was sustained until the collapse of the USSR.

Denmark responded to the crisis with restrictive policies. The full
employment commitment was abandoned, and Denmark has since
suffered from the European syndrome of mass unemployment.[14] Two
main factors explain this. Firstly, the fledgling manufacturing sector
suffered from the high raw material prices earlier than industries did
in the other Nordic countries, because of the lack of a significant
proportion of raw materials and semi-processed production in Danish
industry. Secondly, the 'red and green waves' of the new left were
accompanied by a particularly strong populist, hyper-liberal 'blue
wave'. The rise of right wing populism led to a party realignment
which facilitated an end to welfare reform and restrictive policies.
But hyper-liberalism has been contained in Denmark as well, and
in the 1980s Denmark extended and deepened state intervention in
wage determination in order to contain wage costs (Nielsen and
Pedersen, 1989: 347–62). Moreover, the Danish Right–Centre coalition government as well as the Finnish Conservative–Social Democratic coalition government have expanded the role for selective
industrial policy. Paradoxically, their Social Democratic counterparts
in Norway and Sweden have retreated from such policies (Andersson,
1989: 378–80).

The Social Democrats in Norway and Sweden have run into serious
legitimation problems because of their policy-shift. As they have
engaged in more direct incomes policies, and infringed upon collective
bargaining, they have tended to lose working class support. Such
policies have tended to fragment the union movement (Ahlén, 1989;
Fagerberg *et al.*, 1990: 86–8). This increased the scope for a more
hyper-liberal agenda. An impasse in the implementation of wage-and
industrial policies in Denmark, caused by divisions both within the
parliamentary and interest intermediary processes, have also led to
demands for more hyper-liberal solutions (Nielsen and Pedersen,
1989: 359–68). However, governments with hyper-liberal aspirations

(i.e. the Schlüter and Willoch governments in Denmark and Norway in the 1980s and the Bildt government in Sweden in the 1990s), have shown themselves to be incapable of challenging the 'hard core' of Nordic welfare capitalism, namely the *general principles* of trade unionism and the principle of institutional welfarism.

The Nordic countries also experienced serious problems of capital accumulation. Since popular acceptance of regulatory mechanisms such as incomes policies is predicated on future prosperity and full employment these problems feed into the legitimation problematic. Although Norway continues to enjoy the 'natural advantages' of its oil sector, the reliance on this sector has made Norway's economy more vulnerable to commodity price fluctuations. The oil sector has also crowded out state-promotion of innovation in other industrial innovation in other industrial sectors. The private financial sector has not managed to facilitate the development of new export sectors (Mjøset, 1987). Swedish devaluations, in connection with a more statist incomes policy, generated higher profits in industry, and thus actually reduced the transformation pressure associated with the traditional Rehn–Meidner strategy.

As a result, however, the Swedish industrial structure has not been progressively revitalized. Instead it has been locked into a dependence upon primary and semi-processed commodity producers, and mature industries whose strategies involve corporate take-overs on a global scale and internationalization of production (Erixon, 1989; Ryner, 1993: 20–5). Finland seemed to have had a more favourable development in its export sector. As in Sweden, this sector was based upon the performance of a few large private conglomerates. But Finnish firms produced commodities in an earlier phase in the product cycle, and were still setting oligopolistic prices. In addition, state industrial policy seemed to have created significant product and process innovations. This seemed promising in terms of entering a new growth trajectory (Andersson, 1989: 37–89). But the massive problems of the Finnish economy, including very high unemployment partly associated with the collapse of the Soviet economy, puts this assessment very much in doubt. The Danish manufacturing sector of small niche-producing firms, on the other hand, seems to have regained dynamism. Despite an unfavourable development in relative unit labour costs *vis-à-vis* Sweden, Danish firms increased market share more than Swedish firms in the 1980s. Nevertheless the size of the industrial export sector has remained a problem (Andersson and Mjøset, 1987: 236–37).

Central to the problems of accumulation, then, is a tendency towards massive capital outflows of foreign direct investments, associated with the globalization of production of Swedish and Finnish firms,[15] and with the crowding out resulting from the oil sector in Norway. Consequently, there is a strong tendency towards deindustrialization and peripheralization in these countries as the 'spatial fix' of capital changes. As in the post-war Danish Model, but on a much larger scale, this deindustrialization endangers the ability to sustain current levels of domestic public and private consumption. This is somewhat ironical since Danish corporations are more 'national', and the other countries are now faring worse than Denmark in this regard.

It would be tempting to stop the analysis here and draw a number of general conclusions. One might be that Nordic welfare capitalism may have been an attractive model as the most progressive and far-reaching form of welfare national state in the era of *Pax Americana*. But in the emerging global political economy it is dysfunctional, and therefore those who hold this model up as an alternative to hyper-liberalism are mistaken. But to draw this conclusion would be to over-generalize. Crucial to the failure of both the attempt to extend the welfare state in the 1970s and to retrench it through compensatory liberalism in the 1980s was the inadequate performance of the export sector. The former failure coincided with the Fordist crisis, and the latter with the tendency of peripheralization that characterizes the Nordic political economies.

The Nordic countries are relative losers in the present restructuring of the global division of labour. But that does not necessarily imply some abstract notion of 'inefficiency' of the Nordic economic regulation. Nordic collective bargaining and co-determination regimes seem to have the potential for a good micro-economic performance within the new post-Fordist production-technological constraints (Standing, 1988), and the institutional welfare state does not 'crowd out' the competitive sector (Erixon and Frazer, 1984). Indeed it may be that aspects of Nordic welfare capitalism, such as co-ordinated wage policy, and labour market policy would be worthwhile emulating for alternative accumulation strategies in the capitalist centre.

One should not too hastily draw the overly determinist conclusion that the crisis of the Nordic Models in the emerging global political economy is essentially structural. To do so would be to assume that the compensatory liberal policy responses of the 1980s were somehow optimal responses to the new circumstances. Evidence from at least the Swedish case, suggests that these responses were based on subjective premises that were in sharp contradiction with the terms of legitimation of Swedish civil society. These subjective premises did also not primarily concern themselves with an economic restructuring compatible with a universal welfare state and solidaristic bargaining. The most important policy initiatives to consider in this context are the 'norms based' monetary policy declared in 1985, and the marginalization of the 'wage earner fund' strategy.

THE POLITICS AND IDEOLOGY OF SWEDISH COMPENSATORY LIBERALISM IN THE 1980s

In 1985 the Swedish government adopted a 'norms based' monetary policy to enforce macroeconomic aspects of its 'substitution strategy' for recovery. The central bank deregulated capital markets, and, more importantly, declared that it would no longer borrow abroad (that is, issue bonds in foreign currency) to finance the public debt. Since Sweden has a negative payments balance, this implied that private borrowers had to borrow from foreign lenders willing to hold debt in Swedish crowns via international capital and currency markets. This maximized the exposure of the Swedish interest rate to short term arbitrage speculation, and the interest rate would increase as the 'devaluation risk' was seen to increase. The devaluation risk was a function of the perceived tendency of the Swedish economy to overheat.

Rather than attempting to minimize the exposure of the Swedish economy to global financial markets, this exposure was maximized. The intention was to change the state/market boundary in regulation to exert maximum market discipline upon trade unions and the social welfare ministries in the wage and public budget bargaining processes. 'Excessive demands', increasingly defined by market actors, would be punished by an increase in Swedish interest rates (Bergström, 1993: 159–60; Hörngren, 1993).

This policy shift amounted to an actual abandonment of the government's commitment to the union movement's de-commodification strategy. Previously the Ministry of Finance had represented union interests by pursuing a macroeconomic policy consistent with solidaristic wage policy, through moderate counter-cyclical measures that maintained full employment in recessions, and put a lid on excess profits in booms. Excess profits decreased the negotiated component and increased the market component in wage determination through the resulting 'wage drift'. But now the government actively increased market discipline on wage development. This put exceptional strain on the unions since they had already accepted wage restraint in the context of the uneven increases in profit rates, as implied by the devaluation of 1982. As a result, an ideological rift developed between the Social Democratic Party (SAP) and the union federations (LO and TCO). Previously, tensions would arise from their different functional roles in the mode of regulation. These tensions would arise within the context of an overall agreement on the principles of such regulation.

However, as a *conflict over the principles of regulation*, the unions were less inclined to agree to the terms of the implicit incomes policy. Furthermore, as capital deregulation and the substitution effect of the devaluation created an uneven boom, the 'moral economy' of nego-tiated collective wage determination, that cements wage solidarity among unions (Swenson, 1989), was undermined and fragmented the collective bargaining regime (Ahlén, 1989; Ryner, 1993: 10–12, 25–7). Unions in the export sector were offered high wage increases by expanding multinationals. Other unions were expected to show restraint. But in a context with an 80 per cent union density and a breakdown of corporatist consensus, these unions managed to enforce compensation. The norms based policy, then, had the opposite effect of what was intended. It fuelled rather than contained wage push inflation.

Capital deregulation and the borrowing strategy also had detrimen-tal effects on long term aspects of the devaluation strategy. Capital deregulation stimulated consumption, contributed to an overheating of the economy and resulted in demand pull inflation. The increased export revenues, resulting from the devaluation, and the increased competition from foreign banks and equity markets, created a 'recy-cling problem' for Swedish banks. Thus, they lowered their criterion of credit worthiness and gave attractive loans for consumption and real estate investment.

Here one discerns a contradiction in the government policy mix. The devaluation was supposed to generate earnings in the short run that would be channelled into productivity enhancing investments in the long run. But government credit and monetary policy actually undermined the capacity of the credit system to facilitate such 'dynamic efficiency'. The devaluation strategy presupposed long time horizons for investment return, but the exposure of the Swedish economy to the privatized, multi-centred global financial system short-ened the time horizons. The process of internationalization of production is intimately intertwined with these processes of finance and government policy. The primary cause of credit deregulation was the impossibility to effectively control transnational corporate capital flows (Feldt, 1991: 281). Moreover, the recycling problem of Swedish banks was primarily a function of the increased possibility of transnationalizing Swedish firms to borrow from foreign banks and to raise equity capital on foreign and Swedish stock markets.[16]

The effect of this combination of policy was a breakdown in solidaristic wage determination, and a disarticulation of productive and financial capital. The Swedish economy overheated in the late 1980s. This resulted in a run on the Crown in global financial markets that led to an incredible overnight interest rate of 500 per cent in late 1992, before the Central Bank gave up and let the Crown float. The Crown rapidly lost 40 per cent of its value relative to the Japanese Yen. As the economy rapidly entered a recession in 1992, the real estate market plummeted, leading to the virtual collapse of the Swedish bank system as borrowers defaulted on loans. In the summer of 1993, only one Swedish bank (Handelsbanken) could survive without a state transfusion of liquidity that now is matching total social expenditure in its magnitude.

Were there alternatives to this economic strategy? Clearly, the government could have refrained from pursuing a 'norms based' monetary policy. As LO's economists have argued, the government could have financed its deficit by issuing bonds in foreign currency. This would have radically decreased the sensitivity of the Swedish interest rate to global financial markets, which would have led to a lower and more stable interest rate (Edin, 1993). This would, in turn, most certainly have meant that the awesome momentum of imbalance that developed with the recession of 1992 could have been avoided. Lower and stable interest rates may also have improved the conditions for the implicit incomes policy. Most importantly, the ideological rift between the unions and the government may have been avoided. This would have improved the prospects of containing wage-push inflation. Although the transnationalization of Swedish corporations made capital deregulation more likely in the long run, the implications of deregulation should have been anticipated. If the government had timed deregulation differently in relation to the business cycle, it may have been possible to contain demand pull inflation.

Such measures, however, would not have addressed the long term contradictions of the Swedish Model that emanate from the transnationalization of Swedish corporations and the attendant peripheralization of the Swedish economy. In particular, such measures would not have addressed the need of ensuring productivity generating investments, as the Rehn–Meidner model had done during the Fordist phase by generating 'transformation pressure'. The economic policy of the 1980s indicates that such investments will not be realized through deregulation. However, there were alternative strategies contemplated by the labour movement in the 1970s, that would have increased public regulation of investment that may have made it possible to channel profits into long term, strategic investments.

LO's radical proposal for 'wage earner funds' may have been the basis for such regulation. It could have provided the necessary financial mediation required for industrial policy to be strategically innovative and for not degenerating into defensive pork-barrel politics (which Swedish industrial policy did in the 1970s). The wage earner fund strategy would have been well suited to the Swedish circumstances, because it was geared towards making compatible solidaristic wage policy, co-determination, strategic investments and the increased requirements for equity capital of a small state in the global economy.[17]

From the point of view of industrial policy, the initial 'Meidner Plan' proposal of 1976, was problematic.[18] But it is important to note that the 1976 proposal was intended as a bargaining position, to be worked out through the normal process of tripartite public commissions, and through deliberations between the Social Democratic party and the unions. The very fact that a public commission was set up, that the SAP and LO radically modified the initial LO proposal in a direction more congenial to industrial policy, and that even the employers' federation, SAF, internally worked out a response to the LO proposal (the Waldenström Report), indicates that the elements for bargaining and compromise were there (Åsard, 1985). Why was this potential alternative policy orientation, which would have built on and reinforced the 'state capitalist' institutions of the Swedish Model, marginalized and ultimately rejected in the late 1970s and the early 1980s? Moreover, why did the Social Democratic government decide to pursue a 'norms based' monetary policy in 1985? Are (and if so how) the marginalization of the wage earner fund proposal and the adoption of the norms based monetary policy related?

No doubt, further careful research is required to reconstruct in detail this political struggle over economic regulation. However, a number of central propositions can be made.

First, although the wage earner fund proposal of 1976 was promising in terms of making the social welfare expansions compatible with economic regulation and accumulation, it clearly went beyond the 'social welfare' discourse which cemented the post-war Swedish power bloc. By challenging private ownership of the means of production, the wage earner funds opened up latent divisions within the SAP regarding the transformation from capitalism to socialism. Simultaneously, this was an issue around which the otherwise divided non-socialist parties could articulate a common agenda and effectively challenge the Social Democratic party (Pontusson, 1987).

Second, the wage earner fund issue served as a catalyst in changing the balance of forces and interest within SAF (Schiller, 1987; de Geer, 1989). The 'red wave' had seriously undermined the legitimacy of the strategy of compromise and co-operation within SAF. There were competing outlooks of confrontation and continued corporatist co-operation within SAF on the question of how to respond, and the flurry of Social Democratic reform initiatives, especially in the area of co-determination, that followed. (The very existence of the Waldenström Report indicates this.) But when the LO-proposal of 1976 was perceived as a threat to private property, the balance of forces within SAF tilted decisively in favour of a confrontational hyper-liberal strategy. The initiative for such a strategy was taken by representatives for small scale firms and representatives of corporations in the Wallenberg/SE-Bank sphere of interest. SAF's 'old guard', groomed in the mould of the Swedish Model, with their strongest support in the Handelsbanken sphere, was removed from leading positions.[19] Consequently, SAF took on a role of leadership in 'fighting the funds'. Internally, the Waldenström Report was rejected, and SAF pursued a strategy of categorical non-accommodation in the Public Commission process. As a result the Commission collapsed in 1980 (Åsard, 1985; 102–26). SAF also orchestrated a massive propaganda campaign against fund socialism and for the virtues of free enterprise (Hansson, 1984). This enabled a united campaign of the non-socialist parties against the funds.

Thus, the Social Democrats were isolated. The ideological coherence, and massive scope of the SAF-campaign, in contrast to the hesitancy and internal divisions within the labour movement, made the wage earner fund initiative hopeless for SAP to pursue. Although the SAP and LO managed to reach consensus on a fund proposal in 1981 that was satisfactory both to the union, and the party, including the future Minister of Finance, Kjell-Olof Feldt, the capacity of their opponents to politically mobilize on the issue, made the government back down. A symbolic wage earner fund bill (intended to appease

LO) was passed through Parliament in 1983, but because of the limited size and clout of these funds, they were to have no significant macro-effect on the economy. The limits set by social welfare ideology had been severely felt by the labour movement.

The containment of the wage earner funds can be understood with reference to the ideological limits of the popular discourses of 'social welfare' and the 'Cold War' (Sainsbury, 1980: 48–81, 82–115).[20] The non-socialists, led by SAF, successfully exploited the terms of these discourses, while the labour movement lacked certainly the capacity and strategic sense, and maybe also the will to change the terms of these discourses. But how is this political outcome related to the economic policy of the 1980s? It is related since the policy dilemma the wage earner funds were intended to resolve – to make compatible solidaristic wage policy, economic restructuring, macroeconomic balance, and an institutional welfare state – would now be addressed through the devaluation/substitution strategy and the norms based monetary policy.

This substitution strategy was formulated by a joint SAP-LO 'crisis group'. However, the report of this group (SAP, 1981) is ambiguous. It can be read as a manifesto of moderate reinforcement of state capitalism, where wage earner funds and industrial policy will play a limited yet significant role. But it can also be read in a 'compensatory liberal' manner, as a manifesto for a straightforward incomes policy, without significant regulatory innovation to facilitate solidaristic wage policy. The union movement would continuously insist on the former interpretation, while the Ministry of Finance consistently moved in the direction of the latter interpretation. The limited nature of the wage earner funds bill of 1983, and the norms based monetary policy cemented this course.

How should one make sense of the political process behind the norms based policy? Contrary to the wage earner fund issue, one cannot primarily refer to the popular-political level, since this policy hardly was discussed beyond the inner circle of senior officials in the Central Bank and the Ministry of Finance. There was no consultation and debate in unions, riding associations, and party conferences, and public commissions that typically precede major Social Democratic policy shifts in Sweden. It even seems as if the Prime Minister, although consulted, was excluded, or more to the point, excluded himself, from this policy shift (Feldt, 1991).[21]

Thus a number of factors seem pertinent. Above all one must recognize that there actually is an elective affinity between the doctrine of a moderate Keynesianism subscribed to by Social Democratic officials in the Ministry of Finance, and this brand of monetarism. The Social Democratic policy makers who entered the Ministry of Finance balked at the structural deficit generated by 'vulgar Keynesianism' in the 1970s, and sought a means to redress this imbalance. But why was it assumed that a norms based policy would be the best means? There was a vacuum of knowledge among Social Democrats of the workings of finance, a type of knowledge which becomes crucial when one deals with a structural deficit.[22] The result was that policy advice was only available from 'academic', non-partisan intellectuals in the universities and the Central Bank. These intellectuals had no organic link with the labour movement. Rather, their links were with fora such as the Bank for International Settlements (BIS), academic networks of economists and business sponsored think tanks such as the Policy Studies Institute (Britain), the Committee of Economic Development (USA), and their Swedish counterpart, SNS,[23] such fora were informed by the increasingly dominant monetarist discourse. Indeed the Ministry of Finance had always prioritized external competitiveness and full employment over solidaristic wage policy, and it seems as if the terms of the 'moral economy' were never quite understood by the Ministry (Martin, 1984: 212).

CONCLUSION

This chapter has probed the prospects of Nordic welfare capitalism and the case of Sweden.

The first part of the argument discussed the emergence of the 'global political economy' which provides the context for restructuring. The socio-*economic* forces involved in restructuring include the shift away from Fordist mass production and mass consumption to an emphasis on flexible specialization, internationalization of production and finance, and a reduction of turnover time. The socio-*political* forces involved in promoting this change include a transnational hyper-liberal power bloc, strengthened by the defeat of the left and the crisis of the welfare state. However, there are contradictions and forces of resistance to this development.

The chapter also discussed the Nordic modes of regulation that synthesized international competitiveness with predominantly institutional welfarist, de-commodified distribution, and the socio-economic and socio-political context in which this mode of regulation was embedded (disarticulated Fordism, and the 'red- green' coalitions). In the third section it was argued that the Nordic Models did not escape the international economic crisis of the 1970s. Attempts to extend welfare reform could not be integrated into the mode of regulation. As a result, fiscal and competitiveness crises developed. Hyper-liberalism, challenging the welfare state, gained force at this time. But the Nordic countries responded to the crisis with 'compensatory liberal' policy: with fiscal moderation, monetarism, and reliance on an increasingly explicit incomes policy. Compensatory liberal convergence in the 1980s was but another phase in the organic crisis. The tendency towards peripheralization in Sweden, Norway, and Finland was identified as the most important aspect of this phase of organic crisis.

An important implication of the evidence presented in this chapter is that one should be wary of abstract explanations of the crisis of the Nordic Models, for example those that emphasize 'inefficiency' and 'sclerosis'. One should also be wary of interpretations that simply conclude that crisis can be reduced to an institutional incompatibility with the emerging global political economy. It is important to recognize that there were alternatives to the economic strategies pursued in the 1980s. It is an open question whether these alternatives might have been more compatible with the socio-economic imperatives of the global political economy.

In Sweden some of the policy choices made, particularly the norms-based monetary policy, were themselves primary causes of the severity of the economic crisis of the early 1990s. Some policy alternatives, such as wage-earner funds, were marginalized. These might have counteracted the peripheralization tendency and may have managed to restore both competitiveness and redistributive imperatives. The wage earner fund initiative went beyond the limits of Swedish social welfare hegemony by threatening certain rights of private property. Adoption of a norms-based policy can be explained with reference to the knowledge orientation of Social Democratic personnel in the Ministry of Finance. The dilemma of managing a fiscal crisis in the context of the ideological defeat of the wage-earner funds created a space where monetarist policy advice gained prominence. Monetarism was primarily advocated by the central bank and academic economists. Many of these economists were connected to transnational élite networks.

After the collapse of the Social Democratic strategy, the Conservative-led coalition government of 1991 tried to move in a hyper-liberal direction. However, its success was limited. In part this was because at least two of the coalition partners, the Liberals and the Centre Party (formerly the Agrarians of the old 'red-green' coalition) were wary of market fundamentalism. But the most important terrain to consider in this context is collective bargaining. Since the mid-1980s, SAF pursued rather successfully a strategy of decentralizing wage determination to the level of the firm so as to maximize firm wage flexibility for globalizing corporations (Pontusson and Swenson, 1993). But given Swedish union density, such a strategy has inherent limitations. For example, the wage round of 1993 pointed to these limitations. The move of the employers to ensure firm level bargaining was effectively halted at the branch level by alliances of unions, overlapping the traditional white collar–blue collar divide. Faced with the prospects of strikes, or even work-to-rule, at a time when the depreciation of the Crown had increased export orders, Swedish employers put aside hyper-liberal principles, and agreed to branch level agreements.

Thus, if it can be said that compensatory liberalism thus far has failed in Sweden, it must be said that hyper-liberalism has had even less success. A brief comparison with Thatcherism indicates why this is so. It is not sufficient that hyper-liberal ideas gain a foothold at the level of intellectual debate and policy, it must also permeate some of the 'common sense' of popular discourse. For Thatcherism that required a well prepared, decisive victory *within* the Conservative Party, and general political questioning of some of the principles of welfarism, and other reformist forces that sustained the existing 'common sense' of British civil society (Hall and Jacques, 1983: 19–39; Hall and Schwartz, 1988: 95–122). By contrast, the principles and programmes of the institutional welfare state were (and are) still highly popular among Swedish wage earners (Svallfors, 1989). Insofar as the welfare state draws criticism, it is because it does not provide enough services. Finally, Swedish hyper-liberal forces still have to contend with the resilience of post-war Social Democracy, that is still a considerable force in terms of defining political ethics and symbols.

However, the counter-forces to hyper-liberalism have yet to devise a coherent alternative accumulation strategy. But there are tendencies towards such a strategy. There are union initiatives to reformulate solidaristic wage policy to take into account the post-Fordist labour process, and to make work-time an issue for collective bargaining ('solidaristic work policy') (Mahon, 1991). Tied with this is a tendency to overcome the white collar–blue collar divide that has characterized the Swedish labour movement. But such a wage policy has to be connected to macroeconomics, industrial policy and welfare state development and to international economic policy. There has been little development in terms of macroeconomic ideas. The only new development is the embrace by the trade union movement of the European Union. Social Democrats would like to see themselves as playing an ideological leadership pressing for 'Social Europe'. This was expressed by the call of their leader, Ingvar Carlsson, for European-level Keynesian 'walls', to make viable the European 'house', where the Single Market is the floor, and the Social Charter is the 'roof'. However, given the severe obstacles to a Social Democratic vision of the EU, this is a shaky strategy. It would seem that participation in European macroeconomic institutions and policy would make it difficult to revitalize solidaristic wage policy. It is also unclear how EU-membership will address peripheralization tendencies of the Nordic economies, since market proximity, rather than lack of membership is the primary factor behind such peripheralization.

ACKNOWLEDGEMENTS

I would like to thank Anders L. Johansson, Director of the Swedish Centre for Working Life, and the Scandinavian-Canadian Academic Foundation for their logistical support, and Lennart Erixon, Rianne Mahon, Rudolf Meidner, Bernt Schiller, Bengt Sundelius, and policy makers interviewed in Sweden. I thank Carolyn Bassett, Stephen Gelb, Katherine Scott and the participants of the Oslo MUNS symposium, especially Björn Hettne, for comments on earlier drafts and Robert Cox, Stephen Gill and Leo Panitch for their advice on methodology. I gratefully acknowledge financial support of the Social Sciences and Humanities Research Council of Canada and the Swedish Women's Educational Association.

Notes

1.   *Ex ante* integrated wage norms imply that wages for a given turnover period of capital are set before the production process begins, minimizing risk and stabilizing demand according to anticipated productivity increases. This type of wage determination is said to have been pioneered by Henry Ford.

2. Embedded liberalism was a compromise between economic nationalism and free trade liberalism, predicated on domestic interventionism. For that purpose, the international monetary order of the Bretton Woods was based on the principle of the double screen. Expansion of international trade would be facilitated by the gradual abolition of exchange controls, and fixed exchange rates. However, to ensure that these imperatives did not debilitate the full employment commitment, the IMF system would finance short term payments of deficit countries from funds provided by membership contributions. (Due to the reluctance of the US administration to provide the IMF with adequate funds, this function would in reality be performed unilaterally by the US.) In addition the norms of the IMF stated that if 'fundamental disequilibrium' developed, exchange rates could be altered with IMF concurrence. Finally, in this system, governments maintained the controls on capital markets that had been implemented in the 1930s and 1940s (Ruggie, 1983: 209–11).

3. For an analysis of relationships between unions, the technocratic élite of Social Democratic parties, and new social movements, see Jenson and Ross (1986). For an account of issue-based radical groups, see McCann (1986).

4. This is, of course, an inadequate characterization of the rise of hyperliberalism, which in fact entails a complex of socio-political processes and strategies both in civil society and in the state and on both the domestic and global levels.

5. Reagan's economic policy, combining monetarism and a reflation of effective demand through increased military expenditures (military Keynesianism) resulted in high US interest rates, and an overvalued dollar, and thus provided both for cheap imports and capital inflows to finance the budget and balance of payments deficits. This order can still be considered hegemonic, since it has, in the main, been sustained through consent (Cafruny, 1989: 118–20). For global perspectives on the social implications of Reaganomics, see Davis (1984) and Lipietz (1989).

6. This is as long as a stable macroeconomic environment, supervision of international financial activity, and international lender of last resort functions are present to avert endogenously produced financial crises. According to Helleiner (1994) the 'weak regime' of the BIS is sufficient in this regard.

7. This relies upon Mjøset (1987: esp. 410–11).

8. This is not to imply that the Nordic Models are the only existing examples of 'disarticulated Fordism'.

9. This distinction was originally formulated by Titmuss (1974: 30–1, cited in Korpi, 1983: 190–1). In the institutional welfare state, social policy is considered an integrated part of society, not an emergency substitute to the market and family in the provision of need, as in the marginal/residual model typical for other Western welfare states in the post-war period.

10. Compare Matti Alestalo and Hannu Uusitalo's account of Finland's welfare state development with that of Sven E. Olsson (Sweden), Stein

Kuhnle (Norway), and Lars Nörby Johansen (Denmark) in Flora (ed.) (1986).

11. Wage costs did not increase more in Sweden than in the other Nordic countries, but its export performance was worse. Thus, there has to be an alternative explanation. According to Erixon, the key causes of the cost crisis was the revaluation of the Crown (as Sweden entered the European monetary snake), increases in employers' contributions in the financing of public sector expansion, and poor productivity development. The latter points to the importance of the particular product composition of exports. The first factor points to the importance of the crisis of the international monetary order. The second factor points to an increase of the public sector that could not be granted within the balance of payments constraint.

12. Swedish export industry consisted of firms in previously oligopolistic markets that in the 1970s came to face price competition. Exports in special steel made up a significant portion of exports, and Sweden was also affected by the particularly severe world crisis in that sector. For an exposition of the product cycle theory, see Vernon (1971: 65–77, 107–09).

13. See *Economic and Industrial Democracy* Volume 15, Number 3 (1994).

14. Denmark has however, a comparatively generous unemployment insurance system.

15. The continued tendency towards a drain of productive capital is indicated by the acceleration in foreign direct investment, without corresponding inflows in Finland and Sweden (IMF, 1990). Of the world's top 10 most 'stateless firms' (% sales and assets abroad) in the world, three are Swedish (one is Swedish–Swiss, ABB), three are Swiss, one Dutch, and two are British (Fagerberg, 1991: 208). Market proximity is the most important factor, motivating foreign investment for Swedish firms (Bergholm and Jagrén, 1985: 71–160).

16. I am grateful to Professor Ulf Olsson for this point.

17. Given the disproportionate financial capacities of the Swedish investment bank and the global reach of Swedish transnationals, it would be virtually impossible for Sweden to achieve effective steering through bank capital as in Japan and France. Pontusson's (1992) account of the failure of Swedish industrial policy in the 1970s points to these types of steering problems. However, by intervening at the profit augmentation stage, and by mediating through strategic portfolio capital on the stock market, wage earner funds might have achieved effective steering. By cutting off 'excess profits', and channelling them to special funds, wage earner funds would also have eliminated the dilemma of solidaristic wage policy to raise sufficient profits for investments without risking wage drift (Martin, 1984: 271–7).

18. There were competing, and potentially contradictory, objectives of structural revitalisation and labour representation in this wage earner fund proposal. And, if anything, labour representation was emphasized (Åsard, 1978). Although this is not incompatible with structural revitalization, it was unclear how revitalization would be ensured.

19. Corporations of the Wallenberg/SE-Bank sphere, with liberal affinities emanating from an ethos of 'family ownership', had always been reluctant participants in capital-labour accords.

20. In the elections of 1982, SAP was re-elected mainly because they were believed to be able to ensure full employment. Yet their commitment to wage earner funds was highly unpopular (Lewin, 1992: 371–2). The lack of ideological resonance between full employment and wage earner funds is striking, considering that the wage earner funds were a means to rescue the Rehn–Meidner model.

21. Memoirs of the Minister of Finance between 1982 and 1990, Kjell-Olof Feldt, describe how Prime Minister Palme, reacted to pressure from the Central Bank and the Ministry of Finance to deregulate capital markets. In meetings, Palme's body language became increasingly negative and hostile. Just as Feldt expected Palme to reject the proposal, Palme snapped, 'You do whatever you want, I don't understand any of this anyway' (Feldt, 1991: 260, my translation).

22. Based on interview with Per-Olof Edin, Chief Economist, LO, Stockholm, 16 April 1993. According to Edin, '[In the post-war period] finance had been held in check so that it could be our faithful servant.' This created an 'open flank' in the Social Democratic movement when the problem of dealing with a structural deficit in the new global financial environment arose.

23. See Söderström (1989). Bergström (1993) points to the importance of the intellectual leadership of the SNS in the advocacy of a norms-based monetary policy in Sweden.

3 Finance, Production and Panopticism: inequality, risk and resistance in an era of disciplinary neo-liberalism[1]

Stephen Gill

'The most anxious man in a prison is the governor.' (George Bernard Shaw, *Man and Superman*, 1903)

Recent growth in the power of capital relative to labour and in the way it reconstitutes certain ideas, identities and interests, and forms of state, is the primary political content of the processes of globalization, but this content is always localized and refracted through various social and cultural forms. The globalization process is a hierarchical one, and is associated with economic constraints and political pressures – or forms of discipline in society. One way to understand the functioning of aspects of power and discipline in the specific conditions of North American civilization – and to a degree in other OECD societies – is with reference to the Panopticon: the blueprint for the perfect prison that Michel Foucault (1979) took from the utilitarian social engineer Jeremy Bentham (1859).

The Panopticon can be taken as both a form of social myth and an exemplar of important political practices by some of the forces of large-scale corporate capital and associated elements in the G-7 states to attempt to institutionalize pervasive and perhaps all-encompassing forms of social control. It is a myth because it poses the issue of the possibility and desirability of politically constructing and maintaining a certain form of order whilst advocating the efficiency and welfare of a commodified economic system that is in principle based upon spontaneous and self-regulating forms of economic activity, co-ordinated through markets. Nevertheless, the practices of what we call here 'panopticism' are growing, and largely based upon the gathering of large amounts of personal data on individuals through transactional and other activity. The main purpose of these practices is to categorize, construct and channel the behaviour of individuals and groups so that these people can be monitored, normalized and manipulated for purposes of profit or avoidance of loss.

Nevertheless, in North American civilization (and in somewhat different ways in the OECD nations more generally), the Panopticon relates principally to those individuals and populations that are integrated into the privileged, corporate circuits of production, consumption and finance. In the context of the wider global political economy, these people represent less than 10 per cent of the world's population. The rest of the world's population – that is its vast majority – is in effect excluded from these islands of normalized affluence, since they do not represent opportunities for exploitation and profit. There people, however, may pose a threat to the privileged circuits and as such the systems of policing and military organization are in part configured to prevent them from threatening the basis of the social order that underpins the global political economy as it is defined here.

In North America, levels of not only unemployment, but also household indebtedness rose, especially in the 1980s. These developments, along with reforms in social security and tax administration, had the effect of binding workers to the disciplinary structures of not only the workplace, but also the finance and credit structures, and the global political economy, under the general and intensified surveillance of the state, especially as risk was gradually de-socialized for a majority of the population. At the same time, the use of surveillance and sorting techniques for maximising knowledge about, and influence over workers, savers and consumers – for example credit-card holders – appears to be growing in those parts of the private sector which are associated with what has been called the 'culture of contentment' (Galbraith, 1992), a phenomenon known in Western Europe as 'two-thirds society' (the other third of the population is increasingly marginalized).

Indeed, such techniques are part of a broader process of social transformation involving a widening of inequality and a process of marginalization. A type of social triage, especially noticeable in the sphere of finance, internally ranks those deemed to be sufficiently profitable consumers or workers, as well as effectively excludes those who have no value in terms of this particular form of Bentham's *felicific calculus*. What Bentham called the goal of maximizing the 'happiness' of the greatest number is therefore achieved at the expense of the immiserization of a large and growing minority of the population. In this way, the post-war social contract that existed in many OECD nations has begun to disintegrate in the shift towards a more disciplinary form of neo-liberal order, not only in the Anglo-Saxon nations but elsewhere, as the recent case of Mexico illustrates.

However, this situation is unsustainable politically since it intensifies the polarization of societies, heightens the forces that make for pronounced social conflict, and provokes resistance. Indeed, the indignation of the population is magnified when it becomes clear that as panoptic practices increase at the level of the individual and for the majority of the population, the mechanisms of surveillance and accountability in the world of high finance – for example in the exotic derivatives markets – seem notable by their absence. Indeed the lack of oversight and authoritative regulation of large parts of the global financial markets raises the question whether we will in the not-too-distant future see a major global financial collapse.[2] What is needed is a growing democratic consciousness of the nature of the global financial system and the collective risk that is posed to world society by the peculiar and Panglossian reliance on self-regulating market mechanisms for the majority of economic agents, whilst allowing for a socialisation of risk of a privileged minority (for example oligopolistic corporate capital and large institutional investors).

THE POLITICAL ECONOMY CONTEXT FOR CONTEMPORARY PANOPTICIST PRACTICES

The Panopticon is a Greek composite term which means 'sees all'. Foucault described the principle of panopticism as 'ensuring a surveillance which would be both global and individualizing whilst at the same time keeping the individuals under observation' through the illumination of space (Foucault, 1980:6). Bentham's (1859, Vol. IV) blueprint for the *Panopticon, or Inspection House*, is well-known. It was intended to ensure, through the all-seeing and dominating eye of the warder from a central watch-tower, a transparency which would also cause the inmates of the prison to exercise self-discipline, that is to act, as it were, as surrogate warders. It depended on the actuality, or possibility of constant surveillance, a method which made the technology of surveillance apparently both economical and effective over a large subject population. The Panopticon was never built – it was, like the economics of Adam Smith, more of an 'imaginary

machine', designed in the spirit of Newton. As Foucault understood
it, the Panopticon made power both visible and unverifiable. However, some Foucauldians have suggested that things have gone further,
to the point where increasingly surveillance is being built into the
labour process as well as the financial (or actuarial) structures: it has
become, in this context, both more visible and more verifiable.

Of course, in no society is there, or can there be, an Orwellian all-
seeing eye, although there are some historical precedents for attempts
to approximate this capability – for example the Janissaries of the
Ottoman Empire or the imperial bureaucracy of ancient China, that
used capillary forms of surveillance that pervaded the smallest village
or hamlet. Nevertheless, there seems to be a growing tendency
towards the increasing use of surveillance capabilities by the liberal
democratic state to regulate the new market society and to exercise
social control in a period of rapid social change. One possible explanation is with reference to the interplay between fiscal crisis and the
globalization of financial markets. The rapid globalization of finance
from the 1970s onwards occurred in the context of the recycling of
petrodollars in the Euromarkets following the first oil crisis in 1973,
and the onset of 'stagflation' and general economic slowdown in the
1970s. In this context, there was a growing tendency world-wide
towards fiscal crisis of the state, as tax revenues rose more slowly
than the cost of government expenditures (such as unemployment and
social insurance). This situation was manifest at all levels of government, from municipal to federal (the first major instance of the fiscal
crisis of the state in the USA was in New York City in 1975). The
counterpart to this development in the Third World was the so-called
debt crisis. Personal indebtedness also rose in the USA during this
period for a growing proportion of the population (see below).

Partly because of the growth in the international mobility of capital,
governments – of various political complexions – were pressured into
providing an investment climate judged attractive by global standards.
The 1980s saw a period of competitive tax-cutting initiated by the
supply-side policies of the Reagan Administration that forced other
states to respond by cutting their taxes or risk losing investment or
financial services business to lower tax jurisdictions. In the 1980s this
has gone with attempts to raise funds by the state through privatization and attempts to save money on services by charging user fees (for
instance, for medicines) or by instituting competition in the supply of
government services (for example, for cleaning and maintenance of
buildings; weapons procurement) as American leaders sought to 'rein-

vent' government (Osborne and Gaebler, 1992). Moreover, as economic stagnation continued, governments have had to pay increased attention to collecting tax revenues (and raising cash through privatization) in an age where the ideology (but not the reality) of the balanced budget (or of 'financial stringency' and 'prudence') has come to prevail in economic discourse. This has, according to Steinmo (1994), created a more 'activist tax state', and traditional forms of state intervention in the economy to promote redistribution have declined in OECD nations. Indeed, much of the work which has gone into the 'reform' effort in the former Soviet Union by the international financial institutions and the western governments has been concerned with the construction of more effective databases and population profiles, and methods of tax collection. More generally, the world-wide trend has been to attempt to introduce more 'business-like' approaches in public administration, with the neo-liberal governments of New Zealand in the 1980s and 1990s at the vanguard of the new thinking.

Another antipodean nation, Australia, like New Zealand, is also a typical liberal-democratic society (along with Canada, the UK and the US), and in different ways to its southern neighbour, illustrates aspects of the general trend I have noted. Australia has recently experienced fiscal crisis and the change in the political landscape, especially as political discourse shifted away from social democracy towards conservatism and neo-liberalism. Whilst the economy was liberalized over the last 20 years, the law enforcement, taxation and government benefits agencies gained increased power within the state apparatus (one impetus was the growth in violent crime and crimes against the person, as well as white collar crime). The social security ministry shifted to more rigorous monitoring of its clients, in a return to the type of method akin to the reforms which Bentham and other utilitarian liberals advocated for paupers, that is premised upon 'inspectability' of claims and obligations. In other nations it has become part of the normal discourse of government to speak of 'workfare programmes', in part because of the growing resentment of many taxpayers towards the unemployed and those who are the recipients of welfare payments.

Noteworthy here is that private firms in various countries also have massive centralized databases, much of which contain public information, and thereby the difficulty of separating public and private aspects of data-gathering, coding and surveillance – a difficulty which has also arisen in the USA as a result of the proliferation of private security agencies and guards, which now significantly out number 'public' police (official law enforcers often rely on their private counter-parts for effective urban policing in the USA).[3] A notable example of such private information corporations is TRW, a US-based credit-rating and marketing organization which claims to have detailed economic and social data on 170 million American citizens (the US population is about 254 million). Another important example which shows that there is, at the same time, a struggle over the proliferation and potential decentralization of control over data-bases was in 1990 when the Lotus Corporation withdrew its plan to market a product called *Marketplace: Households*. This product was withdrawn because of 30 000 protests from an angry public concerned that such a decentralized system was a grave threat to personal privacy. The product had detailed information on 80 million US households (120 million people), including name, address, and significant detail on shopping habits and income (phone numbers and credit-ratings were omitted in anticipation of privacy complaints) (Gandy, 1993).

THE LABOUR PROCESS: TECHNOLOGY, POWER AND EXPLOITATION

Bentham's Panopticon, conceived in 1791, was modelled on a factory run by his brother Samuel in Russia, and was based on, and sought to rationalize, the practices of asylums, schools, monasteries and hospitals, as well as factories and work-houses for the poor. Later, when we observe the emergence of Taylorism and scientific management, we can note the use of similar systematic technologies of worker control in capitalism, to place not only shop-floor workers, but also supervisors and managers under surveillance and thus to constitute, objectify and exploit labour more systematically. One might argue that the technical capacity to carry out these forms of hierarchical surveillance has increased with the advent of new technologies. Thus surveillance and 'disciplinary power' has been built more firmly into the labour process, especially in the computerized 'office factory' with its banks of video screens, and in assembly lines where managerially defined work rhythms and tasks are embedded in the machinery.

In other words, a change in technology does not necessarily mean a change in the fundamental social relations of capitalism, for example alienation and exploitation. The key issue is power and the control over the conditions under which the technology is used, and the purposes of its use, since labour-saving technology can be a potential or actual source of emancipation (from the washing machine to the internet). More generally, some surveillance technology may be quite beneficial and is needed to ensure the supply of global public goods – for example in the verification of arms control agreements, in monitoring the ecosphere, depletion of rain forests, climate patterns, etc.

Thus the introduction of such techniques is often banal and some studies have suggested that new information technologies in the workplace are not really any more intrusive or degrading than face-to-face surveillance, although computers do create new occasions for monitoring by generating more information which is of use to managers. On the other hand, there is clearly a great deal of resentment and anxiety in the ranks of middle management, as the new technologies are introduced in ways which make their own positions much more insecure. Not all of the new technological developments are as 'carceral' as the panopticist metaphor implies – some are liberating, but ambiguities abound. A recent example of industrial restructuring using advanced technologies in ways which are premised on mutual, and relatively non-hierarchical forms of organization is Asea Brown Boveri (ABB), the Swiss–Swedish engineering giant. In the early 1990s ABB sought to transform its production organization in what it calls 'a new industrial revolution'. According to Robert Taylor, this strategy was inspired by a text written by the Boston Consulting Group, *Competing Against Time* (1990). Restructuring along these principles is advanced in Sweden, where work responsibilities have been decentralized into work teams at the same time as worker skills have been enhanced in order to cut production cycles from 86 to 35 days. This strategy to boost productivity is based on blending so-called 'lean production' methods pioneered in Japan, with 'Swedish work culture', premised on a coalition between management and unions. This has allowed the distinction between administration and production to be largely abolished. However, the plan means that 25 per cent of the labour force will be made redundant.[4]

On the other extreme, however, the new technologies can be, and are being used in an ultra-exploitative and coercive manner to not only increase the intensity of work but also to control the actions and rhythms of workers and to keep them monitored genetically and biologically. Gramsci (1971: 279–318) noted the seeds of this development in his analysis of 'Americanism and Fordism', where the innovation of new means of accumulation required the creation of a new type of worker. A contemporary example of this is the way production tasks are redesigned so that they can be performed by robots, so that the role of humans in the factory is reduced to filling in for the robots when the robot malfunctions – a development akin to the nightmare of Fritz Lang's *Metropolis*. New auto assembly lines run by General Motors embody this idea, and they are accompanied by mandatory drug testing and urine analysis which in effect, are designed to mandate the elimination of workers who, it is claimed, are unfit to work to the technologically and managerially defined rhythms (Sakolsky, 1992: 115–26). Indeed, it can be argued that for the vast majority of workers in the OECD since the mid-1970s there has been an intensification of work, and new managerial strategies have been combined with new technologies to increase the direct and indirect forms of surveillance and control. Stress and anxiety levels have increased. As the power of capital has grown, relative to labour, workers have found that their real incomes have stagnated, and for many during the 1980s, have fallen and continued to fall.

This is part of the broader climate within which to consider new forms of workplace surveillance. According to the US Office of Technology Assessment, such technologies are intended not only to improve the performance of workers (through monitoring output, use of resources and communication), but also to monitor their behaviour, location, concentration levels, and predisposition to error (for instance, through drug testing). Now 98 per cent of the Fortune 200 largest corporations in the USA screen potential employees by drug testing. Indeed, the number of major US corporations that use drug-testing to screen applicants and workers has risen by 277 per cent since widespread testing began in 1987. About 30 million US workers are subject to annual tests. In addition, Federal regulations mandate testing of about 8.5 million workers, including government contractors (*Guardian Weekly*, October 6, 1996). Moreover, their personal characteristics, including not only their 'truthfulness' but also their predisposition to health risks are tested in many US firms. Other examples of the coercive and carceral use of what are called 'dual use' technologies – those which can be both socially useful but also potentially, socially repressive, are the use of electronic tags to monitor the location of workers (and which are also used to monitor prisoners either within the penitentiaries or when they are on parole). Genetic screening techniques plus lie-detector and other tests are coupled to credit-ratings and criminal checks made on individuals as part of the hiring process in a growing proportion of big US corporations, as well as in various (not just sensitive) areas of the state bureaucracy. In the case of US corporations, efforts are made to sort out potentially 'risky' workers in the hiring process – that is to avoid hiring those who may become 'sickly' workers and thus place a financial burden on the corporate health care plan (Draper, 1991).

The trend in North America is towards a surveillance process which increasingly focuses on the worker (for example, the worker is viewed as a risk, as well as a tool of production). Occupational risk is equated with the susceptibility of the worker rather than (hazardous) workplace conditions, especially in North America (Draper, 1991). This explains why there is such an increased interest in, and use of genetic testing, health, insurance, credit-worthiness and criminal history checks. For example, the numbers of Fortune 500 companies which use genetic screening for hiring decisions has doubled over the last decade, with now over 15 per cent using such techniques.[5] The key economic force driving this process in the USA is the combination of increasing health insurance costs and the lower costs of the genetic technologies. Elaine Draper (1991) argues that this form of the social construction of risk is linked to a broader tendency in the OECD countries – the rising use of genetic explanations for social phenomena.

All of these measures have prompted different forms of resistance, either passive or active, including strikes, work stoppages and go-slows, and even collusion between workers and line managers to escape surveillance from above. Other techniques include 'anticipatory conformity' and 'appearance management' (Sakolsky, 1992: 117–18). These forms of resistance had their precursors prior to the onset of industrial capitalism, for example weavers' riots in London, and peasant revolts and poaching in Britain, after the enclosure of agricultural lands and the appropriation of the traditional commons in Britain in order to capitalize agriculture in the seventeenth century. Such struggles continued in the eighteenth century (Hill, 1961).

'TRIAGE' AND THE RECONFIGURATION OF SOCIAL AND FINANCIAL RISK

Oscar Gandy (1993) traces the origins of panoptic surveillance and normalizing techniques to pre-industrial times, and to the notion of *triage*, a French expression which means to pick or to cull: to sort out the good apples from the bad. In English it means 'the grading of marketable produce'. The term *triage* has more frequently been associated with medical decision-making, for example, in a situation of mass battlefield casualties, where only those most likely to survive and fight are given treatment.

The bulk of the informational bases for modern panopticism are everyday transactional activities that leave traces which can be (electronically) recorded, stored, sorted and evaluated, in part according to the application of statistical and other evaluation principles.[6] Much of this is premised on techniques associated with insurance: the avoidance of risk. Examples of this are numerous, but they include credit and financial companies, insurance and health firms and marketing corporations. This kind of information gathering, and its sorting into categories is now so routine that it is built into the process of everyday life – this is elaborated below.

Modern *triage* techniques – in the context of market forces – are used to marginalize or eliminate 'unproductive' and high risk individuals, and to identify those who can be 'constructed', normalized or captured as workers and consumers. In the USA, this type of direct and indirect sorting process is applied across a range of activities by bureaucracies of government and large corporations. This has meant that, for example in the medical field, perhaps 30 per cent of the total population has no effective health care insurance, because state provision is inadequate and in the private sector they are considered too 'risky' to cover or to treat.

When risk-avoidance rules are applied (some by computer programme) to credit and insurance/health applications, high-risk individuals may be automatically eliminated from authorization of credit, from private health insurance, or, as an implicit condition for future insurance cover, women may be coerced into pre-natal screening. The process of credit-rating affects the conditions under which loans are extended, and the rate of interest which is paid. To obtain credit means giving access to a great deal of personal information and this is in turn manipulated into sorting categories, as well as sold on the marketplace. The credit-rating process is intimately bound up with the production process, not only in terms of the rating of corporate bonds which price the interest rate for loaned funds for investment in plant and machinery or for research and development, but also, as noted, in terms of the recruitment of labour. Companies increasingly refer to credit information agencies when considering new employees: those who have demonstrated their ability to service debts are more likely to be hired, *ceteris paribus*, than those who have faulty records. Moreover, many poorer people cannot gain proper access to credit, and when they do, they pay much higher real rates of interest. This category means those who are poorest and most vulnerable, such as new immigrants, the poor, single-parents, the unemployed.

These changes are also bound up with the reconfiguration of civil society, in so far as certain aspects of risk (both market risk and credit risk) have, at least since the Second World War, been largely socialized in the OECD countries. What is emerging is contradictory. On the one hand, risk is shifted increasingly down to the personal level and hedging of risks takes a predominantly market form (such as the provision of private health care arrangements, private security guards, and so on). On the other hand risk is increasingly generalized (for instance, the environmental risks or market risks, such as a fall in the stock market undermining the life-savings of people, that is their pension fund investments). A key aspect of social life in the late twentieth century is the growth in the prominence of 'manufactured risk' (as opposed to natural risks and disasters, such as earthquakes), and this provokes attempts by individuals to provide for such risks (Giddens, 1990: 112–50). I would add to this that all of this is occurring in an era of state budget cut backs and the reduction of the socialization of risk provision for the majority of the population – and thus a greater privatization of the risk calculus at the level of the individual. Many people enter into information grids (such as in the case of credit provision) to facilitate their lives and obtain access to a valuable resources (credit and insurance). Indeed, some use cards to offset certain risks that they encounter in their everyday (financial) lives. Credit card use means that transactions are recorded; credit cards often provide insurance against counter-party risks, such as flight cancellations, faulty products, car accidents, and so on.

Moreover, in the USA – despite the apparent hegemony of market forces – there is some form of socialization of risk – but it seems to benefit an affluent minority of the population. Coincidentally those who benefit are the most politically active members of a society characterized by extreme political alienation and electoral absenteeism. Approximately half of the eligible voters do not participate in Presidential elections, and thus a President can be elected with less than 30 per cent of the potential vote; when the Republican Party led by Newt Gingrich gained control of the House of Representatives and the Senate in 1994 with the intention of pushing through their 'Contract with America' in 100 days (designed to decentralize government and to radically redistribute income from the poor to the rich) this victory was built on a narrow electoral majority that consisted of a little over 20 per cent of the potential vote. By contrast the electoral turnout in the October 1995 referendum on the sovereignty of Quebec in neighbouring Canada was 94 per cent of the eligible vote. This peculiarity of American politics may help explain why, for example, and as J.K. Galbraith (1992) notes, the US Federal government insures depositors for up to $100,000 per bank account: by definition, the poor (few of whom ever vote) will not have such large savings in a bank. When the Savings and Loans collapse occurred, it cost the US taxpayers over $250 billion to pay compensation to those with S & L accounts, that is mainly to the members of the 'culture of contentment'. Another phrase which reflects this state of affairs is the idea of 'corporate welfare' payments, at a time when social entitlements for the poor and needy are being reduced world-wide.

FINANCE, CREDIT-WORTHINESS AND CREDIT-CARDS

The 1980s was a period of tremendous change in the sphere of finance. One dimension of this change was a huge growth in indebtedness and credit expansion at all levels: from corporate to individual, from federal to local government. In the 1980s, access to credit became a key determinant of the reproduction of not only economic, but also governmental activity. This process has been commonly understood to be an indirect one, conducted within the context of the forces of supply and demand in the marketplace. However, especially from the early 1980s, the poor credit conditions and heightened competitiveness of the global political economy began to give more prominence to the role of credit-rating agencies, concerned with the monitoring and surveillance of firms and individuals, as well as municipal and national governments. Credit-rating agencies such as Moody's and Standard & Poor's became more influential. A good credit-rating became the *sine qua non* of economic status in United States society. In what former Librarian of Congress Daniel Boorstin once called 'the great democracy of cash', access to credit on reasonable terms means access to economic resources and indirectly to political power.

In North America, and in the US in particular, the materialism of liberal democracy means that the substantive conception of citizenship involves not only a political–legal conception, but also an economic idea. Full citizenship requires not only a claim of political rights and obligations, but access to and participation in a system of production and consumption. Central to the contemporary definition of participation in this system is access to the financial system, and, in particular, to the credit allocation process. Those who gain access to credit are ranked hierarchically (for instance, holders of American Express Cards, which are either Green, Gold or Platinum). Moreover, each 'cardholder's' behaviour profile is scrutinized on a daily basis, according to over 450 separate categories. Companies rank people according to financial and social status, employment record, criminal and health records, and so on. Not all of these records are integrated: but some are, apparently for private insurance, credit and health.

Today about 70 per cent of US families have at least one card, up from 50 per cent in 1970. Holdings of bank cards (such as VISA, MasterCard, Optima) has also risen quickly, and 54 per cent of all US families held these in 1989, up from 16 per cent in 1970. Bank card holding has increased further since 1989. In 1990 credit cards were used to purchase some $455 billion of goods and services, and credit card charges accounted for 13 per cent of all consumer expenditures, up from 10.8 per cent in 1980 (Canner and Luckett, 1992: 655). Credit growth dropped dramatically in 1991 as the so-called 'credit crunch' hit the USA after the excesses of the 1980s came home to roost.

Credit cards are used for two reasons: as a means of payment and as a source of credit. Interest rates are more critical for those who use the card for credit: as a debt instrument. Dependence on the use of cards for these purposes is increasing. Revolving credit (which is mainly unpaid balances) rose from $60 billion at the end of 1980, 19 per cent of all consumer instalment debt, to more than $240 billion at the end of 1991, which represented well over one-third of all consumer instalment debt which was outstanding (Canner and Luckett, 1992, Table 2: 656). Most credit of this type is unsecured, but increasing numbers of borrowers have to turn to a recent innovation, secured accounts: those with low incomes or poor credit histories (as with the case of Byron, discussed below). These accounts require borrowers to deposit a sum ($500–$1000) in a savings account, at low interest to gain a card and thus perhaps to rebuild a credit rating.

This reflects the higher losses associated with poorer people generally, with recessionary conditions and the search for greater profits in an increasingly competitive credit card industry. A study of the effects of deregulation in US banking for the American Management Association found parallel trends – indeed compelling evidence of a trend towards the segregation of banking services to create a three-tiered, hierarchical structure with the poor effectively marginalised out of mainstream banking facilities. The poor paid higher fees and received lower rates of interest on their deposits. The author found that these trends exacerbated their poverty (Jorgenson, 1986). Since that study the same trends have accelerated.

Despite relatively low profits (for example, when compared with mortgages and other types of lending) as the credit card industry was becoming established on a mass basis in the 1960s and 1970s, by 1984 the profitability of credit cards had risen above that for most other forms of lending, as personal indebtedness levels rose. Nevertheless, surveys indicate that in 1989 32 per cent of cardholders owed less than $500, and an additional 18 per cent owed between $500 and $1000, and most cardholders are relatively insensitive to interest rate levels (which in real terms have been very high for much of the last decade). Spreads between credit card rates of interest and those paid on deposit or other interest-bearing accounts were wider in 1995 than they had been for 20 years. At the same time delinquency rates did not rise any faster in the early 1990s than in previous recessions. This allowed the companies to increasingly nuance their operations:

> For the most part, card issuers have lowered rates selectively. In some cases, they have targeted their solicitations to individuals deemed to have certain desirable characteristics, an approach made more feasible by the development of extensive data bases and improved techniques for screening potential cardholders. Some of the largest national issuers have segmented their cardholder bases according to risk characteristics, offering reduced rates to a select group of existing customers who have good payment records; higher-risk late-paying customers are charged still higher rates.

The hierarchical sorting of credit card holders seems set to continue:

> In the future, segmented rate structures will probably become more widespread as lenders continue to try to categorize accounts by their profitability and price them accordingly. (Canner and Luckett, 1992: 666)

ECONOMIC CITIZENSHIP AND THE DEBT TRAP

Let us now try to describe how this process originates, and then look at a specific case.

In North America civil society prepares its future citizens for the moment when they attain the age of economic citizenship, in so far as this is reflected in the possession of credit cards. For example, a recent TV series, produced by the public service broadcasting network, TV Ontario (TVO), and shown in 1992, was an educational course in creating the conditions for obtaining a credit rating. To obtain a credit rating, as illustrated in the first programme, teenagers needed to realize that this is only possible through incurring debt (alone) and by carefully and consistently servicing the debt. Over time, this would establish a clear and documented record of financial rectitude. However, the first problem was access to the initial loan, since this would require a guarantor, who, almost inevitably, would be a parent.

Nevertheless, upon successful servicing of a relatively small, initial loan, this particular shackle of parenthood could be sundered, in anticipation of a larger loan, for example, to buy an automobile. The question is, how does a young person service such a loan? The TVO programme emphasized that teenagers should take full responsibility for servicing the loan, for example, by obtaining weekend or evening employment in a grocery store. This would have the combined effect of showing their ability to be good employees as well as maturing, responsible adults.

In this way, young adolescents are groomed for entry into not only the consumer-credit economy, but also, the production structure. Thus, the ability to gain access to the credit system in some ways anticipates the realization of their economic citizenship. In other words, the acquisition of relatively independent access to financial resources means that North American adolescents begin to develop a capacity to transcend the more traditional forms of discipline associated with the family and the school. In so doing however, one form of discipline is penetrated and transformed by another: market discipline. In a sense, generational conflict belonging to the sphere of the family is transcended by a common subordination to the laws of the market.

Of course, the capacity to enter the credit system in this way is not equal for all, since the initial point of entry into the credit system rests upon the credit-worthiness of the initial guarantor of the first loan.

A recent article in the *New York Times* examined the case of a forty-year old hospital administrator who was striving 'to restore a tarnished credit-rating'. 'Byron' had accumulated more than $30,000 in debts, mainly through use of credit cards for tuition bills, furniture loans, and other household expenditures. Hounded by creditors,

Byron sought help from 'a local consumer credit counselling service. The service interceded with the creditors and now Byron is paying $649 a month to satisfy the last of his debts.' Byron kept to the schedule of repayments and is now repairing his credit-rating. The article pointed out the costs of doing nothing to deal with the credit problem. The article quoted Jewell L. Bailey, vice president for education with the Consumer Credit Counselling Service of Oregon, which handled Byron's case:

> Without a good credit rating, you may not be able to find an apartment or even get a job...Many more employers are ordering credit reports, and a good report is often the deciding factor when a company must choose between one candidate and another.[7]

Information is routinely gathered and stored by credit bureaux on major credit card expenditures, or for loans to finance purchases such as automobiles or houses. Credit bureaux gather information on credit users and sell it to banks, private companies and retailers. The information includes what each account holder owes, or has paid, and whether the payments are up to date. It also includes whether debt collection agencies, or other methods, have been needed to secure payment for bills. Other information, which is within the public domain, such as bankruptcies, or failure to meet taxation payments, are also routinely included. Negative information is usually kept on these records for up to seven years and bankruptcies for ten. Moreover:

> And, in three special instances, negative information may be reported indefinitely: if you apply for $50,000 or more in credit, if you apply for a life insurance policy with a face amount of $50,000 or more, or if you apply for a job paying $20,000 or more (and the employer requests a credit report).[8]

In the case which has just been outlined, the repair of Byron's credit rating was a painful but necessary process, for him and his family. The burden of servicing is one thing, the black mark against his ability to be part of the productive economy is another. His future access to credit and employment may have been permanently jeopardized even after he has fully repaid his debts. To repair Byron's credit required not only harder work and longer hours on his part, but also on his wife's, since she was forced to take up part-time employment. In this way, the debt burden mandated an additional labour supply, in much more coercive conditions than might have otherwise been the case. It is common in North America for blue-collar and white-collar employees to have more than one job and it is increasingly rare that such second jobs are regulated by unions.

THE RISKY BUSINESS OF GLOBAL FINANCE

Global finance is part of the transnational historical structures which intensify the pressures and constraints felt by Byron and the children of North America (and elsewhere) in their everyday lives. Yet it is a system which lies in part outside of national structures of governance and systems of accountability. It operates in a situation of absence of, or under-regulation, partly caused by the competition between financial centres, with the leaders being New York, London, Singapore, Tokyo, Paris and Frankfurt, with Chicago the leader in financial and commodity futures. For example, by 1994 the *daily* flow of foreign exchange transactions world-wide may have exceeded $1 trillion or about the total foreign exchange holdings of all the central banks of the major industrialised nations (Miller, 1995), and London is the leader in this sector. This is despite the fact that perhaps no more than 10 per cent of all financial transactions are ultimately related to real economic activity (that is to finance trade flows or capital movements). Much of the rest is related to speculative activity, money laundering and tax evasion, as well as the offsetting of risk, for example in the derivatives markets. This does not mean, however, that somehow we are seeing the emergence of a 'casino capitalism' (Strange, 1986) where finance has become detached from production. Rather the situation is a more complex and changing one.

Part of the context for the globalization of financial markets was the explosive growth in the so-called Euromarkets and offshore centres, plus the intensification of financial innovation in the 1970s. Moreover, since the early 1970s, rentier interests in the USA and in other OECD nations (for example the UK) have been at the vanguard of efforts to liberalize global finance, efforts which accelerated in the 1980s (and included ongoing pressure on Japan, for example in the Yen–Dollar negotiations). The USA has also used its influence within the G-7 and the multilateral financial agencies such as the IMF and the World Bank, to press for financial and wider economic liberalization in the Third World and in the former communist countries.

US-based financial power, then, is at the centre of the transnational structures associated with the 'G-7 nexus', but in the sphere of finance other financial centres and sets of interests are important.

Much of contemporary finance (including the financing of manufacturing or agriculture) has taken a quasi-prudential form, given the propensity to speculation which the system offers and because of the financial risks associated with unstable swings in prices, currencies and interest rates. Nevertheless, the global financial system now seems to be under-regulated and may be vulnerable to collapse. For example, a review of the recent annual reports of the International Association of Securities Regulators (IOSCO) reveals the rapid strides being made in the integration and automation of stock markets world wide, and a growing concern – especially since the 1987 world stock market crash – over the adequacy of surveillance mechanisms and the monitoring of traders by supervisors. Impetus for the introduction of ever-higher levels of technology in finance has come from the USA and Canada, with the US NASDAQ market a leader in 'automated market surveillance facilities' (Bröker, 1988). Linked to this was growing competition in financial services which was a major trend of the 1980s. Because of the fungibility and mobility of financial forms of capital, holders of such capital respond to changes in information very rapidly indeed (in many cases this response is automated through computerization).

Increasingly, global finance is characterized by the explosive growth of exotic financial instruments (such as derivatives) which, it is argued, are designed to offset or hedge various risks in a market-based system. These risks include vulnerability to market risk (involving price fluctuations); counter-party credit risk (threat of default by the other party to a contract); liquidity risk (when one financial instrument is difficult to replace quickly at something approximating its 'fundamental' value); operational risk (for instance, failures of internal control, perhaps involving fraud, human error or computer malfunctions). There are, in consequence, derivatives for equities, for hedging credit risk and for foreign exchange options, as well as for agricultural commodities, retailing, and the so-called 'emerging markets'. Very few people, however, know exactly what derivatives are, other than that they are financial products that are derived from other products and flows – that is, apart from the few individuals that actually create them.[9] More to the point, however, is that these instruments were initially introduced to maximize financial profits in an era of stagnation in the OECD. Moreover, much of their explosive growth in the early 1990s, as in the 1980s, was driven by greed. As a result, many of the new financial products were very highly leveraged – in ways that have parallels with the junk bonds of the 1980s.

In the early and mid-1990s there was growing international concern at the degree to which such derivatives might be, as the noted financial journalist, John Plender put it, 'a multi-billion dollar accident waiting to happen', caused by overconfidence in market growth, loose regulatory or internal controls over dealers, and of course, ignorance about the products. Some companies lost huge amounts in derivatives trading, for example Metallgesellshaft of Germany lost at least $1.4 billion in oil derivatives (futures and over-the-counter swaps) in 1993, and was bailed out by Deutsche and Dresdner Banks at a cost of $2.43 billion. Kashima Oil of Japan lost some $1.5 billion in foreign exchange derivative trading in early 1994. The same fate has befallen local governments, for example in the UK, Hammersmith and Fulham, which had entered the sterling interest rate swap market as early as December 1983, on the advice of City of London brokers. Orange County, California, declared bankruptcy at the end of 1994 in the mother of all municipal defaults, caused by speculative losses in derivatives (in plain English, gambling with taxpayer's money). Since off-balance sheet derivatives trading is not only a kind of modern-day equivalent to alchemist's gold, but also, assumed to be a largely zero-sum game, these losses were, it is suggested, offset by the gains of others. Nevertheless, a 1993 Bank of England study, quoted by Plender, had concluded that the trading by largely unsupervised hedge funds was a 'a supervisory hole at the very heart of the derivatives markets', partly reflecting the absence of a panoptic or surveillance capability in the derivatives industry:

> In this twilight world everyone depends heavily on the rating agencies. Yet Moody's, for one, admits that a large proportion of outstanding contracts are too new for it to feel sure that the risks are low... [moreover] risk-shifting instruments also have a way of pushing risks on to those least able to absorb them... The real problems, both for individual banks and for the system, are about opacity, leverage and lack of managerial competence. Central bankers will have to be on their mettle if that potentially lethal combination is not to lead to trouble.[10]

A widely-publicized example of the lax forms of supervision practised by the authorities and by the headquarters of the parent bank was the collapse of Barings Bank in 1994, with losses in the region of £860 million in early 1995. These losses were linked to the gambling exploits of Baring's star trader, 28-year old Nick Leeson. Based in Singapore, Leeson made bets on the Singapore and Osaka derivatives exchanges on expected upward movements on Tokyo Nikkei 225 Index, with futures and options contracts, but failed to sufficiently hedge his positions since he was after a huge profit. His strategy came unstuck because investor sentiment began to turn against Japan because of fears of a potential banking collapse; the Nikkei fell further because of the Kobe earthquake. Barings – once the subject of a bail out 100 years earlier in the era of *haute finance* – was then bought by Nederlanden Group for £1.[11]

Nevertheless, the story is not just one that involves so-called 'rogue' traders like Leeson or lax internal controls as manifested by Barings (and poor supervision by the Bank of England). Many of the world's biggest players (and speculators) in the global financial markets are pension funds and insurers, as well as the large hedge funds who compete to increase their post-tax rate of return, to assure fund growth and attract more customers/savers. There are some signs that these institutional investors, as well as 'small' investors are becoming more cautious in light of these huge losses, pressing for more conservative, risk-averse financial products. However, what is still needed are attempts to raise the awareness of *all* pension contributors/holders as to what is, or might be, really happening to their life savings, and to alert them to the potential dangers of their savings being linked to many of the exotic financial instruments.

Despite the surveillance capacities of the regulators and the private credit-rating agencies, for example much of US investment banks' derivative dealings are carried out through unsupervised special-purpose subsidiary firms, who, paradoxically, are often given higher credit-ratings than their parent bank. Moreover, little information is disclosed about the counter-parties to the contracts issued, so that the creditors of Kashima Oil might have thought they had holdings in an oil company, when in fact its business was really foreign exchange dealing. The global financial system is only as strong as its weakest link. Is this in Japan or is it in New York or Singapore? In the summer of 1995, regulators from the world's 10 major financial centres agreed to increase mutual information flows and pressed banks and institutional investors to develop better 'in-house' risk assessment systems. It remains to be seen whether these will be sufficient.

Indeed, one possible danger in a systemic sense is that, derivatives *are* ultimately based on the provision of real goods, services, resources and commodities, although often at many times removed from the point of production. Moreover, there are signs that the futures exchanges that sell the bulk of derivatives are linking up, electronically to facilitate mutual trading and create new products, thus making regulation more difficult and maximizing the possibility of what bankers call 'contagion effects'.[12] It is also worth noting that derivatives operate not just at the level of world capitalism in a Braudellian sense – amongst the large transnational corporations, institutional investors and hedge funds that operate within and raise funds in the wholesale financial markets – they also have begun the pervade the economics of everyday life, although most people are totally unaware of this:

> The fixed-rate mortgage would not be possible without the use of derivatives, for example. Offers by shops of interest-free finance to buy goods such as cars or washing machines also rely on derivatives. Small businesses, too, use derivatives, chiefly to protect themselves against adverse movements in interest rates and exchange rates . . . such as an interest rate cap, which puts an upper limit on the rate of interest a borrower has to pay, an interest rate swap which allows the client to swap his floating interest rate payment for those tied to a fixed interest rate. Small investors also benefit from the increased use of derivatives by pension funds and other institutional investors in which they have a stake. Potentially, derivatives can enhance the performance of the fund, hence providing a higher return for each individual investor.[13]

What is important then is both the way in which financial innovation increasingly permeates every day life and the processes of consumption and production (few people are able to buy a car or a house by paying for it with cash) and how expectations concerning the future are shaped in part by the new financial structures (for instance, the likelihood of an adequate pension on retirement). Whilst much of this situation rests upon the self-regulatory capacity of market agents and market forces, many liberal economists point out that derivatives traders may be taking imprudent risks in anticipation of a government bail out, for example where the central bank acts as a lender-of-last-resort: a type of socialization of risk. However, structures of production (and the savings for pensions) involve longer-time horizons than those promoted in a climate of opinion which validates the get-rich-quick mentality of the 1980s and 1990s. Senior central bankers and regulators (many of whom move to the private sector they are regulating on retirement) seem to validate the present situation where there is an imprudent and myopic lack of oversight. Thus the longer time horizons of the archetypal small saver, Marx's famous 'English shop-keeper' (Marx, 1967: 609, and p. 609 fn. 1) can be contrasted with the short-sightedness at the highest levels of corporate capitalism and government. Increasingly, corporate finance officers (and the treasurers of public funds) seek to hedge risk with products they do not understand, and G-7 leaders do little about this.

CONCLUSION

This essay has sketched some of the normalizing and disciplinary trends principally within North American society, and shown how these serve, in a contradictory way, to systematically include and exclude individuals and groups from its peculiar forms and symbols of economic and social citizenship. The United States case, in some senses, reflects the global situation with regard to the nature of financial power at the micro-level of the individual, and how this relates to macro-financial structures, national and global. It also illustrates the complex links between finance, production and consumption in the processes of capital accumulation. It is not simply the case that finance hangs above the rest of the political economy, as it were, as a dominating and abstract force, since the interrelations are more complex whilst forming part of an order that I have called one of 'disciplinary neo-liberalism' (see also the chapter by Fantu Cheru and Stephen Gill for a more global application of the concept). Indeed, partly because of the centrality of the USA in the global political economy, especially in matters of finance, the United States case in some senses interrelates with those of other nations, as well as being one that can be used to indicate the logic of some of the more ominous of current trends. Such trends highlight the need for democratic and comprehensive re-regulation of money and finance and an attempt to socialize risks on a more democratic basis. However, it may take much bigger and more significant financial collapse than the 1994–95 Mexican peso crisis to trigger global action on this front.

Further, this chapter introduced certain Foucauldian ideas but repositioned them within an historical materialist framework so as to better account for those who are included and those who are excluded or marginalized in the political economy. The concept of panopticism, understood in terms of both surveillance and the normalization of the individual through disciplinary practices, may apply most intensely to those who are integrated into the production, finance and consumption structures of the corporate sector, for example to members of the 'culture of contentment' and to those who are attuned to and in harmony with the norms of the mass consumption culture.

Yet not everyone is willingly incorporated, and resistance to such normalizing practices is also occurring. Indeed, the intensification of surveillance in the work place and in the streets may be taken as signs of a crisis of motivation, social order and government legitimacy – signs that all are not equally contented in the democracy of contentment. Indeed the marginalized may have forms of knowledge that are not amenable to rationalization and discipline in the sense of Foucault's bureaucratic and corporate 'regimes of truth'. Some of these forces may be aligned to progressive movements, whereas others may be more reactionary and violent.

Thus, a strategy of incarceration and surveillance – linked to market discipline – may not be enough to sustain the prevailing forms of dominance and domination. Marginalized groups may actively seek to develop counter-hegemonic forms of power/knowledge, for example in that archetypal 'panoptic' society, apartheid South Africa, a society that incarcerated Nelson Mandela and other ANC leaders for decades. Here, state violence and surveillance could not prevent change, or indeed the possibility of communication between Nelson Mandela and his comrades even when they were kept in solitary confinement on Robben Island. Thus where Foucault represents a cry of outrage at the taming of the individual and a purely defensive strategy of localised resistance, historical materialism goes much further in an attempt to theorize and to promote collective action to create an alternative form of society – even from within a prison (where Gramsci sketched his famous notebooks on fragments of paper that were smuggled from the jail).

Notes

1.	This chapter substantially adapts and draws upon an essay originally published as, 'The Global Panopticon? The neo-liberal state, economic life and democratic surveillance', *Alternatives*, Vol. 20, No. 1 (1995) pp. 1–49, to whom acknowledgement is made. I would like to thank participants in the Vikersund symposium for comments, especially Robert

Cox for his criticisms of the first draft, and Randy Persaud for useful comments.

2. A failure of IMF and World Bank surveillance of Mexico's domestic economic developments in 1994 was part of the bungled devaluation that led to a plunge in the value of the peso in December of that year. The ensuing 'shock therapy' programme to stabilize the economy shaped by the IMF has led to a massive plunge in output, a huge growth in unemployment and widespread social misery and chaos. Here the bail-out led by the IMF and the United States government effectively socialized the losses of the large banks and wealthy individuals in Mexico, the USA, and elsewhere, that is losses associated with the assets held mainly in short-term Mexican public securities. At the same time, the costs of the bail out have been shifted onto the backs of the bulk of the Mexican population.

3. Ralph Blumenthal, 'As the Number of Private Guards Grows, Police Learn to Enlist Their Help', *New York Times* 13 July 1993; Clare Collins, 'Hiring Private Security Guards to Cut Neighborhood Crime', *New York Times*, 18 August 1994.

4. Robert Taylor, 'Resetting the clock', *Financial Times*, 10 February 1993.

5. Priscilla Regan, 'Surveillance and New Technologies: Changing Nature of Workplace Surveillance', paper to workshop, 'New Technology, Surveillance and Social Control', Queen's University, Kingston, Ontario Canada, 14–16 May 1993, pp. 8–9. There is a difference between genetic monitoring (for example to ascertain if workers are exposed to damaging health risks at work and which may therefore be of benefit to workers and to employers) and genetic screening, which smacks of the survival of the fittest. Moreover, genetic changes may occur as a result of processes unconnected to the workplace.

6. According to Gandy, in the USA, people who are less well educated and who watch a lot of TV are more likely to assume that the unrestricted provision of personal data, especially to private firms is a good thing, leading to better products and services. These people tend to have the jobs that are most routinized, predictable, calculable and controlled – they do not quite approximate the typical members of Galbraith's culture of contentment who on the whole are somewhat better educated and affluent, with more control over their time at work. The Canadian Federal Privacy Commissioner's report for 1993 stated that most Canadians were in a 'technological trance' and they were, on the whole, very complacent about the implications of the new information and other technologies (such as genetic screening). Geoffrey York, 'Privacy report warns of "Big Brother" computer', *The Globe and Mail*, 14 July 1993.

7. Deborah M. Rankin, 'Rehabilitating a shattered credit rating', *The New York Times* 16 January 1993.

8. Rankin, 'Rehabilitating a shattered credit rating'.

9. For example, a *Financial Times* Survey, 'Derivatives: evolution in the shadow of disaster' 16 November 1995, defined derivatives as 'a contract the value of which changes with the price movements in a related

or underlying commodity or financial instrument. The term covers standardised, exchange-traded futures and options, as well as over-the-counter swaps, options and other customised instruments.' The survey contained a glossary of terms for the uninitiated; these included 'barrier options', 'contangos', 'hybrid securities', 'quanto options' and 'swaptions'.

10. John Plender, 'Through a Market, Darkly', *Financial Times*, 27 May 1994.
11. It is said that futures and options contracts require a reasonable degree of mathematical sophistication and computer programmes. Their value changes on an hourly basis according to shifts in market indices, exchange rates and so on, and many options can be traded at very short notice. Leeson, who was authorized by the parent bank to make trades of up to £50 million without prior central authorization, had left his high school in the UK at the age of 18 having failed his 'A level' examination in maths.
12. The top 10 futures exchanges in terms of millions of contracts in 1994–5 were (1) Chicago Board of Trade 109.7; (2) Chicago Mercantile Exchange, 103.9; (3) BM&F, Brazil 71.7; (4) Liffe, London 68.9; (5) New York Mercantile 39.2; (6) Matif, Paris 36.6; (7) London Metals 24.3; (8) DTB, Germany 23.6; (9) Tiffe, Tokyo, 23.0; (10) Meffe, Renta, Spain 19.3. Source: *Financial Times* Survey, 'Derivatives: evolution in the shadow of disaster', 16 November 1995.
13. *Financial Times* Survey, 'Derivatives: evolution in the shadow of disaster', 16 November 1995, p. vi.

4 Restructuring the Global Division of Labour: old theories and new realities[1]

James H. Mittelman

Of all the great changes involved in restructuring the world today, the single most important force may prove to be globalization. A market-driven and multidimensional process, globalization renders obsolete invented divisions of the world into developed and developing countries, industrialized and industrializing nations, and core and periphery. The familiar imagery of a core, semi-periphery, and periphery no longer applies to a new structure that envelopes both vertically integrated regional divisions of labour based on the distinctive comparative advantages of different locations, and horizontally diversified networks which extend their activities into neighbouring countries as part of corporate strategies of diversification and globalization. The old categories do not capture the intricacy and variability of the integration of the world economy as well as the ways it constrains all regions and states to adjust to transnational capital. The global transformation now underway not only slices across former divisions of labour and geographically reorganizes economic activities, but also limits state autonomy and infringes sovereignty.

In a notable attempt to explain vast changes in the global political economy, Karl Polanyi (1957) held that the socially disruptive and polarising tendencies in the world economy were generated by what he called a self-regulating market, not a spontaneous phenomenon but the result of coercive power in the service of a utopian idea. He traced the tendencies in the world economy that caused the conjuncture of the 1930s and produced – in the context of a breakdown in liberal-economic structures – the onset of depression, fascism, unemployment, and resurgent nationalism, collectively a partial negation of economic globalization, leading to world war.

Like the global economy of the 1930s, the contemporary globalization process represents unprecedented market expansion accompanied by widespread structural disruptions. While escalating at a world level, globalization must be regarded as problematic, incomplete, and contradictory – issues to be taken up below. By globalization I mean the compression of the time and space aspects of social relations, a phenomenon that allows the economy, politics, and culture of one country to penetrate another (for an elaboration of this argument, see Mittelman, 1994a). A hybrid system, globalization intensifies interactions among, and simultaneously undermines, nation states. Although globalization is frequently characterized as a homogenizing force, it fuses with local conditions in diverse ways, thereby generating, not eroding, striking differences among social formations. Fundamentally an outgrowth of the bedrock of capital accumulation, this structure embraces and yet differs in important respects from trends posited by theorists of the International Division of Labour (IDL) and the New International Division of Labour (NIDL), two theses which provide both a point of entry for analyzing global restructuring and an opportunity for developing an alternative formulation.

To examine major facets of global restructuring, inquiry must revisit, even if only sketchily, previous attempts to come to grips with novel systems of production, the distribution of rewards, and the political and social consequences. Briefly reviewing classical theories of the IDL, though not allowing us to explore the far more complex features of contemporary capitalism, offers a fruitful way of posing relevant theoretical questions for later discussion. Plainly, it will be important to understand why and how classical authors understood and defined the IDL. Even from a short synopsis, it should be apparent that there are serious disagreements not only about what engenders the division of Labour, but even about what constitutes its essential characteristics. The IDL interpretation must be supplemented by the idea of a NIDL, which seeks to explain the shift of manufacturing from advanced capitalist to developing countries – a spatial reorganization of production in the second half of the twentieth century. After subjecting the NIDL thesis to critical scrutiny, I will propose another perspective, which might be called the Global Division of Labour (GDL).

My main argument is that the GDL involves a restructuring among world regions including their constituent units, notably states and export networks. This approach focuses on the interpenetration of global processes, regional dynamics, and local conditions. One element of reordering this hierarchical system is massive transfers of population from the Third World, eastern Europe, and the former Soviet Union to the advanced capitalist countries, though there are also significant migratory flows within the South. Acting as magnets attracting imports of labour, global commodity chains form networks that interlink multiple production processes as well as buyers and sellers. Mediating among these macro political and economic structures are micro patterns rooted in culture–family, communal, and ethnic ties.[2] Culture becomes a switch on the tracks of regulation and segmentation of the labour market.

Since prior meanings assigned to the term division of labour underpin my argument about the GDL, the first section of this paper examines the concept of IDL in classical political economy, while the second turns to the NIDL hypothesis. Next, by focusing on the interactions among levels of analysis – regionalism, migration, commodity chains, and cultural forces – in a globalizing division of labour, I will attempt to offer an alternative explanation of restructuring. On the basis of a juxtaposition of these three formulations – IDL, NIDL and GDL – the conclusion identifies trends and notes major aspects of an integrating and yet disintegrating world order, today marked by both the persistence of the nation-state system and a challenge from different types of non-state actors. Whereas states are increasingly subject to internal pressure for accountability to the governed, the agencies and forces of economic globalization are largely unaccountable to any group of citizens. The contradiction between the emergence of a clear preference for democracy in national political units and the lack of means to ensure accountability in world markets is a central feature of global restructuring.

THE OLD DIVISION OF LABOUR

Classical political economy

As first studied by Adam Smith, David Ricardo and Karl Marx, the division of labour refers to novel forms of specialization separating the production process into compartments, each one performing different tasks, with varying rates of profit and implications for comparative advantages in trade. Smith's 1776 treatise on the division of labour concerned the wealth of all nations and became the seedbed of modern theories. Positing a 'propensity to truck and barter' innate in humankind, Smith provided the first major attempt to examine the potential for the emergence of a complex division of labour that later developed during the industrial revolution and on the Continent.

The emerging industrial form of production, Smith argued, entailed the erosion of artisan skills and their replacement not by collaboration among several craftsmen but by co-ordination among a large number of people carrying out specific, assigned activities, enabling any one person to do the work of many. The combined labour of a work force in a single establishment outstripped the total effort of individual workers in the old system. Productivity gains were attributable to increases in dexterity because of the reduction of tasks to discrete operations, savings in time lost passing from one activity to another, and inventiveness stemming from intimate familiarity with and attentiveness to a single function. This specialization was paralleled by differentiation in other spheres as well – politics and society – as outlined in Smith's first book, *The Theory of Moral Sentiments*, published in 1759. Although classical political economists are frequently portrayed as positing that society is in large part driven by self-interest, Smith in fact also stressed that in civil society, social propensities constrain egoism and help to avert discord. *The Theory* contains ample discussion of 'fellow feeling', personal conduct, rules of justice and morality.

Smith remained optimistic that the evolving division of labour would be a propellant for higher standards of living and thus offer enormous benefits, but was not unaware of the disruptive and deleterious consequences of repetition and over-specialization. Notwithstanding the dehumanization of work in factories, he was sanguine about economic society insofar as the state provides public goods (notably in the realm of culture and education) to facilitate commerce, sufficient justice to protect from oppression and to secure property rights, and security from invasion. While market society necessitates a relatively autonomous state to sustain *laissez faire* and the division of labour, the scope of the domestic market is an inherent limitation. Whereas in inland, scattered, or scarcely populated areas, individuals retain the need to be able to do many kinds of work, it is trade that increases the reach of the market.

Entering the conversation at this juncture, Ricardo argued that commodities are valued according to the quantity of labour required for their production and can be enhanced through foreign trade, for the rules which govern the relative value of commodities in one country do not regulate the relative value of commodities exchanged among countries. Through the efficacious use of 'the peculiar powers bestowed by nature', each country 'distributes labour most effectively and most economically: while by increasing the general mass of productions, it diffuses general benefit, and binds together by one common tie of interest and intercourse, the universal society of nations throughout the civilised world' (Ricardo, 1932: 114). Hence, Ricardo's basic law of comparative advantage, which undergirds a good deal of contemporary theory, may be summarized as follows: the pattern of international trade is dependent on the principle of comparative labour costs, which holds that if two countries engage in trade relations, each one producing the same commodities, one country would sell the commodity in which its relative (rather than absolute) cost was lower and, similarly, the other country would sell the commodity in which its own cost was low. Like Smith's concept of division of labour, Ricardo's theory of comparative advantage presupposes the notion of civil society and the separation of politics and economics.

Viewing the division of labour as the 'prevalent characteristic of capitalism', Marx did not share Smith's and Richard's faith in the beneficial consequences of the division of labour in manufacturing, where tasks are partitioned and repartitioned, and of the division of labour in society as a whole. Marx maintained that the division of labour in manufacturing brings the labourer face to face with the material power of the production process, cutting down the worker to a detail labourer. Knowledge, judgement, and will are formally exercised only for the factory as a whole, often crippling the worker's body and mind as well. The detailed division of labour – subdivisions of tasks within industries – is thus distinguished from the social division of labour, which sets off whole groups from one another in society. Both criticizing and building on the theoretical foundations laid by Smith and Ricardo, Marx thus sought to recast their arguments and to make explicit a political dimension of division of labour theory.

Sociological theory

Notwithstanding the attempt by classical political economists to interweave economic theory and what is now regarded as industrial sociology, there were only minor advances in the theory of division of labour between the nineteenth century and the second half of the twentieth century, save the interventions of Max Weber and Emile Durkheim. Raising very different questions from the debate over the costs and benefits of increases in productivity surrounding the IDL, sociologists have given specific meaning to the notion of division of labour. Emphasizing 'specialisation of function' as a motor force in history, Weber held that 'functions may be differentiated according to the type of work, so that the product is brought to completion only by combining, simultaneously or successively, the work of a large number of persons' (Weber 1947: 225). To develop this basic proposition, he focused on aspects of the social relations engendered by the division of labour, and established a sociological typology applying to historical cases though not to the division of labour or the economy in general. Weber none the less envisaged the advance of the division of labour in tandem with the centralization of the means of administration – an overall trend toward bureaucratic specialization in all spheres of social life.

For Durkheim, the major issue is the structurally disruptive and cohesive tendencies in the division of labour, which ultimately furthers social integration or what he calls organic solidarity. Unlike mechanical social orders held together by common beliefs and values, modern organic societies rest on the complementarity of different specialized functions. In transitions where the division of labour replaces mechanical solidarity without yet developing the morality (that is, solidarity) to mitigate social tensions, an increased volume and density of interactions entail a prevalence of crime, economic crises, conflicts between labour and capital, and emigration. However, these forms of anomie would lessen, while flexibility and individual freedom would accompany an increasing specialization in the division of labour, which in turn promotes an integration of society.

Old theories, new realities

From this brief overview of the classical writers, it is clear that IDL theory provides a springboard for understanding modern capital accumulation, the expansion of the market presently manifest in economic globalization, and the social consequences of these processes. What is lacking in the theory, however, reflects the general limits to the classical tradition and has important implications for the contemporary period. Although the classical school allowed for the state to be the guarantor of the division of labour in a *laissez faire* economy, democratic or liberal forms of state were not deemed necessary. (Utilitarians like Jeremy Bentham and, later, liberals such as John Stuart Mill were concerned with forms of state. Conservative reformers like Bismarck and mercantilists, most notably Friedrich List, regarded the state as central to capital accumulation.)

The risk in stressing the logic of capital and labour costs while underrating the role of the state lies in invoking economism linked to the rising power of capitalism, a tendency somewhat corrected by the followers of Weber who emphasize divisions of labour by age, race, ethnicity and gender (Cohen 1987: 231–2). Though not silent about the role of culture, classical authors said relatively little about the attitudes, beliefs and habits of different strata in the international division of labour. Nowhere did they analyze, say, the constraints that some cultures place on the mobility of labour (as do contemporary Islamic communities in rural Malaysia, for example). In fact, classical political economy is not explicit about the spatial dimensions of the division of labour – a curious deficiency addressed in the NIDL thesis.

THE NEW INTERNATIONAL DIVISION OF LABOUR

Apart from contributions by Weber and Durkheim, the concept of division of labour remained largely dormant until the beginning of a spatial reorganization of production involving the formation and expansion of a world market for labour and production sites in the 1960s. Varying in emphasis from a neo-Smithian focus on changes in the world market to a neo-Ricardian one on capital exports, NIDL theorists sought to explain the shift of manufacturing from advanced capitalist to developing countries, with the fragmentation of production and the transfer of low skill jobs while the bulk of R & D activities is retained in the heartlands of world capitalism. Fröbel, Heinrichs and Kreye hold that the traditional international division of labour in which the Third World was relegated to the production of raw materials has markedly changed (Fröbel *et al.*, 1980; Lipietz 1985). Transnational corporations have established a global manufacturing system based on labour-intensive export platforms in low wage areas. This move toward industrialization in the Third World and a decline in manufacturing relative to Gross Domestic Product (GDP) in the West and Japan are driven by the structural capitalist imperative to maximise profits under conditions of heightened global competition.

With new technologies, especially space-shrinking systems of transport and communications, the sites for manufacturing are increasingly independent of geographical distance. Capital now searches not only for fresh markets but also to incorporate new groups into the labour force. Initially through the 'global assembly line' of textiles, many Third World women have become part of the international working class. It was the electronics industry which developed the first truly integrated world assembly line.

Contributing powerfully to understanding dramatic changes in the division of labour, Fröbelians clearly identified the growing power and sophistication of transnational capital and its ability to optimize differing opportunities for profit by decentralizing production across the globe (see Gordon, 1988, for qualifications to the NIDL argument). This approach also provides an important angle for studying North–South relations, especially large-scale migrations of capital to the Third World and specific linkages that increasingly differentiate countries at various levels of development.

The NIDL thesis, however, overstates the significance of cheap labour as the propellant of capital around the globe. Surely, low wages do not explain decisions of transnational corporations to touch down where labour is relatively costly (Fernández and Patrichia, 1989: 150–51). Locational decisions represent a mix of considerations and often favour countries such as Singapore where labour costs exceed those in neighbouring countries. Hence, a 1993 study of 47 countries by Business Environment Risk Intelligence (a private association with headquarters in Geneva, Switzerland, and operations in the United States) shows that on the basis of a weighted composite index, which measures the number of skilled and technically trained people against market requirements, the Singaporean labour force ranks

Table 4.1   Business environment risk intelligence: labour force evaluation measure (*points scored in brackets*)

Country	1993 position	1992 position
Singapore	1 (78)	1 (79)
Switzerland	2 (74)	2 (75)
Japan	3 (72)	3 (73)
Belgium	4 (71)	4 (71)
Taiwan	5 (68)	5 (69)
Germany	6 (65)	6 (66)
Netherlands	6 (65)	7 (65)
United States	6 (65)	8 (64)
France	9 (63)	10 (61)
Norway	10 (62)	9 (62)

Source: Singapore Economic Development Board, *Singapore Investment News* (May 1993), p. 8.

best in the world in productivity – ahead of its counterparts in runners-up Switzerland, Japan and Belgium (Singapore Economic Development Board, 1993: 8). Below is a labour force evaluation which reflects four indices: legal framework (a weighted average of 30 per cent), relative productivity (that is, output per worker day against wages – 30 per cent), worker attitude (25 per cent), and technical skills (25 per cent).

Another difficulty with the NIDL thesis is that the old international division of labour (for example, in agriculture) has not disappeared but coexists with the new division, forming what might be regarded as an articulation of the old and the new or a redivision of labour. If indeed the issue is to identify continuities and discontinuities, it is appropriate to ask exactly what is new about the New International Division of Labour. The claim that industrialization in the Third World is new neglects the establishment of import-substituting industries in Argentina, Brazil, and Mexico in the 1930s and 1940s. Actually, industrial growth in some parts of Latin America dates to the inter-war period (Gereffi, 1990: 3). The structuralist logic embraced in the NIDL perspective leads analysts to glide over historically specific conditions prevailing in individual countries, regions, industries, and sectors that form a pattern of incorporation into a global mosaic.

Moving beyond economism the key questions are (1) what conditions in respective zones of the world economy are propitious for entry into this division of labour? and (2) on what and whose terms? In other words, what are the political dynamics that both join and separate global linkages in production, exchange, and consumption?

THE GLOBAL DIVISION OF LABOUR

Regionalism and globalism

What is new about the contemporary period is the manner and extent to which domestic political economies are penetrated by global phenomena. There is no single wave of globalization washing over or flattening diverse divisions of labour both in regions and industrial branches (Henderson, 1989). Varied regional divisions of labour are emerging, tethered in different ways to global structures, each one engaged in unequal transactions with world centres of production and finance and presented with distinctive development possibilities. Within each region, sub-global hierarchies have formed, with poles of economic growth, managerial and technological centres, and security systems.

It would be fruitless to seek to define a single pattern of regional integration, especially a Eurocentric model emphasizing legal principles, formal declarations, routine bureaucracies, and institutionalized exchange. This would be an inadequate guide for infrastructural and production-based orientations – to some extent a reality and certainly a goal among the members of the Association of South East Asian Nations (ASEAN) and the Southern African Development Community. Regional divisions of labour are of course not static but change rapidly, reflecting expansion and contraction in production in different locales, the instantaneous movement of finance, the coalescence of production and trade networks, as well as the consolidation of production and distribution systems.

Though a diminished actor relative to global forces, the state facilitates the reorganization of production, and the interstate system remains an important point of reference in an integrated world society. With proper timing during a period when the world economy was robust, state interventions promoted remarkable economic growth in East Asia's Newly Industrialising Economies (NIEs) – Hong Kong, Korea, Singapore, and Taiwan – marked to varying degrees by fragmented and weak indigenous capitalist classes which have allowed the military and bureaucracy to control state apparatuses.[3] By such activities as coaxing foreign investors, ensuring ample quantities of scientific and engineering labour power, and offering a generous tax policy, the state in Singapore has played a key role in the country's 'free market' economy. To industrialize and attain upward mobility in the GDL, the state in East Asia has deliberately gotten the prices 'wrong' through incentives and subsidies to local business (Amsden, 1989; Gereffi and Fonda, 1992).

The state has also taken a hand in reconfiguring labour processes, sometimes through repression, partly to keep down the cost of labour, and also, as in Japan, by encouragement of experimentation with the 'just-in-time' manufacturing system. Calling for synchronized and continual supplies to reduce storage and overhead costs, this method can reduce the size of the labour force otherwise required to maintain production levels. The leading economic power in the Asia–Pacific, Japan has exported its 'just-in-time' system to neighbouring countries, demonstrating that regional hierarchies can contour patterns of labour supply within various zones of the global economy and exercise transnational influence over the bargaining power of workers.

Regional hierarchies form patterns of *inner globalization* and *outer globalization*. Although globalization is not a matter of choice, the former is inward looking and places greater emphasis on the regional market; the latter's outward focus seeks to reap maximum benefit from the world market. Whereas inner globalization enhances interactions within a region and may divert transactions from without, an open globalizing policy may in fact limit regionalism. In Asia, there are attempts to employ both strategies and, also, to combine them.

Within the Asian Regional Division of Labour (ARDL), a highly stratified hierarchy – Japan, China together with the other areas comprising 'Greater China' (Taiwan and Hong Kong–Macao), Korea and ASEAN, and Indochina – varies by industry and sector. The economic growth generated by the Japanese-led 'flying geese' pattern of regional integration, involving countries at quite different levels of development, suggests important distinctions among generations of countries to have penetrated global markets in diverse branches of industry (see Henderson, 1989, for a study of the semiconductor industry; Doner, 1991, on automobiles; and Dixon, 1991).

While the ARDL developed partly in response to different labour costs, today sub-regions play an important role as intermediaries between transnational corporations and the supply of cheap labour. Two 'global cities' in the ARDL, Singapore and Hong Kong, are regional hubs for concentrations of direct foreign investment. In an attempt to overcome limitations stemming from economies of scale, these regional centres have adopted a strategy of 'twinning', a type of co-ordination which is but one form of linkage.

Another blend of state initiative and private entrepreneurship is the concept of a Growth Triangle comprised of three nodes: Johor in peninsular Malaysia, the Riau Islands of Indonesia, and the city-state of Singapore. While Johor offers land and semi-skilled labour, Riau also has land and low-cost labour, and Singapore is distinguished by high quality human capital and a developed economic infrastructure. A propellant for economic growth, the Growth Triangle creates a wide manufacturing base with different factor endowments in each node and, thus, an incentive for transnational corporations to consider the region as a whole for investment. Introduced in 1990, there are signs that the triangle is attracting foreign investment and causing the migration of industries in search of specific factors of production. Problems associated with integration, however, include the potential widening of disparities in income and the emergence of a shanty economy on the fringes of industrial townships, especially with an inflow of workers of diverse ethnic backgrounds in Indonesia and of young female workers to staff assembly operations. Moreover, the Growth Triangle seems to rest on two legs, Singapore–Johor and Singapore–Riau, without a viable third link between Johor and Riau, both providers of cheap labour and land. To the extent that Singapore suffers an industrial hollowing out, with an exodus of industrial investment exceeding the rate of entry, there will be an increasing need to replace an ageing population with foreign workers (Kumar and Lee, 1991).

Given integrated, cross-border industrialization, both labour markets and capital markets reflect regional momentum within the ambit of economic globalization. In fact, the Growth Triangle shows signs of enlargement. The more ambitious concept of outer globalization, known as a 'crescent of prosperity', is a sub-regional scheme for joint utilization of resources. A bigger version of the Growth Triangle, the crescent would encompass Korea, Japan, China, Taiwan, Vietnam, Laos, Cambodia, Myanamar, and the six ASEAN countries (Vatikiotis, Rowley, Tsuruoka, and Shim, 1991).

With the emergence of integrated regional production and trade networks, a triangular pattern entails industrial relocation from Japan and the NIEs to ASEAN. The ASEAN countries import machinery, equipment, parts and supplies from the Asian home countries of foreign investors, using them to manufacture goods which are then exported to Western markets. Added to this triangular form of trade, other types of growth triangles are developing. Launched in 1992, a second sub-regional growth triangle within ASEAN links the Malaysian port-city and industrial centre of Penang (known as 'Silicon Island' in light of its sizeable semiconductor manufacturing base) along with its peninsular hinterland in Malaysia, the city of Medan and north Sumatra in Indonesia, and southern Thailand up to the city of Phuket. Another triangle under consideration would comprise the southern Philippines, Sabah in Malaysia, and north-eastern Kalimantan, Sulawesi and Maluku in Indonesia. Outside ASEAN, a triangle will join Yunnan, China, in a cross-border zone with parts of Laos and Vietnam. The formula in establishing these zones of inner globalization is to utilise small-scale, decentralised negotiations among fewer parties committed to locally based and relatively informal arrangements rather than to involve the cumbersome and time consuming bureaucracies of full regional groupings (Lim, 1992).

In contrast to autarkic forms of regionalizm in the 1930s, today there is considerable hostility to the formation of exclusionary trading blocs. Out of a commitment to *liberal multilateralism*, Japan is reluctant to support measures which bolster regional economic alliances and favours a policy of *de facto* economic integration with limited formalization (as for example, with the East Asia Economic Caucus.) From a liberal perspective, multilateralism may be defined as an 'institutionalized form which co-ordinates relations among three or more states on the basis of "generalized" principles of conduct' (Ruggie, 1992: 571, building on Keohane, 1990). Even including scholars like Ruggie (1993) who reject an orthodox realist interpretation and give credence to an 'extranational realm', the prevailing paradigm in academic journals on international relations acknowledges yet fails to theorize the role of new social movements in multilateralism and, therefore, is of limited use in explaining the extent to which economic globalization reinforces or undermines the neo-liberal order. Quite clearly, globalization suggests the need for global economic management, but existing international institutions were designed to co-ordinate a system of nation states in which each state was supposed to be sovereign over its own domestic economy (Emmerij, 1992: 8). There is thus an inherent disjuncture between the process of globalization and international institutions, establishing the potential for a transformation of global governance.

An alternative concept of multilateralism stems from both the notion that as the process of globalization is now unfolding, no one can be held accountable for the direction of events in the world economy, and a normative preference for inclusiveness, or empowerment, of less privileged groups in the restructuring of global institutions. *Transformative multilateralism* therefore implies the articulation of non-state forces in the process of international organization. In this sense, Robert Cox views multilateralism as 'a commitment to maximum participation in a dialogue among political, social, economic, and cultural forces as a means of resolving conflicts and designing institutional processes' (Cox, 1991: 4). An emancipatory project, this approach calls for a significant opening to popular movements during a period of global restructuring. As yet, however, there is insufficient evidence to suggest that participatory channels are becoming both accessible to and genuinely representative of different elements in the global division of labour.

What appears to be emerging in the near term is *truncated multilateralism*: not a world of competitive trading blocs but of states locked into global regions in very different ways, trying to optimize their positions, and encountering resistance from social groups and movements adversely affected by globalization. Three regions – North America, the European Community, and East and Southeast Asia – form 'megamarkets' as well as dominate global production and trade. They generate 77 per cent of world exports and produce 62 per cent of world manufacturing output (Dicken, 1992: 45). One of the principal challenges to this and other concepts of multilateralism in recent years is massive displacement of labour, an aspect of global restructuring that accentuates differences between sending and receiving countries.

Inter-regional and intra-regional migration

With the simultaneous restructuring of global production and global power relations, the growth poles of competitive participation in the GDL are drawing large-scale and increasingly diverse imports of labour from their points of origin. Seeking to escape a marginalized existence and repression, population transfers within a stratified division of labour reflect a hierarchy among regions, countries, and different rates of industrialisation (Mittelman, 1994a).

While migratory flows are as old as history itself, the dimensions of the contemporary upsurge are staggering. The United Nations Population Fund (1993) estimates that there are at least 100 million international migrants living outside the countries in which they were born. Their annual remittances to families at home amount to $66 billion, more than all foreign development assistance from governments. By 1987 New York City alone had 2.6 million foreign-born residents, representing 35 per cent of the city's total population. The projection for the year 2000 is that the immigrant population (foreign born and second generation) will account for over 50 per cent of the city's population (Sassen, 1991: 316). Europe is also one of the areas particularly vexed by numerous new 'birds of passage', including environmental refugees propelled by natural disasters, elements of North Africa's middle strata fearing Islamic resurgence, and countless asylum seekers. According to the United Nations Economic Commission for Africa, 30 per cent of Africa's skilled work force was living in Europe in 1987. It is also estimated that today, one out of 18 Africans resides outside his or her country of origin (Keller, 1993). Among European countries, Germany is host to the largest number of foreigners – 5.2 million. Next is France with 3.6 million, followed by Britain with 1.8 million and Switzerland with 1.1 million, or 16.3 per cent of that country's population (Kamm, 1993).

What is new about this influx of migrants is the direction of flows from sending to receiving countries as well as the spatial dispersion of growth poles, forming a distinctive territorial division of labour. The more dynamic economies act as magnets attracting mobile resources primarily from the South and the East to the West. The redistribution of labour within and across regions also includes migratory flows within the South, although a large portion of these transfers become South to North movements. Many locales in the South or on the fringes of the North (for instance, southern Europe) are merely stopovers or way stations as the newly arrived leapfrog to their countries of destination.

Although market dynamics are the galvanizing force in the extensive movement of peoples from their homelands to other areas of work and settlement, this propellant is not merely a by-product of a structural tension between capital and labour. To be sure, capital is forming large unregulated markets, and labour is less capable of transnational reorganization. Capital is increasingly globalized, but trade unions still imagine their identities primarily in national terms. With calls for 'borderless solidarity' and for the eventual establishment of regional trade union structures (Lambert, 1992), international solidarity is an ever important motif, but the nation-state remains the key point of reference.

The salience of class thus lies in its integration with non-class categories. At issue are the interactions of production and the formation of multiple identities. Insofar as employers exercise vast control over the conditions of labour, identities are very largely constructed in the realm of leisure – that is, in the community or household – where work experiences are given meaning. Often, activities such as sports, neighbourhood associations, or festivals provide the milieu for the formation of identities. In this sense, a changing global division of labour is situated at the cross-roads of class and cultural differences.

At this juncture, the regulation of migrant labour is performed less by the state or formal multilateral processes than by informal monocultural and multicultural mechanisms. Liberal multilateralism may constrain immigration, yet the capacity for and record of inter-governmental co-ordination are quite limited. In Europe, for example, pressure is mounting for a common policy on immigration, but the European Union (EU) lacks judicial authority in this area. Although the EU subscribes to the principle of free movement of persons, permanent immigration and the right to grant asylum are reserved for national governments.

The presence of distinct immigrant cultures has posed problems for the identity of a number of host countries. In France, the immigration issue became highly politicized in the 1960s and 1970s when it became evident that waves of labourers were of decidedly different origins from those of their predecessors. Not only did the duration of stay increase, but workers brought their families, settled and produced second-generation immigrants, many of whom do not conform to a national identity imagined as a unitary French culture impervious to race and ethnicity. In fact, new elements of the French population who maintain their own languages, religious traditions, dress codes, and dietary practices encounter employment opportunities restricted to persons of indigenous culture or to those who have assimilated local culture (Zinniker, 1993). The case of immigration in France suggests that as multiracial and multiethnic societies evolve, culture becomes an instrument in the regulation of labour.

So too, after 1945, Germans invented a myth of 'cultural cohesiveness' to replace 'racial cohesiveness' as a defining identity. This imagery was not problematic as long as the original guestworker system brought in a modest number of foreigners from southern Europe to provide cheap manual labour for the German economic miracle. The idea of 'Germanness' – ethnic and cultural homogeneity – is a myth that is widely embraced and one that cannot measure up to the test of history. In fact, German culture is an accretion of polyglot European influences. For instance, many residents of the Ruhr area are directly descended from Poles who came to work in the mines in the nineteenth century (Wettern, 1993).

Setting aside the question of veracity of identity, a series of wildcat strikes among foreign workers in 1973 made it clear that Germany would have to invest substantially in housing and education for migrant workers and their families. A supposedly disposable labour reserve emerged as long-term residents. As the Swiss author and playwright Max Frisch said of the receiving countries, 'We asked for workers, but human beings came' (quoted by George, 1992: 123).

A naturalization programme would require a redefinition of German citizenship, which is inherited from one's parents (*ius sanguinis*) and is not based on a person's place of birth (*ius soli*). Hence, only children of at least one German parent are legally entitled to German citizenship. The sole exclusion from this rule are the descendants of ethnic Germans who settled in eastern Europe in the eighteenth century, a group persecuted during and after the Second World War. Many new arrivals from the east have few or no ties to Germany, but are thus able to circumvent the stringent regulations applied to other immigrants, including guest-workers' children born in Germany. The maxim that 'Germany is not a country of immigration' means that some Germans even consider naturalized immigrants to be still Italians, Greeks or Turks. They may have resided in Germany for all of their lives, may speak only German, and are none the less viewed as outsiders (Wettern, 1993).

Notwithstanding a multicultural work force, monoculturalism remains the dominant identity among Germans. Thoroughgoing assimilation does not guarantee equal access to a slot at the work place but is a possible route to employment, for multiculturalism would require a reinvention of German identity.

What directly impinges on the lives of migrants is informalization of labour supply and the emergence of new linkages between North and South: smuggling networks and international gangs have become important conduits largely outside the reach of multilateral regimes. In the chains connecting the United States and Mexico, a 'coyote' escorts clandestine entrants across the border. Highly sophisticated, illegal systems of labour supply actively recruit potential migrants, some of whom slip into the United States while others remain in servitude in Mexico, often in brothels with Central American women forced to pay off the coyotes. Transnational criminal organizations also set up voyages from Fujian Province in southern China and Taiwan, with numerous stopovers, and deliver undocumented immigrants to New York and other American ports, where new arrivals are frequently greeted by hostility and hardship.

Working underground, especially if they do not speak the language of the receiving country or lack specialized skills, illegal immigrants typically subsist in the informal economy – for instance, in sweatshops, peddling, gypsy taxicabs, and industrial homework. A burgeoning illegal market for low-cost labour provides entry-level jobs through family and communal networks. Meanwhile, in the smaller towns and villages of the sending countries, migration has had a profound impact. In a Polanyian sense, the extension of the labour market tears the social fabric and inserts new polarities between those who receive remittances and can now purchase a variety of consumer goods and those who do not have such largess. In countries with a large portion of the male population holding jobs overseas, a nation-wide shortage of workers boosts salaries but also makes the lives of countless people more desperate and deprived. The separation of families, a generation of orphans, and the introduction of AIDs into rural areas by returning emigrants are but some of the tangible consequences of a changing division of labour. Enmeshed in a complex structure of dependence, migrant workers and their families are commodities like other commodities bought and sold on a global market, and are thus one part of a chain of commodification in modern capitalism.

Global commodity chains[4]

Labour flows are integral links in global commodity chains, serving as rough locators of position in geoeconomic structures. As originally defined by Hopkins and Wallerstein (1986: 159), a commodity chain is 'a network of labour and production processes whose end result is a finished commodity'. By tracing these chains, one can delimit the division of labour and the transformation of production systems. For each commodity, one focuses on different nodes from distribution to marketing, production, and the supply of raw material. These chains not only join multiple production processes but also reflect the totality of production relations in an extended social division of labour.

Inasmuch as other authors have provided detailed case studies of the organization and geography of commodity chains in a variety of industries (shipbuilding, garments and apparel, footwear, automobiles, and so on), I will not rehearse their work here (see, most notably, Gereffi and Korzeniewicz, 1994). Empirical research shows the diverse ways in which the evolution of networks of complex industrial, commercial, and financial ties has created distinctive nodes that link raw material supply, manufacturing operations, and trade flows into commodity chains in an increasingly integrated global economy. These chains cut across the geographic and political boundaries of nation-states, and are explained in part by social and cultural patterns.

Cultural formation

Transnational linkages are essentially stateless and held together not only by flows of commodities but also by marriage, clans, and dialects – in short, a common culture. Indeed, the impact of culture is perhaps the most neglected factor in division of labour theory (Munck, 1988: 101). What is often overlooked is that class ties are formed by both impersonal economic forces and shared beliefs and values; lives are shaped and meanings are formed in distinctive cultural contexts. Hence, class is overlaid by ethnic, racial, and sexual divisions of labour. With the impetus toward globalization, cultural responses to the expansion of the market provide intersubjective meanings and intermediate inequalities arising from a changing division of labour.

There are varied manifestations of regional and global networks in which culture and the division of labour are intertwined. A notable illustration is the Chinese transnational division of labour, a vitalizing force in the remarkable rates of growth experienced by East Asian and Southeast Asian economies in recent years. A powerful regional network – an informal though pervasive grouping – comprises the combined wealth of 40 million overseas Chinese in Southeast Asia, estimated at $200 billion, the worth of Hong Kong's seven million residents (another $50 billion), Taiwan and the People's Republic of China (PRC) (Sender, 1991). Taiwan now represents the world's four-teenth largest economy and commands the biggest accumulation of cash reserves – more than $80 billion – of any country in the world. What the World Bank refers to as the Chinese Economic Area (CEA or China, Hong Kong and Taiwan), also known as Greater China, has had an average growth rate of more than seven per cent a year since 1962, and by the year 2002, will have a GDP ranking ahead of that of France, Italy and Britain and approaching the United States' output (World Bank, 1993: 66–7).

Table 4.2 GDP comparisons for four economies: market price and standard international price estimates (trillions of US dollars)

Country	At market prices		At standard international prices		
	1991	2002	1990[a]	2002[b]	Per capita income[c]
Chinese Economic Area (CEA)	0.6	2.5	2.5	9.8	7,300
United States	5.5	9.9	5.4	9.7	36,000
Japan	3.4	7.0	2.1	4.9	37,900
Germany	1.7	3.4	1.3	3.1	39,100

a. The source of these estimates is World Bank, *World Development Report 1992* (except Taiwan, China). Estimates vary widely, however; the Summers and Heston (1988) estimate for 1985 was $2.6 trillion for china alone.
b. This growth rate is an upper bound for the CEA because projections at standard international prices tend to rise more slowly than market prices at official exchange rates as relative income per capita rises (reflecting the higher relative price of services in high-income economies).
c. Per capita income is in thousands of US dollars.
Source: World Bank, *Global Economic Prospects and the Developing World* (1993), p. 67.

Table 4.2 compares the CEA's economic size – the 'fourth growth pole' of the global economy – to that of other leading economies.

With PRC growth in Gross National Product exceeding 15 per cent in the first half of 1993, there are even fears that market reforms have generated a runaway train – an overheated economy that the state cannot cool without considerable political ferment (Walker, 1993).

The Chinese transnational division of labour originated with various waves of migration from the mainland to neighbouring territories and Southeast Asia. One of the important functions that Hong Kong served was to assemble Chinese emigrants for shipment to other areas as contract labourers. Singapore provided a trans-shipment point for most workers destined for Southeast Asia's plantations and tin mines. When the Chinese settlers had established themselves in receiving countries, they filled a vacuum in trade, marketing, commerce and service occupations. The indigenous populations had access to land but not to capital and growing international markets. Despite perceptions identifying ethnicity with particular types of economic activity (namely stereotypes of middlemen), the Chinese minority has established superior access to capital and credit through family associations, dialect groups, clans, and places of origin in China. Throughout Southeast Asia, Chinese big businesses have dominated the national economies, notwithstanding state assistance for indigenous entrepreneurs, and have constituted family firms traditionally controlled by one man or one family. Their formation and economic role reflect Chinese immigrant and minority status in receiving countries, for these groups and associations in China exist mainly for rural–urban migrants in commercial centres (Lim, 1983: 2–3).

Once settled, ethnic Chinese in Southeast Asia sent funds home through remittance brokers. Typically, brokers aggregated these monies and transferred them through Singapore and Hong Kong, which had the sole free-exchange market for remittances after the Second World War. Those in the remittance business diversified their holdings, using the funds they had collected to purchase goods for export to China and channelling the proceeds from sales to pay off the remittances (Wu and Wu, 1980: 91–2). Clan and especially linguistic ties provided the channels for funnelling the funds, with capital moving through the network in circuitous ways.

Major changes in the circuits of capital reflect structural shifts in the economies of Asia related to the relative decline of entrepôt trade and the rise of domestic manufacturing. The drop in entrepôt trade led to a reduction in the activities of import–export agents acting as middlemen between the mainland and Southeast Asia. There followed the development of international financial centres in Hong Kong and Singapore, which have become conduits of funds for foreign investment as well as well as sources of capital for other Third World countries. In Southeast Asia and Hong Kong, ethnic Chinese own and manage many banks as well as their foreign subsidiaries in Japan, the United States, and elsewhere. Flush with refugee capital and short-term funds parked for placement, these banks are able to perform vital services for their Chinese customers and have made them attractive partners for financial and trading institutions in the United States, Japan, and Europe (Wu and Wu, 1980: 90–107).

Faced with the political challenge of economic nationalism by local ruling classes, large-scale Chinese traders dispersed control of their firms among relatives, trusts, and shelf companies in such locales as Panama, Vanuatu, and Liberia. There emerged a labyrinthine complexity of family interests and numerous cross-shareholdings (see Cottrell, 1986, for a detailed mapping of the extensive holdings of the Kuok family). Chinese tycoons, as they are known, have also established myriad joint ventures with foreign interests, many of them ethnic Chinese in other countries. The business ties of the Kuok family, for example, emanate from the group's offices incorporated in Singapore and Hong Kong to all of Southeast Asia, Fiji, China, and Australia (Heng, 1992: 131). Another strategy for repelling the challenge of economic nationalism is to form alliances with non-Chinese capital in ways acceptable to local power brokers. Thus, a new generation of Chinese business leaders has sought political patronage in countries such as Malaysia while maintaining communal business ties at home. The new breed identifies closely with the interests and needs of the Malay capitalist class and the imperatives of a Malay-dominated state. The two-pronged strategy of building ties to Malaysian and non- Malaysian capital is based on a realization that political alliances are crucial to capital accumulation but also that the patrons of Chinese clients can be submerged by changing political currents (Heng, 1992: 142).

Similarly, in Indonesia, following a number of anti-Sinitic riots, Chinese businessmen have sought protection from the authorities and have aligned their economic fortunes with those of the local ruling class (Robison, 1986: 317). To reduce their risks as a politically vulnerable minority at home, many overseas Chinese families are also remitting investment capital to their provinces of origin in the 'motherland' not only for sentimental reasons but also because of economic performance there.

As noted, evidence suggests that the Chinese transnational division of labour is emerging as an epicentre for economic growth in Asia. Greater China is a sub-regional triangle whose axes are the economic links that informally join the southern Chinese provinces of Guangdong and Fujian with Hong Kong and Taiwan. Asia's newest and most dynamic economic force, this triangle of 120 million people has a combined GDP of almost $400 billion.

The Greater China Triangle emerged during the 1980s when Hong Kong and Taiwan, bolstered by investment from ethnic Chinese around the Pacific Rim, moved their manufacturing bases to the People's Republic in order take advantage of cheap labour, low rent, and an enormous potential market. Opening to external capital, Guangdong Province has integrated its economy with Hong Kong, many of whose residents or forbears emigrated from there and speak the regional dialect, Cantonese. In the provincial capital of Guangzhou, efforts are underway to establish contacts among the 20 million overseas Cantonese all over the world (almost 40 per cent of an estimated 55 million Chinese outside the mainland). With 63 million people, Guangdong itself is more populous than any European country except Germany, and increasingly operates as a single entity with the six million people of Hong Kong, even before it officially becomes part of China in 1997. Guangdong also draws on the neighbouring provinces of Guangxi, Hunan, and Sichuan for much of its labour supply, raw materials, and markets. Urban areas in Guangdong attract large numbers of Chinese labourers looking for work and wages, which are low in comparison to the pay in Hong Kong and Taiwan but exceed those on state farms and state-run factories (Sun, 1992).

In one of Guangdong's consumer electronics factories, for example, the average take-home pay of its 4000 workers is 4000 yuan per month, about $72 or twice the average pay of a worker in a state-run factory. Producing remote-control toy cars for Hasboro, telephones for Radio Shack and hair dryers for Conair, this factory is one of the 30 000 enterprises in Guangdong managed by Hong Kong businessmen; together, these firms employ nearly four million workers. The factory noted above is part of the Grande Group – a microcosm of the Greater China Triangle. Most of the production is on the mainland; R & D is carried out in Taiwan; and its managers and corporate headquarters are based in Hong Kong (Sun, 1992).

In a classic Polanyian pattern, the expansion of the market is a disruptive and polarizing force in China – a country of 1.15 billion people with the world's largest surplus labour pool and without an effective framework for regulating mass migration to booming micro-regions along the coast. With direct foreign investment concentrated in the coastal region, socio-economic differences with the vast interior are widening. From 1981 to 1988, the gap between gross industrial output in the coastal provinces and the nine western provinces grew 2.7 times. Young women from all over China flock to the south to work in female-intensive industries such as prostitution; some become mistresses to foreign entrepreneurs or local millionaires, easily identified by their fancy luxury cars and associations with thugs crossing the border into Hong Kong. Income inequality, criminal activities, environmental degradation, the incidence of venereal disease and fear of AIDs are on the rise. In southern China, there is none the less a long tradition of redressing grievances, peasant unrest and rebellion when disparities grow too far out of line with what is politically tolerable. Approaching the second phase of a Polanyian double movement, an evolving and countervailing source of power represents a potential challenge to Beijing.

While Guangdong attracts migrants, Taiwan faces serious labour shortages and greater worker militancy, which prompts national capital to invest more rapidly in the People's Republic, and following Singapore, to import foreign workers. Transcending the micro-region and sub-region, further extension of Chinese-owned or controlled multinationals includes syndication and co-operation in joint ventures with western and Japanese capital. While clan and especially linguistic ties continue to reinforce business interests among ethnic Chinese, traditional family linkages are increasingly integrated with professional management practices. Generational divergence within the Chinese networks has challenged the customary, intuitive style of the ageing patriarchs. Modern English-speaking, MBA-toting managers, many of them financial technocrats, reflect the tenets of liberal-economic globalization transmitted by business and law schools not in their ancestral villages but in western countries where they now invest, trade, and borrow.

Clearly, Chinese culture mediates the institutional arrangements in the regional and global divisions of labour. Broadly speaking, it is an adaptive, flexible, and dynamic culture. It is responsive to market forces, the requirements for business success, necessary interactions with the local population, and transnational opportunities. It is also employed selectively as a business strategy where it is advantageous to demonstrate minority characteristics to mobilize an investable surplus and engage in trade. But the use of cultural identity is not limited to the minority community. For the general population, intersubjective meanings attached to the interactions between culture and economic activities supersede or mask their objective significance, promoting conflicts within the ethnic and racial divisions of labour – to a large extent, a transnational phenomenon in East and Southeast Asia – and leading to state policies which only contradict stated government goals and accentuate societal tensions (Lim, 1983: 20–3).

CONCLUSION

Division of labour theories are a valuable tool for examining global restructuring, especially because they identify major trends that constitute the changing social geography of capitalism. However, classical theory and its neo variant are economistic, underrate the role of culture, and fail to allow for the possible reversal or interruption of contemporary restructuring; these interpretations do not offer a theory of transformation. The future is not best understood as more of the present – straight-line projections – for change in a post-cold war and post-hegemonic world is a spasmodic process.

Neither the economism of division of labour theory nor the political primacy argument engrained in realist and neo-realist approaches to liberal multilateralism are an accurate guide to an emerging world order. The problem with primacy arguments is that they presuppose a separation between an interstate system grounded in a territorial division among sovereign powers and an economic arena in which divisions are mediated by the market. By delimiting politics and economics as separate spheres, the dominant conceptualization of globalization rooted in liberal economic theory serves the interests of the beneficiaries of an expanded market. The challenge is to provide an alternative to the terms of reference employed by the enthusiasts of economic globalization.

From another perspective, globalization does not sideline the state but, rather, forces it to accommodate domestic policies to the pressures generated by transnational capital. State initiatives represent attempts to manoeuvre and achieve *national* mobility within the GDL, often by seeking to build productive capacity and to gain a technological edge. In the fastest growing regional economy – Southeast

Asia, having overtaken the East Asian NIEs in the late 1980s – state policies are adopted to establish centres of innovative R & D so as to move toward higher value-added activities.

Nevertheless, the state is outflanked by transnational forces, for it aggregates the energies and synergy of human activity at a political and territorial level that does not correspond to evolving flows of labour, capital, and technology.

Links are increasingly developing between *region states* and the global economy. Formed by parts of states, as in 'the third Italy' and Baden-Württemberg, or by economic patterns that overlap state boundaries, such as in the cross-border zone radiating across the Straits of Malacca joining parts of Laos, Vietnam and Thailand, region states hook into and seek to derive advantage from market expansion in a global division of labour (Ohmae 1993). In this configuration, the seeds of conflict are planted by leaders who contest the reality of globalization and either try to fan the flames of economic nationalism or build competitive trading blocs (Mittelman, 1994b). Another response is to accept the brute fact that no country can escape the effects of globalization. If so, it is necessary to define interests in terms other than the imagined 'nation' and avoid merely defensive strategies. *Global regions* may then seek to navigate the currents and ride the tide of market expansion in a global division of labour (Sadler, 1992).

These patterns suggest that the GDL reinforces and transforms the NIDL; the emerging structure is an articulation of the GDL, distinctive regional divisions of labour, and the texture of local conditions. The key elements in this structure are embedded in the globalization process, understood here as a shrinking of the time-space aspects of social relations. Beyond an appreciation of a realignment in the role of the state and technological innovation, explaining the GDL requires attention to (1) evolving regional formations in their institutional and informal aspects, (2) intra-regional and inter-regional migratory flows, (3) the complex web of interlinkages among global producers, their outputs and specified markets, and (4) the ways in which cultures are historically constructed, emerge from and help to shape the economy of a region.

The region provides the starting point for analyzing a changing GDL, for it is the site of distinctive divisions of labour and a major arena for large-scale transfers of population. Competition and the fear of extinction drove firms and enterprises to expand and produce on a scale wider than a national market. With technological innovations, the transnational mobility of capital, and space-shrinking advancements in transport and communications, a new and more intensive phase of accumulation integrated production processes is linking the nodes in commodity chains. Manufacturing activities forming classic production sequences – with the outputs of one being the inputs for another, while also interrelated to other components of the global economy (finance, trade, and marketing – have deepened the accumulation process. Lubricating commodity chains so as to facilitate flows of capital and labour, culture eases the tensions generated by the GDL.

As the global economy changes, the role of each region varies. Quite clearly, globalization is an uneven process forming what Durkheim might have termed *supra-organic solidarity*. At the world level, there are multiple structures of specialization binding and yet acting as spacers among zones of the global economy. Given the disparities between global regions and marginalized regions, there are different globalization narratives. While the former are riding the waves of globalization, the latter are driven by its currents and have lost control. No longer socially embedded in a national political economy, market forces are increasingly unaccountable and disembedded, less dependent on the social structures that gave rise to them. To the extent that modern society is dominated by economic relationships, the challenge is to identify and enlist the agents of social change for re-embedding the unprecedented productive capacities of economic globalization in the interstices of world society.

Although Polanyi (1945) conceived market expansion as a global phenomenon, he also believed that regionalism offers an alternative to the universalist attempt 'to make the world safe for the gold standard'. Contrary to a universalist conception of capitalism based on the principles of liberal economy, the regional characteristics of globalization suggest another strategy for market-ridden societies. Not a panacea, regionalism may be a remedy for the by-products of the utopian conception of the market. Within the mega-structure of globalization, the adoption of new regional instruments for managing large-scale flows of labour, economic non-co-operation, and intolerant nationalism may be a way toward achieving social justice. Moving beyond market-determined, private-sector-led forms of integration, regionalization programmes can be developed to curb the anti-social tendencies of transnational capital. Corporate and statist regionalization strategies should not go uncontested. While the enthusiasts of economic globalization-cum-regionalization will defend social privilege, regionalism also provides space for fresh forces to spring up, align, and look more to a future of post-globalization.

At the end of the day, does this emancipatory possibility constitute anything other than a utopian vision? Unlike the embedded world economy of the 1930s – the raw material of Polanyi's analysis – the contemporary form of disembedded globalization defies his attempt to subsume economics under sociology. Economic globalization congeals the material power of capitalism on a world scale. The asymmetry between capital and labour will not be resolved by the imminent unity of a global working class. Not only is the bourgeoisie of the world uniting more rapidly and more effectively than is the proletariat, but also labour is predominantly particularistic and local. Working class identity is not primordial but one of several mobile identities deriving from the economic, racial, ethnic, and sexual divisions of labour. Forging a political culture of resistance – a counterhegemony – draws on the salience of class and requires a reinvention of the interactions between production and identity.

Notes

1. A preliminary version of this chapter appeared as 'Rethinking the International Division of Labour in the Context of Globalisation', *Third World Quarterly* (1995) Vol. 16, No. 2, pp. 273–95. I also owe a debt of gratitude to Edmé Dominguez and Stephen Gill for thoroughgoing and helpful comments in a preliminary draft.
2. For provoking ideas on the nexus between production and identity, I am indebted to the collective discussion at the Symposium on 'Work, Class and Culture' hosted by the University of the Witwatersrand's History Workshop and the Sociology of Work Unit, Johannesburg, South Africa, 28–30 June, 1993. Particularly valuable from the standpoint of the text that follows is the examination of the dilemmas of a 'shift from the political culture of resistance to one of reconstruction, from social movement unionism to strategic unionism' in a paper on 'South Africa's Industrialisation: The Challenge Facing Labor' by A. Joffe, J. Maller, and E.C. Webster.
3. The categories of East Asian NIEs and ASEAN overlap, for Singapore is generally regarded as a member of both groups.
4. In the present context of considering the GDL, I will say less about commodity chains than about other themes, and mention this dimension mainly for the sake of completeness. Paralleling the discussion in this section, I am writing a case study of a key commodity chain – textiles and the garment industry, with emphasis on the southern African regional division of labour – and will not recapitulate my research findings for the purposes of this chapter.

5 New Global Migration Dynamics

Hélène Pellerin

Global migration is not a historical novelty. Today its importance stems from its place in a context of a 'massive historical transition' (Meissner *et al.*, 1993) in the structures of world order. The challenge to policy and to the 'old multilateralism' stems not necessarily from an unprecedented size of human migration taking place across borders as many would argue (Garson, 1992), but more from its character, and the contradictory objectives of the various players involved in this issue. Consequently, the implications of global migration for a 'new multilateralism' are ambiguous and contradictory.

Migration participates in and is a consequence of, other changes in world order. Such changes entail processes of restructuring in production, in state structures and in configurations of power among various social forces. These transformations determine the conditions under which migration is occurring. As part of the global restructuring of social practices global migration extends beyond national boundaries, and connects with economic, political and cultural dynamics otherwise more or less divided (Mittelman, 1994a). The recognition of the impact of migration upon local and global processes and structures implies that the phenomenon involves complex social relations between migrants and the societies of origin and of destination:

> Migration is not an act – a single event, such as crossing a border. It is a process, which involves various stages, and which may take a lifetime – or more! ... The process starts with capitalist penetration and changes in the region of origin, and leads on through labor migration, family reunification and settlement to social, cultural and political transformation of the country of immigration. The culmination of the process is the development of permanent and multifaceted links between the country of emigration and the country of immigration. (Castles, 1989:107)

The form global migration is taking in the present period is conditioned by processes of socio-economic restructuring in ways that both foster and restrict the movement of people. The development of social links and networks that the movement of people is inducing suggests that the conception of migrants which prevailed in the post-war period, that is as mere factors of production, mobile and disposable in the dynamic of the global labour market, no longer holds (Lim, 1992). Yet, the active participation of migrants in the interstices of both the interstate system and the world economy does not provide for the improvement of their situations, let alone the constitution of a counter-movement, in a Polanyian sense, of a global civil society that would represent anti-market forms of organization (Zolberg, 1981). Because migration is subjected to the forces of global restructuring, its role in a counter-movement of global politics is to be queried. But for an effective multilateral form of regulation of global migration to emerge, some dimensions of migrants' networks and institutions would have to be added to states' bi-or multilateral measures.

Before we can come to this conclusion, an assessment of some of the reality of migration is necessary. With this in mind, the substantive focus of the chapter is on those forces of migration which cut across 'North–South' dimensions, and I use examples from the textile-apparel, automobile and agro-industrial sectors to illustrate my argument.

EMERGING TRENDS IN GLOBAL MIGRATION

The Continuous Observation System of Migration of the OECD, that gathers information on migration flows from all OECD members, has referred lately to the intensification of migration involving widely disparate geographical areas (Garson, 1992). The United Nations High Commissioner for Refugees, Sadako Ogata, declared to the media in 1992 that every day more than 10 000 refugees are forced to flee their homes. Despite these references, the number of migrants in the world has not increased significantly in the last twenty years. In the early 1990s, it is estimated that less than 2 per cent of the world's population were on the move (Bloom and Brender, 1993).[1] The current period can thus be compared to other, more ancient flows, such as the Huns moving from Mongolia to ancient Gaul and Italy in 150 BC, or the Europeans migrating to North and South America from the sixteenth century on (Davis, 1974). In all these instances, migration flows have involved disparate geographical areas, for long and short periods. If there is a singularity in the current period, it is related to the forms migration is taking, rather than in the scale of migration flows.

The composition of global migration in the current period is changing with the increasing importance of new categories of migrants. The UN Secretariat refers to the rise of new forms of migration, humanitarian in nature, that is, composed of refugees and asylum claimants, illegal or undocumented migrants, and family members being reunited (UN, 1992a). An increasing importance of woman among migrants is one indication of this shift in the composition of migration flows. Together with new categories of migrants, women are taking a larger part of the total migration figure since the 1970s. Developments also indicate that the phenomenon is becoming more transnational than international in nature.

The emergence of new categories of migrants is directly related to the forces regulating global migration. Greater restrictions imposed by states of destination on the entrance of foreigners have led to the search for new avenues by prospective migrants. Thus the increasing number of asylum claimants and undocumented migrants is closely related to the greater restrictions put on the entry of migrant labour. However, the conditions that lead to the migration of people, namely the 'push' and 'pull' factors in regions of origin and of destination have remained the same, and even intensified with the process of global restructuring.

GLOBAL RESTRUCTURING AND NEW CONDITIONS OF MIGRATION

The new face of migration can be considered as the other side of the coin of a more global economy. It is part of the process of global restructuring which affects at least three interrelated dynamics of social order: the division of labour, geographical and functional; the relations between capital and labour, and the relations between the state and society, that is the management of society (Ross and Trachte, 1990).

The financial revolution of the last two decades has allowed for the freer movement of capital from one region, one enterprise or one currency to another. The hyper-mobility of financial forms of capital is redefining the strategies and the terrain of capitalist rivalry (Moreau Defarges, 1993; O'Brien, 1992). It is accompanied by other global tendencies, such as the development of new 'productive systems' that integrate various industries and regions in a corresponding if not unitary logic of accumulation (Verhaeren, 1990; Petrella, 1989). The dynamics of capitalist competition have expanded to regions that were previously either closed or unattractive as a whole for capital accumulation, respectively eastern-central Europe and the former Soviet Union, and many Third World countries. In this context, there has been an intensification of global migration since the 1970s, related to the process of restructuring and of capitalist expansion in various regions. These changes are not solely economic in nature, but affect the social and political fabric of societies, with a direct impact on migration dynamics.

The way in which societies and economic sectors are integrated into the global division of labour through foreign investment is one determinant of global migration and can also influence the direction of the flows (Sassen, 1988). By destroying the traditional means of livelihood, and by proletarianizing a greater part of the population in some regions, foreign investment encourages the movement of people, very often in the direction where capital is coming from. This logic is illustrated in many regions of the world that are related to the three main poles of economic power: North America; western Europe and east Asia. In each of these poles, migration follows particular economic paths and is tied to specific countries. France, one of the leading poles of attraction for foreign workers in Western Europe, has attracted numerous new migrants in the last two decades. Two of the largest groups of foreigners who came to France between 1982 and 1990 were North Africans (particularly from Morocco), and Turks. Likewise, through the 1980s French investment in these areas increased (for information on Morocco see El Mellouki Riffi, 1989; and for Turkey see OECD 1992b). Other areas such as the African Franc Zone or sub-Saharan Africa also supply labour to France, despite a decrease in foreign investment (Economou et al., 1992)[2] In the latter cases, special economic, political and cultural linkages were developed which encouraged migration, such as a monetary union, military assistance and educational patterns for the élite (Hugon, 1993).

In other parts of the world economy, a similar phenomenon can be observed. Mexican and Filipino migrants have been moving to the United States for a very long time, and in particularly large numbers since the 1960s. These movements correspond to opposite movements of capital, from direct investment in off-shore production, such as the

Maquiladoras in the north of Mexico, or in key industrial sectors like the agro-food industry in the Philippines, to indirect involvement in shareholdings of some industries (Sassen, 1993; Martin, 1993). Japan and other Asian 'dragons' are reproducing similar patterns of mobility. Japanese investments in south and southeast Asia have increased in the last ten years, focused mostly on the automobile and electronics industries (Sassen, 1993). In overseas development assistance, Japan has become one of the largest donor in the region, with a significant impact on models of social organization and economic development. Japan meanwhile has recorded an inflow of migrants from these regions; between 1982 and 1988 the number of registered migrant workers increased from 34 000 to 81 000 and this does not include the large number of undocumented migrant workers (UN, 1992). Countries such as South Korea, Taiwan, Hong Kong and Singapore have also become zones of immigration in the last decade, thanks to the creation of migration channels joining them to regions of investments in Southeast Asia, that is from Bangladesh to Malaysia, or the Philippines. Another factor promoting these migration patterns has been Japanese and other foreign investors directing their strategy in these countries' labour-intensive industries (Fong, 1993).

Patterns of capital mobility and foreign investments suggest that a greater integration in the world economy tends to intensify the process of migration, rather than slow it down as neo-classical economists tend to argue. This suggests that the social and economic organization of society is more determinant in the process of migration than the absolute gap between poor and rich regions, or than levels of foreign investments. The process of global restructuring involves different forms of articulation of local economic activities with global industries, and encourages changes in socio-economic organization prevailing in the societies concerned.

The forms foreign investments take, the sectors involved, and the ways in which they articulate with other sectors of the economy can create new 'push' and 'pull' factors for migration. One concrete historical case can clarify this point. French investments in Morocco increased substantially in the 1980s, and two sectors received much of the incoming capital: the automobile and the textile-garment industries. For the automobile industry, Renault in particular adopted a strategy of internationalization of its production, involving mostly assembly activities and component production. Simple and standardized production methods have been introduced in Latin America, East Asia and Tunisia and Morocco (Chanaron de Banville, 1985). In

Morocco this entailed the development of an enclave, isolated from the rest of the economy (with export rates as high as 85 per cent of the parts and systems assembled) draining local capital and labour. The price competition that governed the vertical segment of the automobile system in Morocco meant that low wages and labour flexibility were necessary. Migration represents here a solution for an increasingly large number of people unable to find work in this skewed labour market.

In the textile industry, Morocco has developed a specialization over the last 10 or 15 years, with a 20 per cent increase in the total merchandise exports of the industry between 1965 and 1989 (World Bank, 1991). Morocco became the second trading partner of France in textiles, after Italy, in the 1980s. Mainly European foreign direct investment in the textile industry articulates with the indigenous process of production, through branch plants and subcontracting (Boussemart and Rabier, 1983). This form of investment led to a restructuring of the labour market, with a significant impact on labour practices. The textile industry in Morocco employs both regular workers, and a self-employed work-force composed mostly of women working at home. In the 1980s, unpaid female family workers in the manufacturing industry represented 7 per cent of the active population of the sector (ILO, 1989). The development of the manufacturing sector, and the integration of the textile industry into the world economy have not destroyed other forms of labour practices, rather they have articulated them with global forms. This articulation has encouraged competition over labour costs in the industry, while favouring particular categories of workers, self-employed women. Many people have lost jobs in this process, while those who did find work became connected to other production sites in the world, notably in France itself. Migration channels have developed around this globally fragmented industry.

The issue of refugee movements, often explained by narrow political factors, can also be related to movements of capital, and economic restructuring. Capital's movement and changes in the social organization of production act as push factors in many 'refugee producing countries', by affecting states' set of priorities concerning strategies of development in favour of foreign capital and the use of land, labour and natural resources for export production. This is done partly to curry favour with ruling élites and some domestic factions of capital in the countries of origin. However, the consequences of open investment and trade-oriented policies are often disastrous for local populations:

ecological degradation, internal displacement of people, social unrest, and political repression. Countries like Angola, Zaïre, and the Congo saw large outflows of population in the 1980s. For African countries, the reliance on export earnings results in increasing needs for large areas of land, at the expense of small, subsistence farming. This has the effect of displacing a large number of people to urban centres in search of work. Some of these internal migrants will eventually cross borders, while others, a large majority, will strive to survive in increasingly degraded social and ecological conditions.

The dynamics of financial restructuring and integration act on 'push' factors through states' management of local social and economic situations. Conditions for new credits are generally translated by skewed spending priorities of states and they result in the exclusion of large sectors of the population. The dynamic triggered by such policies constitutes the background of many refugee situations (Pellerin, 1993). Indeed, the adoption of austerity measures and structural adjustment plans require states to adopt specific social policies to cut public spending in areas such as food subsidies, education, health care, public transport, and so on. At the same time, efforts are made to attract foreign capital by introducing measures which would ensure stability and profitability for such ventures. Such a policy agenda tends to worsen the precariousness of some sectors of the population, while state repression is often used to force social practices into the logic of global capital accumulation. The contradictory forces of integration and exclusion contribute to foster the climate of violence that is constitutive of the refugee experience (Zolberg, 1988). The situation has worsened with the growing external debt of many African countries, forcing austerity measures and additional restrictions on local development efforts. Under these conditions, some social forces mobilize to change the course of development, either by transforming the relationship between the ruling élite and fractions of capital, or by empowering groups within civil society more generally. But they often meet with strong resistance from state authorities, often supported by the army.

What the above discussion suggests is that the integration of production at the world level in more or less fragmented processes according to the strategies of enterprises (Ruigrok and Van Tulder, 1993) has led to the socialization of capitalist relations of production and the expansion of its logic to a growing number of sectors and regions, with a direct impact on the dynamic of global migration. But the connection between the socialization of capitalist relations and international–transnational migration is not accidental or contingent. Migration in the contemporary era is not a mere consequence of the process of restructuring, an 'externality' of the world economy in transformation. It is in fact central to the process of restructuring, and particularly in the new offensive of capital to subordinate the power and organization of labour, with important consequences for the management of society. Restructuring has increased the flexibility, the fungibility and the mobility of capital, and strengthened its power over labour. Global migration in its present form reinforces this dynamic.

MIGRATION AND THE INCREASING POWER OF CAPITAL

Whereas the post-war period saw in the OECD a strengthening of labour and improved working conditions thanks to social struggles in a context of economic growth and strong state interventionism; and whereas in other parts of the world the dynamics of decolonization and nationalization were subordinating both capital and labour to state management, the current period is witnessing an unleashing of the power of capital. The latter has progressively globalized its dynamics (Madeuf and Michalet, 1978) and it has increased its mobility and flexibility beyond the confines of the national economy, at the expense of nationally-organised labour movements (Ross and Trachte, 1990).

The global restructuring of the economy was triggered by the search for new ways of preventing economic stagnation and declining profitability for many large corporations. Two strategies have been particularly used: the search for new economic inputs and resources, and the delinking of labour reproduction from the production process. The existence of global migration is not fortuitous in this context; it is both the product and the condition for restructuring to take place.

With regard to the delinking of labour reproduction from labour exploitation, this took the form of a flexibilization of the labour market and the dismantling of social protection. Migrant labour has been instrumental in this process, but not simply in the role of a reserve army of labour as was broadly argued to be the case twenty years ago (Castles and Kosack, 1973), but more importantly by its active participation in the process of restructuring itself. Migrant labour is not in a reserve pool of labour, stagnant or latent. In many advanced capitalist countries, it tends to be employed equally, if not more than the indigenous work-force (Lever-Tracy, 1983).

The contemporary economic function of migrant labour in industrialized receiving societies emerged from changing labour practices in the late 1960s and early 1970s (Verhaeren, 1990). Migrant labour allowed for the coexistence of high levels of unemployment among the indigenous labour force, and economic decline more generally, with significant levels of employment amongst foreign workers, or at least some categories of foreigners in several sectors.[3]

With the process of restructuring, the dichotomy separating a primary from a secondary labour market is becoming meaningless. The last fifteen years have witnessed numerous state policies concerning unemployment, the establishment of a minimum income, training programmes, and legislation authorizing contractually-limited employment in several sectors. The adoption of these various measures resulted in the creation of a national rather than a segmented labour market, in which more and more workers are in precarious positions in terms of employment (Lecler and Mercier, 1990). Global restructuring has led to increasing competitiveness throughout economic sectors. This global competition is based on either low production costs, technological developments, or sizes of markets (Ross and Trachte, 1990). A new model of production is unfolding, with significant variations across countries and sectors; it is what Sabel has referred to as 'moebius-strip organisations' integrating together several forms of production, organizations and labour practices (Sabel, 1991).

Rather than serving to regulate economic cycles, migrants seem to participate in the deregulation of the productive process in many industries; they become a 'vector' of restructuring (Courault, 1990). This also means that their place and role vary according to the multiple patterns of restructuring adopted in several industries or sectors. In the automobile sector in France for instance, the process of restructuring involved the mechanization and the robotization of many of the productive functions, especially in the conception phase. This specialization led to the division of the production process, and to the subcontracting of components fabrication to the best offers in terms of quality and price. Many migrants find work in factories tied by contract to the automobile industry. At the same time, a de-skilling on assembly lines allowed for re-localization of these activities where it was profitable or for the employment of foreigners with few skills.[4]

Traditional market segmentation has been replaced by new social relations of production based on increasing precariousness for workers and subcontractors on the one hand, and access to large markets and strategic alliances on the other. The world textile–garment industry has undergone a different form of restructuring, with correspondingly varied consequences for migrants. It is the sector as a whole which experienced transformation, including the relation between its two poles: the production of textiles and of clothing. New sources of supply were offered from the 1960s onward, with the creation of synthetic fibres. This entailed a re-centring of the world industry towards the industries controlling the new technology (Mytelka, 1991). As a corollary, new fabrication procedures were developed in the clothing industry which entailed very short term and flexible production. The 'ready-to-throw-away' has replaced the ready-to-wear (Montagné-Villette, 1990). These changes have generated new forms of production organization that are not confined to a specific location nor to a region.

Global migration has been conditioned by these changes, while it has been instrumental to the restructuring of the textile industry. The emergence of large numbers of small enterprises, home work and unpaid family workers in the industry are propitious forms of work for many migrants (Montagné-Villette, 1990; McLean Petras, 1992). The networks created and maintained by migrants not only provide a labour force, but also capital and markets for this fragmented industry, thus facilitating its self-reproduction.[5] Ethnic businesses, relying on community resources – financial and human – are particularly successful and numerous in this labour-intensive sector of the economy (Morokvasic, 1991; Ma Mung, 1992; Palidda, 1992). Migrants' close connections with textile networks give them an advantage over more traditional industries.

Many newly created small and medium size enterprises practice a policy of specialization in one segment of the production process. Close contacts and the existence of a network of subcontractors ensure the design, production and distribution of the product within a very short time period. While some subcontractors are located in countries in which certain advantages compensate for the distance from the provision of textile and/or the fashion market (such as Turkey, Tunisia, Morocco and Mauritius) others are located in the OECD. And the presence of foreigners in OECD manufacture should not be overlooked. In France, the textile-clothing sector recorded an increase in employment of foreigners in the last 15 years, from 9.9 per cent in 1975 to 12 per cent in 1990. The sector has become one of the largest employers of migrants, and in the last ten years, it has become the fastest growing in terms of employment. While some foreigners in the sector are undocumented, a large number are legal yet their work is undeclared.

Global restructuring in the textile industry has the effect of bringing to the forefront the interweaving of public and private nexus of social relations of production. In this context migration is a potentially more generalized process, involving the entire family units or segments of a migrant community.

The search for new sources of supply in a modified global division of labour is another aspect of the restructuring of production that is occuring. This search was made possible by important changes in the world order, such as the opening of the Eastern bloc to market dynamics and the formal democratization of state structures in many Third World countries. The agro-food business has been influenced by these changes. Many regions participate in this global industry and in each of them, the integration in the world dynamic for supply, demand and production involves the destruction of small-scale farming. An increasingly mechanized industry has led to a substantial drop in prices against which the small landowners cannot compete even on the local market. Decline in small-scale farming is noticeable in the Sahelian region of Africa or Southeast Asia, as well as parts of the OECD. These changes have meant mobilization and migration of a large number of people who are no longer able to provide for their own means of subsistence. This landless labour force searches for work on large agricultural sites or in cities (Chossudovsky, 1993; Hugon, 1991).

In many of those regions economic hardship is combined with various forms of repression, resulting in even greater outflows of people. Hence the modernization of agriculture in the southern part of Turkey is coinciding with important, and forceful outflows of people, many of whom join the ranks of the asylum seekers in France and elsewhere in Europe (Akgunduz, 1993; Wihtol de Wenden, 1990). The land that is 'freed' is then integrated into the modernized sector (Chesnot, 1993). In the Philippines, military and para-military operations aiming at cleaning rural areas from the supporters of the outlawed communist party and its armed-wing have resulted since the 1980s in massive displacements of small farming communities and the destruction of their houses and livestock. This population has joined the ranks of internal refugee centres in several cities. In many instances their land has then been appropriated or acquired by large sugar cane plantation owners.[6]

What these cases suggest is that far from being a mere consequence or 'externality' of processes of restructuring, forced displacement of populations is becoming an integral part of the many ways in which the economy is restructured. The forced movement of people is now integrated in the process of land redistribution, agricultural reforms and the reorganization of the global agro-food industry. Massive displacements of people in war-torn regions seem to facilitate the redistribution of the land and the control of natural resources according to new configurations of forces in the world economy. It is a modern version of the enclosure movement which began in England in the fifteenth century, resulting in more capital intensive agriculture in the industrial revolution.

THE REGULATION OF GLOBAL MIGRATION: BILATERALISM, MULTILATERALISM OR TRANSNATIONALISM?

The movement of people has been significantly transformed over the last quarter of a century in its direction and in the nature of the flows. In recent history global migration has been restrained by state regulations and workers' movements (Mauco, 1933; Borkenau, 1942). Today, additional forces intervene in the conditioning and regulating of migration's expansion and direction.

States constitute, even today, the most important force of regulation of migration, albeit with different priorities and different forms of control over the movement and insertion of migrants. Among emigration states, there has been a renewed interest in the question of migration over the last 10 years, as this outflow of people proved to bring some benefits in terms of foreign currency and the regulation of the employment situation at home. Many Southeast Asian states have elaborated policy frameworks for controlled emigration flows. Since the late 1970s, such efforts are one component of export-led strategies in the Philippines, Sri Lanka and Bangladesh, just to name a few. Most of the efforts of exporting states consist in encouraging emigration from home, attracting employers abroad, and signing bilateral agreements with labour-importing countries, such as the Gulf states or some Asian countries (Singapore, Brunei, Japan, Hong Kong). But given the framework whereby they are but another production asset contributing to the factor endowment of exporting countries, migrants and their well-being generally get little concern in this kind of regulated arrangement.

Receiving states have done little, in recent years to provide for the protection of the rights and welfare of migrants. The progressive exclusion of labour movements from the formulation of decisions around migration in the 1960s is partly responsible for this shift in attention. Other reasons relate to changes in the forms of labour needs that determine immigration policies and which tend to encourage a flexible labour force. In the last twenty years, many receiving states adopted restrictive policies in terms of the selective entries of foreigners, and in terms of the rights and privileges associated with their sojourn. The first form of restriction is visible through visa requirements in almost all immigration countries. There is a conscious effort made in the three OECD regions of immigration to sign agreements with countries of origins for the flow of specific categories of people, educated, skilled or ethnically closer to societies of destination.[7]

Within the European Union, despite the Treaty of Rome provisions regarding the free movement of people, there are still limits to the mobility of nationals of its member states according to their employment status. The Portuguese were the first to notice the discrepancy between the Treaty and reality. Despite their joining the Community in 1986, and the free circulation of goods and services that this entailed, the complete mobility of Portuguese people was not going to be allowed until 1993, that is until a transition period would reduce the propensity of flows of labour out of Portugal and towards the North of Europe. The transition period led nevertheless to large outflows of Portuguese workers to other EC countries, through indirect sub-contracting practices by employers so as to bypass the law on migration of labour. Employers hired Portuguese workers through private employment services in France, Belgium or outside Europe (Marie, 1988).

As for other European Union citizens, their mobility has been carefully monitored through specific administrative rules, the result of which has been the possible restriction on the movement of unemployed people. Indeed, even though European Union nationals are allowed to look for work in various member countries, the renewal of their European residence papers, a formality in principle, might be rejected in case of unemployment, retirement or double residence (Martin *et al.*, 1990; Prétot, 1990; Bosscher, 1990). The reality of the free circulation of people in the European Union has been disconcerting: according to ILO statistics, workers' mobility decreased in 1989 (Martin *et al.*, 1990). The increasing selection of migrants by governments reinforces the tendency of migrants to use other channels to enter countries of destination. These other channels, such as family reunion, asylum or illegal stay, have been tightened up in the last decade however, in an effort to restrain some dimensions of the migrants' mobility.

This highlights a second aspect of the restrictive trend in immigration policies, namely the restriction on the 'positive' mobility of labour. The positive aspect of labour mobility concerns the possibility of the individual to get the best offer for her or his labour power. This contrasts with the negative aspect of mobility which refers to flexibility in the conditions of work imposed upon workers (Moulier-Boutang, 1991). While the latter has been part of the strategy of much manufacturing capital for two decades at least, the former dimension is starting to receive some attention, particularly with regard to migrants. Several regulations have been put into place intending to reduce the ability of migrants to self-select their own job and location. Some of these control measures involve the delivery of work permits for specific jobs or sectors; others, through the legalization of clandestine migrant workers, aim also at channelling their participation in the economy (Moulier-Boutang *et al.*, 1986). Other measures attempt to prevent the constitution of ethnic enclaves and social networks by migrant labour through restrictions on family or community migration.[8]

The trend towards converging restrictive immigration policies in most receiving states has not been fortuitous. It marks a shift in priority of multilateral efforts in the regulation of global migration. In the first 60 years of the twentieth century there was a concern over migrants' rights, privileges and social reproduction. The liberal credo that permeated the world order referred to the fundamental rights of individuals to come and go as they please (Mauco, 1933) while the ILO was able to codify basic rights for migrants (ILO, 1952). These efforts have been replaced by a greater degree of convergence towards the fundamental right of people to stay where they are (Meissner *et al.*, 1993).

The first signs of this shift appeared in the regional containment of refugees after the Gulf War. From its inception in 1952 the world refugee system has favoured the rights of individuals who could testify to a well-founded fear of persecution directed towards them personally or their relatives. It managed legally to exclude the victims of civil wars, of environmental catastrophes and of generalized structural or physical violence.[9] The latter are not considered refugees, and very seldom do they receive asylum; international humanitarian law considers that these individuals have a right to leave their country but does not guarantee them a right to enter any country (Goodwin-Gill, 1989). Humanitarian status is sometimes granted, a status which indicates the reluctance with which countries of destination open their doors to people who do not fit in the narrow and individual legal definition of refugees. The growing number of situations producing massive refugee flows in recent years brought about changes in the refugee system, namely serious efforts to contain refugees in their region of origin. Already in the 1920s there were attempts to find regional solutions to the problem of forced displaced persons (Skran, 1992). In the post-Second World War period, the regional solution has also been emphasized with the creation of refugee camps near the regions where conflicts, wars or catastrophes have forced populations to flee. Since most of the post-1945 violent conflicts have occurred in the Third World, it comes as no surprise that most of the refugee camps are located in these regions. In 1991, it was estimated that 90 per cent of the refugees in the world were in Third World countries (US Committee for Refugees, 1991). The Gulf War marked the beginning of a new phase in the regional containment of migrants, with the use of military might to ease the immediate conditions of the displaced persons while ruling out the eventuality of their movement outside the region. The large scale movement of Kurds that could not easily be relocated in neighbouring countries induced the search for a local solution, namely a humanitarian–military intervention to protect the displaced population in the conflicting zone itself (Meissner *et al.* 1993; Suhrke, 1993). A similar pattern was found in the former Yugoslavia where most of the displaced population – around 2 million out of a total of 2.5 million – was contained within the territory of the former Republic with the help of a few relief agencies (Meissner *et al.*, 1993).

The objective of containing refugees in specific zones has been progressively extended to migrants in general, as is clear from such regional agreements as the Schengen Convention and the Dublin Accord within the European Union. The Schengen Convention, based on the idea of the abolition of internal borders among European states, tends to impose a heavy toll on those states that are contiguous to the European Union. Moreover, the association of Poland to the agreement, as well as the ensemble of countries composing the

European Free Trade Association (some of which subsequently joined the European Union), has the effect of pushing further away from the European Union migrants as well as the management of their flows. The Dublin Accord, signed among the members of the European Union, determines that the state of entry of an asylum claimant should have the responsibility of examining the claim. By doing so, this agreement has a similar effect, that is, of putting the heaviest burden of migrants' control onto the peripheral and often therefore the weakest member states of the European Union (Meissner *et al.*, 1993).

Other multilateral efforts have been initiated since the 1990s, this time to tackle the long term causes of migration, and find solutions that would curb the movement of people. Outside of its regular clearing house function, the OECD has convened a series of conferences in the 1990s dealing with the problem of global migration and its long term solutions related to development (OECD 1994). A similar approach was adopted by the G-7 at their meeting in London in 1991. And the Trilateral Commission produced a report on existing trends and long term solutions to migration in the early 1993 that sets the tone for states' efforts at curbing the flows of people (Meissner *et al.*, 1993). New ways of looking at the question of migration seem to characterize these recent multilateral efforts; away from the mere function of supplying large economies with foreign labour, and closely related with addressing the problem at its source, that is, in less developed regions of the world. The general focus has been on the interaction between poverty and migration, and particularly between high population growth, lack of democracy, and migration. However, the focus on demographic practices and political institutions contributes to a narrow conception of the problem, thus blaming the poor of 'demographic incontinence' (Meillassoux, 1991) and political immaturity. This approach ignores the complex interaction between the restructuring of production, the globalizing economy, the disarticulation of social relations that feeds the process of migration, and the role migrants themselves play in maintaining flows.

Despite a focus on long term problems and solutions to global migration, most efforts which have been initiated by states are increasingly unable to respond to a growing dimension of the migration process, namely the networks and institutions being created by migrants and other forces around them. These networks operate transnationally and across borders and tend to facilitate the movement of people. The existence of social networks allow migrants to be resilient to a certain extent to policy restrictions and regulations established by states and interstate bodies, sometimes with the assistance of state authorities, particularly sending states (Lim, 1992; Goss and Lindquist, 1995).

If they do not determine the causes of migration as such, migrants' networks influence the conditions under which the process of migration occurs. They encourage the development of ethnic businesses and commercial activities, often connecting regions of origin and of destination. The commercial practices thus developed operate through a combination of official and unofficial channels between various regions. Ethnic networks also influence the organization of work, the division of labour and social relations of production by integrating in global circuits the activities taking place at the micro-level of communities and households. The existence of social networks among migrant communities represents one dimension of the globalization of civil society whereby social practices taking place at the micro-level are projected onto the global arena by the enlargement of the networks' activities and impact. Migrant networks, like other social movements, potentially represent 'real social processes *sui generis* that take roots in [their] own network of actions and power that are globalising' (Breton and Jensen, 1992: 22). There are, however, important limits to the transnationalization of migration and to the unfolding of a global civil society this might entail.

One of them is the difficulty of networks to rely on states for the recognition of protection and rights of individual migrants, since their existence is due mostly to their bypassing of state regulations. Moreover, migrants' networks do not constitute an alternative nexus of empowerment of migrants. One could even argue the opposite, that migrant networks contribute to the further commodification of migrants, due to the exploitative relations that are constitutive of many of them. A growing number of enterprises in the service sector, in commerce or in manufacturing activities that are organized on an ethnic basis are generally characterized by labour-intensive models of organization and by the abusive practices of the labour force. This indicates that hierarchical relations based on ethnic origins, gender, class, or legal status are often at the basis of the organization of the networks (Phizacklea and Miles, 1990). A serious work of democratization of these networks ought to be done if they are to help in the improvement of migration conditions. Labour organizations and human rights movements in many countries are trying to do this, but they are very seldom consulted, let alone included, in states immigration policies. So far, the existence of migrants networks and institutions has been recognized mostly by sending states, but only as an instrument that would foster their export-led strategy of growth. Receiving states, on their part, have tended to consider these networks as a mere nexus of criminal smuggling operations.[10]

CONCLUSION

Contemporary world migration dynamics are related to the changes and specificity attached to the contemporary period. The restructuring of production and finance, characterized by new forms of inter-state rivalry and by important shifts in the configuration of forces between capital and labour, contribute to foster the push and pull conditions of migration. New forms of migration emerge, more transnational in nature. But the existing restrictions on the movement of people, exerted by states and interstate institutions, prevent the global mobility of labour from matching the power associated with the global mobility of capital.

The trends discussed above constitute a large part of an attempt to harmonize state policies with regard to issues of migration. It is also probably the closest approximation of top-down multilateral management that has ever been reached on this issue. Yet the political dimension it reflects falls well short of the ethical and political standards that need to be attached to a more democratic world order. The controls exerted in this relatively *ad hoc* multilateral effort involve mostly the efforts of 'receiving' states. The few 'sending' states capable of, and willing to, manage the emigration process of their nationals focus more on the benefits of exporting labour than on fostering the rights of migrants. Like the UNHCR camps of Indo-Chinese refugees in Hong Kong, the regulations of transnational migration tend to reinforce the power of capital by proletarianizing larger sectors of the world population on the one hand, and by constituting pools of available work-force in various regions of the world where they are needed, on the other (Fong, 1993).

Within this context and despite these constraints, transnational migration can be viewed as a differentiated agency of change in the world order, especially through the contradictions its dynamics entail. Transnational migration affects the social relations of production in countries of origin and of destination, as well as state–society relations and the global division of labour. Some of the forces tend to reproduce the existing order. The financial and human consequences resulting from emigration, and the patterns of investments from migrant remittances for example, tend to reinforce unequal development and the situation of dependence of peripheral regions towards centres of the world economy.

The increasing fluidity of social relations of production and social organizations that transnational migration triggers is escaping the forms of control on which capital has been relying. Thus informal banking networks such as the 'tontine', or reproductive strategies taking place in the underground economy, come to constitute alternative channels no longer confined to local situations (Hugon, 1993). By doing so, they can escape states and official and/or traditional capital channels, thus undermining their ability to manage or to discipline capitalist accumulation. But in order to challenge existing structures of domination, the social dimension of global migration ought to be taken into account in multilateral efforts of co-ordination. New avenues should be considered to co-ordinate the movement of people, with a focus on the conditions of migration rather than on its outcome, as they are experienced by migrants and migrant networks. The pursuit of such a project requires that national strategies of resistance and opposition take into account migrants' experiences, and make room for global concerns and forms of mobilization. This is one of the most pressing challenges confronting movements of resistance to global restructuring in the contemporary era.

ACKNOWLEDGEMENTS

I would like to thank Stephen Gill and Graham Todd for comments and help with this chapter.

Notes

1. This UN Population Fund estimate is based on the comparison of the country of residence with the country of citizenship of people, not their country of origin, thus excluding migrants who have settled and obtained the citizenship of the country of residence.
2. Foreign investment in Africa south of the Sahara has declined steadily since the 1980s, particularly among non-oil exporting countries. Foreign direct investment accounted for 8.8 per cent of the 1981 total net resources flow to Africa, but dropped to 2.3 per cent in 1985. A slight

increase to 5.1 per cent in 1988 corresponds to investments in major oil-exporting countries, which received 83 per cent of foreign investments in Africa.

3. The case of France can provide some nuances on the role of migrants in the receiving economy. The 1990 census recorded a rate of unemployment of 11.1 per cent in France, all nationalities together. Among foreigners however, the rate was much higher, at 19.9 per cent. This figure tends to suggest that migrants constitute a marginal mass in the total labour force. However, the rate of unemployment varies along nationalities and regions. Among European Union foreigners the rate is lower than that of other foreigners such as North Africans and Turks. In the 1990 census, the proportion of unemployed among European Union foreigners was very close to that of indigenous French workers and was lower than the rate of unemployment among those considered 'naturalized French'. The low rate of unemployment of EU nationals can be explained by the restrictions limiting the movement of job seekers across the EU. And if unemployment figures were higher for women in general (all nationalities 14.7 per cent), particularly among foreigners (27.3 per cent) and for young people (15.7 per cent of young active French men of 25 years of age and lower are unemployed, 24.5 per cent among young foreigners), the unemployment duration tended to be shorter for migrants.

4. This dynamic should not obscure the important loss of unskilled jobs in this sector, held in large proportions by migrants. From 17.3 per cent in the automobile sector in 1975, the proportion of foreign workers went down to 10.8 per cent in 1990. At the centre of this policy lies the goal of preventing the politicization and mobilization of workers, of whom many were foreigners.

5. It is often the case that the task of finding jobs and recruiting the workers to go abroad is done by other nationals. The Philippines is one of the countries where this is done in a systematic way and with the support of the authorities (Martin, 1993).

6. Based on observations and interviews with refugees and NGOs representatives during a stay on the island of Negroes in the Philippines in 1990.

7. The latter instance refers especially to the efforts of the Japanese authority to attract migrants of Japanese descent from Brazil and Peru (Kawai, 1993).

8. This does not concern the category of migrants as 'investors', who are on the contrary encouraged to develop any kind of economic activity, even ethnic enclaves. As one piece of research indicates, Canada is emphasizing the need for this type of migrant and is offering important benefits, including permanent residence and thus eligibility for citizenship within four years. Few conditions apply to the type of investments made (Wong, 1993).

9. As Zolberg (1988) argues, this conception of the refugee tends to reproduce the historical experience of Western states in so far as it refers to the persecution of people for their political actions which are legal according to the norms of liberal democracies.

10. Some go so far as to place the phenomenon of contemporary international migration on the same level as other world order problems such as 'environmental degradation, drugs and terrorism, and weapons proliferation' (for example, Meissner *et al.*, 1993: 94).

6 Identity, Interests and Ideology: the gendered terrain of global restructuring

Isabella Bakker

INTRODUCTION

The gendered terrain of transition from the old global order to a yet unformed new order is increasingly evident in the policy debates of international agencies and national governments who isolate gender as both a socio-economic indicator and a policy target. The United Nations Human Development Report now not only presents us with a human development index (HDI) but also acknowledges that gender-based disparities require an adjusted HDI. Various international agencies such as the World Bank have established their own Women in Development (WID) secretariats in an attempt to make the funding, targeting and implementation of projects more effective. National governments, spurred on by active women's movements and the launch of the United Nations Decade for Women in 1975, established women's bureaux and programmes as ongoing monitors in the policy process. More recently, the UNDP's 1995 *Human Development Report* has devoted itself to a consideration of gender equality as has the World Bank's publication, *Toward Gender Equality: The Role of Public Policy*.

These publications represent a shift in discourse from recognizing the invisibility of women's contribution toward a problem-solving approach which focuses on how to enhance women's human capital in order to achieve overall goals of growth and development. Such an approach differs from the critical thinking and practice that is coming from below – from those at the margins of the development discourse such as peasants, women and environmentalists. These groups have forced themselves into 'the space of visibility of development' (Escobar, 1995: 155) which in turn has produced new discourses and created conditions for resistance.

Much of the institutional impetus for seeing women as a constituency for development in both the North and the South comes from the material changes in accumulation and reproduction (Beneria and Feldman, 1992; Bakker, 1994). For some women, such as those from the working class and the majority of women in the South, there are continuities in the current transition because of the centrality of their labour to household survival. Yet the fundamental transformation in global production relations, the increasing instability of global financial markets, and rising populations in the South, are all creating new material pressures.

The shift in the global order and in the social and cultural sensibilities embedded within that order, is however revealing the contradictory effects of what is a dual process of both gender erosion and gender intensification (Haraway, 1991). On the one hand, the shift to a new cultural, economic and political order exposes a greater number of women to direct market forces (whether as workers, traders or consumers). The feminization of work has been one consequence for some countries of the re-regulation of their political economy (Standing, 1989). Feminization of the labour force is a process whereby women, often paid lower wages, take jobs formerly filled by men. The increasing share of service sector employment in many OECD countries also shifts employment towards job categories dominated by women (OECD, 1994). In addition, the informal sector is also responsible for an increased share of female economic activity. The lines between the informal sector and the formal sector are becoming more blurred with deregulation, casualization and the growth of sub-contracting and self-employment in both the North and South (International Institute for Labour Studies, 1994). In general, the informal sector appears to expand and contract according to economic conditions – during recession formal enterprises rely on subcontracting (for example, industrial homeworking or the contracting out of services) or may deregulate and partially enter the informal sector whilst periods of expansion encourage regularization of economic activities in the formal sector to obtain loans and benefits (ILO, 1993). The 1995 World Development Report notes that women workers in developing countries tend to be concentrated in the informal sector reflecting the urgency for stable sources of incomes, at whatever level, for households. These trends in women's contribution to the formal and informal sectors suggest the increasing importance of a gender-based analysis of restructuring.

On the other hand, the process of labour market polarization appears to be de-emphasizing the dominance of gender. As labour markets restructure in the industrialized countries, there is increasing evidence of a polarization of 'good' jobs and 'bad' jobs (OECD, 1992a). This process is revealing emerging class and race differences among women and is seeing more men moving into what were traditionally female jobs as manufacturing jobs are disappearing and labour market standards are being lowered through explicit and implicit deregulation.[1] Rubery (1988) has argued that in the reverse case, where women are entering previously male-dominated spheres, there is evidence that the status and rewards for such employment also tend to decline. In developing countries, micro studies indicate a potential shift in gender relations within households due to women's economic contribution through formal markets. Both shifts seem to suggest a convergence of male and female labour market experiences within what are increasingly polarized labour markets (according to core and periphery jobs).

What these trends suggest is the need to consider gender as an interactive category of analysis in a complete account of the transforming global order. This is not to insist that gender is always the most important factor but that a political economy framework must incorporate the interaction of gender with other agents (other groups or individuals), structural factors (assets, norms), processes (production, exchange, coordination, coercion) and sites (firms, states, markets, families).[2]

However, attempts to incorporate gender as an interactive category of analysis within accounts of restructuring encounter knowledge structures that obscure the inter-relatedness of economics with the political, social and cultural. As Anna Yeatman has argued, social, cultural and moral claims are deligitimized and 'those who belong to the gender category non-productive and non-economic – namely women – are refused admission to the central decision making forums on restructuring' (Yeatman, 1990). It is not surprising that women have been most successful in engaging with those central decision making forums on restructuring when they have adopted a strategy of integration and visibility that does not challenge the webs of power sustaining inequalities between women and men, the North and the South.

The next section will explore various forms of knowledge production, identifying patriarchal power in language and in discursive practices. In particular, I focus on how power plays itself out in the disciplinary expressions of global restructuring and adjustment. Not surprisingly, statements and concepts about adjustment and economic restructuring reflect the interests and experiences of the most organized social actors: employees, employers, institutional investors in the financial markets, major capitalist states responding to the pressures of globalization. The allocation of visibilities or, how women's visibility is organized, will be considered through several illustrative examples from the critical development literature.

GENDER AND GLOBAL RESTRUCTURING: FROM GETTING THE NUMBERS RIGHT TO CHALLENGING THE DISCURSIVE FOUNDATIONS

The feminist philosopher Elisabeth Grosz (1990) has argued that a great deal of knowledge production reflects intellectual misogyny taking different forms, from the most obvious to the most insidious: the first, sexism, refers to the absencing or unwarranted differential treatment of the two sexes, benefiting one at the expense of the other; the second, patriarchy, is a structural mode of organization which positions men and women in superior and inferior positions and grants different meanings and values to them; and, the final, phallocentrism, is 'a specifically discursive set of procedures, a strategy for collapsing representations of the two sexes into a single model, called "human" or "man" but which is in fact congruent only with the masculine' (150). As a form of knowledge, philosophy is implicated in the definition of the masculine and the feminine and 'provides general rules, methods, and procedures linking women and femininity to marginal, ignored, subordinated, silenced, or repressed positions relative to men' (148).

Like all forms of knowledge, economics also reflects and helps produce pervasive social beliefs about men and women and their social positions. The most general critique levelled against mainstream economic accounts of restructuring is that they tend to subsume all experiences under a universal rubric of 'human' that is in fact an expression of the masculine. A fundamental weakness in neoclassical economics and classical political economy according to feminist writers, is that need and production are not situated within an analysis of systemic reproduction *that includes* human reproduction and sustenance. A further critique from writers in the South has been the tendency to view economic, political and social change through Western concepts which leave little room for the mutual recognition of distinct traditions of civilization. Broadly, both sets of critiques challenge universalizations based on variants of hegemonic power.

Feminist responses within economics can to some degree, be seen as mirroring Grosz' three levels of ontological and epistemic constructions that relate to the broader concern of how our understandings of restructuring are shaped.

Feminist empiricism and women's invisibility

Feminist empiricism argues that it is not the tools of the profession that need improvement only their application, corresponds to Grosz' first level of sexism. As Julie Nelson (1993) notes, many economists appear to adhere to the view that a more careful application of existing methods exposing sexist and androcentric (the male-as-norm) assumptions will yield a more gender-sensitive analysis. Essentially, both economic policy and research can be corrected for gender bias once the hidden gender dimensions are revealed (the 'add women and stir' approach).

A wide variety of research has been conducted through the lens of feminist empiricism with the goal of 'making women visible' as subjects: research on non-market activities as a legitimate area of economic inquiry (Waring, 1988; Folbre, 1986); in labour economics, questioning the implicit male identity of the typical worker and questioning male patterns as the norm, or generalizing from those patterns to the whole population (MacDonald, 1994). Finally, feminist empiricism encouraged the documentation and explanation of economic gender inequalities through a gender-sensitive analysis of data and research.

How has feminist empiricism manifested itself in the debates about gender and restructuring? Probably the largest body of literature and the most developed has been that of Women in Development (WID). Initiated in the 1970s by Western development agencies, WID policies were to recognize the significant economic and social costs of neglecting and undermining women's roles in the development process. Early development policy related to women primarily as mothers or would-be mothers; welfare programmes were devised which made women the primary targets of a 'basic needs' strategy addressed to health, education, housing, nutrition and home-based income generating activities. Many studies uncovered the hidden role of women both as agents in development and as recipients of androcentric policies.

They pointed out that most policy experts are male, were trained by male experts and prepared to interact mainly with male farmers and producers. This meant that the social practices of the experts themselves often altered those of the environment they were targeting in a way that had negative consequences for the well-being of women and children. For example, male farmers became the beneficiaries of early technological improvements in agriculture, were allocated the best land and were integrated into local and regional cash economies despite the fact that the FAO estimates that 50 per cent of the world's food for direct consumption is produced by women. Women by contrast, were relegated to subsistence activities or, if technical improvements occurred in an area dominated by women, these activities were usually transferred to men (cited in Escobar, 1995: 172). This led to calls to have more women experts intervene in policy development and application.

However, the WID approach continues to be criticized for its poor record of integrating women into the development process, its limited understanding of the structural rigidities of patriarchal relations and its reliance on masculine constructions of value and knowledge. Careful application of scientific methods, behaviouralist techniques and the methodological individualism of neo-liberalism may make for a more universal science but will not undermine the existing assumptions of a given scientific community that sustain those scientific methods. As Stephen Jay Gould has noted:

> Science, since people must do it, is a socially embedded activity. It progresses by hunch, vision, and intuition. Much of its change through time does not record a closer approach to absolute truth, but the alteration of cultural contexts that influence it so strongly. (1981: 21–2)

These reflections have led to broader epistemological critiques that question the role of WID discourse and its call for integrating women into development. In WID women are seen as economic actors that need to be incorporated into a more inclusive universalism through a stricter adherence to the existing methodological norms of scientific inquiry (Harding, 1986). There is no questioning of the fundamentals of that universalism – it is human, rests on 'a stable, transhistorical subject of knowledge that can formulate true statements and construct objective knowledge' (Grosz, 1990: 166). In terms of restructuring, only that which can be documented from the vantage point of the dominant scientific community (for instance, neoclassical economics and its mathematical tools) will be a legitimate object of inquiry and intervention. As Harding has observed, 'This solution to the episte-mological paradox is appealing for a number of reasons, not the least because it appears to leave unchallenged the existing methodological norms of science' (1986: 25). However, using standardized techniques and statistics erases certain of women's experiences, creates client categories and structured agendas (Escobar, 1995: 180). This may have yielded a wealth of knowledge and expertise in the last fifteen years but it has also led some western feminists to question the very procedures and structures of development as an institution of ruling. The starting place for a new approach, according to these thinkers, would be a situated knowledge that acknowledges standpoint.

Standpoint theory and women's victimhood

In an attempt to come to terms with the male bias in knowledge construction and policy, a second feminist intervention within eco-nomics has addressed itself to the patriarchal structures that bifurcate male and female choices, resource allocations and outcomes. Focusing on the dual systems of production and reproduction, analysts link this to a pre-determined patriarchal division of labour. The practices and relations surrounding this gendered division of labour vary across societies and time periods; the boundary between the public and the private is variable and may shift according to how a society organizes the provision of income between the market, the state and the family. Nevertheless, the sustenance and caring of humans remains largely separated from the 'productive' sphere of economic activity and is assumed to take care of itself.

Labelled 'standpoint theory' this approach originates in Hegel's reflection on the relationship between the master and the slave. As Harding explains: 'Briefly, this proposal argues that men's dominating position in social life results in partial and perverse understandings, whereas women's subjugated position provides the possibility of more complete and less perverse understandings' (Harding, 1986:26).

In the restructuring literature, various representations of standpoint theory can be discerned. Particularly influential have been writings that link the patriarchal standpoint of economics to the Structural Adjustment Policies (SAPs) of the 1980s. Much of the literature rests on the premise that the evaluation of SAPs, the policy instruments chosen and the evaluation of impacts all embody, implicitly or expli-citly, a male standpoint that creates, implicitly or explicitly, a male bias. According to Elson, 'Male bias stems from a failure to take into account the asymmetry of gender relations; the fact that women as a gender are socially subordinated to men as a gender through both social structures and individual practices' (1992: 47).

Broadly, the literature on Structural Adjustment has: 1) shown how development policy backfires or fails due to lack of attention to women's issues; 2) demonstrated the differential impacts of policies by gender; and, 3) revealed the implicit gender assumptions underlying the formation of policy. The Structural Adjustment initiative represented a switch of strategies on the part of the major official aid agencies in the early 1980s away from incremental redistribution to monetarist and open economy strategies. The earliest contributions tended to focus on poor women (and children) as the most vulnerable groups affected by the public sector cutbacks endemic to SAP initiatives (Cornia, Jolly and Stewart, 1987). Implicit in these accounts was a privileged standpoint – one that revealed the true costs of SAP strategies because of women's intersecting roles in the paid and unpaid economies. In Mexico, for example, inflation reduced real incomes and the price increases that followed the devaluation of the peso resulted in a decrease in the urban real minimum wage of 47 per cent between 1982 and 1988 (Beneria and Feldman, 1992). However, a disproportionate burden was placed on women because of the sexual division of labour which means that deep cuts in household budgets and demand reducing policies such as cuts in public services (education, health) or goods and services subsidized by the government (electricity, public transport, basic food stuffs) increase pressures on those who administer the household on a daily basis. The need to stretch the paycheck in order to meet basic needs and the anxiety and conflicts over decisions about which items to cut from diets and household consumption often means an intensification of domestic work: more cooking, changes in purchasing habits, and so on.

Whilst the analysis of impacts of structural adjustment through a gender lens again provided vital knowledge about the inequities of global restructuring, accounts of SAP often reinforced a victimhood of women that denied their agency and strategies of resistance. Chandra Mohanty (1988) for example, criticizes white, Western feminists for their universalizing tendencies ('sisterhood is global') and their process of 'Othering' (Eurocentrism) third world women.[3] Mohanty and other third world writers have been particularly critical of the victimology in western feminist accounts of global restructuring. For example, discussion of international restructuring of manufacturing industries and the rise of Export Processing Zones frequently see Third

World women as the passive victims of multinational capital. Newer approaches originating from writers outside of the western framework examine the interaction of constraining structures and women's varied responses to changing material incentives. For example, Naila Kabeer has demonstrated how women garment workers in Bangladesh have taken the new insecurities and opportunities of the government's active encouragement of garment industries and reconstituted purdah norms and customary practices toward a new definition of women's roles (Kabeer, 1989).

Feminist postmodernism and women's fractured subjectivity

This third paradigm challenges both the inclusive universalism of feminist empiricism and the binary universalism of the standpoint approach. Emphasizing the fractured realities and identities created by modern life, feminist postmodernism deals with overlapping, inter-connected concepts because it is experientially or contextually based (Nelson, 1993: 30). Within economics, feminists have challenged discursive foundations, 'the Cartesian view (that) underlies the prestige given to mathematical models of individual rational choice' (Nelson, 1993: 33) and needs, revealing their masculinist foundations (Pujol, 1992; Sen, 1984). As Grosz notes, phallocentric representational models feed into a framework that entails a two-fold procedure: 'one is a leveling procedure where all differences are reduced to a common denominator implicitly defined by masculine interests; the other is a process of hierarchization where one sex is judged better than its counterpart' (1990: 151).

Feminist economists have illustrated how collapsing femininity into the term 'human' does not recognize the masculinity of this universal term. As Elson puts the point:

> Being a worker, or a farmer, or an entrepreneur, does not overtly ascribe gender; but women and men have very different experiences as workers, farmers and entrepreneurs; and the supposedly gender-neutral terms 'worker', 'farmer', 'entrepreneur', are imbued with gender implications. In fact, the 'worker' or 'farmer' or 'entrepreneur' is most often taken to be a man – creating male bias in both economic analysis and economic policy. (Elson, 1992: 2)

This bias is circumscribed and shaped primarily by the structural separation of 'family' and 'economy' that occurred with the advent of industrial capitalism. In the precapitalist epoch, as Karl Polyani (1957) observed, the economy was embedded in society with most production taking place in one's home and involving most household members. Once the economy became disembedded, separate from society and more specialized, this also changed the way in which a society organizes the interrelationship between paid work and raising children. The separation of 'family' from 'economy' made women's work in the family invisible and created a gender hierarchy in the workplace.

The state played an important role in shaping gender identities through a series of economic and welfare related measures. Through the eyes of policy makers, women were mothers or secondary workers sustained by a family wage system. Women engaged in child rearing did not for the most part have an independent entitlement to resources and were dependent on others (family members, life partners) or welfare state arrangements to meet their needs (Orloff, 1994). States and markets continue to operate without counting the costs of caring (Waring, 1988) and this is reflected in recent economic strategies directed at addressing the dual pressures of globalization and fiscal crisis.

The current round of restructuring is 'reprivatizing' many maintenance and caring activities that, through Keynesian Welfare State interventions, had become public, state sector responsibilities. Activities within the public sector are also being re-shaped to conform to private sector rules and criteria. Programme delivery, for example, is frequently based on a more individualized notion of dependency, with the social and structural foundations of dependency increasingly being cast aside in favour of *individual* solutions to what are perceived to be *individually-determined* problems (Fraser and Gordon, 1994). The struggle for survival in many countries of the South has also become increasingly privatized at the expense of the extended family and community.

These elements of state restructuring are contributing to the reshaping of the economic and political identities of citizens. Keynesianism rested on a notion of social citizenship and assumed that the public could enforce certain limits on the market. However, the new order is reshaping these ideals toward market-oriented values based on self-reliance and competition. As Janine Brodie has noted the new 'ordinary' citizen does not make 'special' impositional claims on the state based on difference or systemic discrimination: 'the ultimate function of this special/ordinary dichotomy is to suggest that we ought not make demands on the state because ordinary people don't require assistance and protection' (1995: 35).

In terms of gender identities, the claiming of the general interest over special interests also serves to re-constitute gender identities and reaffirms the masculine as the referent. By de-legitimizing or isolating gender as both a legitimate interest and identity that influences resource allocation, restructuring discourse is shifting our shared understandings, our notion of 'impositional claims' toward an individualist, self-interested neo-liberal order. Feminists writing in this vein are interested in utilizing Corrigan and Sayer's insight of grasping state forms culturally, of discerning how different state forms regulate and impose acceptable forms of individual and collective identity (1985).

Feminist postmodernism is not without its internal tensions and critics. Some have argued that abandoning a collective 'feminist story of reality' may undermine the political effectiveness of practical gender interests in a world still dominated by strong alliances between science and relatively stable and unquestioned social projects. Others have suggested that overlapping universalisms may simply yield a taxonomy of relativist realities that will be ultimately disempowering.

CONCLUSION

This chapter has suggested that both the discourse and the practice of global restructuring is not gender neutral. A new gender order is in the process of being created based on the quantitative and qualitative feminization of labour markets, a redrawing of public and private responsibilities for human maintenance and reproduction toward individual responsibility, and a withdrawal of the modern state from earlier gender equality measures such as childcare and affirmative action programmes. Analyses lodged within economics have captured this gendered dimension of restructuring and adjustment in a limited fashion because of: (1) the androcentric nature of economic theory; (2) the aggregate nature of much of economic analysis (households, firms, nation states); and, (3) the exclusive focus on the production of goods and services sold in the market whilst the reproduction and maintenance of human resources is taken for granted and the blurring of lines between the informal and formal sectors remains under-analyzed.

Feminists have attempted to write themselves into economic debates on restructuring using different ontological and epistemic constructions. I have reviewed three in this chapter – each yields a different level of analysis. For example, feminist empiricism can be linked to an individual level of analysis with its focus on improving the investigative tools of the individual researcher for the broader goal of a more inclusive, better science. Feminist standpoint theory can be equated with a structural approach to issues that reveals how particular patriarchal forms are embedded within economic representations of restructuring. Feminist postmodernism concurs with analysis at the level of discourse, that is, how gendered economic relations are expressed in universal terms that are in fact male in their construction. Some writers within this tradition have argued that the representation of a universal experience within economics such as the rational economic actor often also writes out a lot of male experience.

A consideration of each of these feminist interventions suggests a certain practical complementarity between the approaches. For example, empiricism and standpoint may be usefully combined to advance an argument based on both practical and strategic gender interests.[4] Some of the accounts of homeworkers are particularly promising for linking a context-based analysis to a grand narrative. Work in this area has focused both on the top-down impact of international organizations' discourse on homework (Prugl, 1994) and bottom-up initiatives that give voice to the local responses of casual workers to the growth of flexible forms of work (Rowbotham, 1993). Such accounts reveal how multinational strategies are articulated with divisions in the labour force based on gender, ethnicity, age and class. In this way, feminists examine how gender is socially constructed, producing subjective identities through which we understand the world and shape our shared meanings, practices and institutions. But in addition to improving the accuracy of our accounts of global restructuring, such feminist analyses also suggest alternative ways of being and knowing that inform our larger project of constructing an ethical world order, one that is based on multi-tiered resistances which include a rejection of knowledge structures as tools of ruling.

Notes

1. Explicit deregulation refers to an erosion or abandonment of formal regulations by legislative means, and implicit deregulation, a process through which remaining regulations have been made less effective due to inadequate implementation or systematic bypassing (Standing, 1989).

2. See Nancy Folbre, 1994, *Who Pays for the Kids? Gender and the Structure of Constraint*, for a fully elaborated model of feminist political economy.
3. In the process of her discursive analysis, Mohanty herself takes the standpoint of third world women in an attempt to refocus the centre of feminist Western feminist forms of knowledge production and conceptions of agency.
4. Practical gender interests are usually in response to an immediate perceived need, and they do not generally entail a strategic goal such as women's emancipation or gender equality (Molyneux, 1985:233). By contrast, strategic gender interests reflect a more critical approach that links women's subordination to a systemic analysis.

7 Structural Adjustment and the G-7: limits and contradictions[1]

Fantu Cheru and Stephen Gill

This chapter analyzes stabilization and structural adjustment programmes and their effects, with regard to the nature of, and limits to, the spread of capitalist 'market society', in the post-Cold War era.[2]

To pursue these aims the chapter draws on the framework outlined in Chapter 1 so as to explore the knowledge, institutional and material structures associated with the 'G-7 nexus'. Indeed, an aim of this chapter is to probe some of the limits and contradictions associated with the material and ideational forces of transnational capital, which are driving G-7 perspectives and policies.

One set of limits relates to various perspectives within the ranks of the G-7, which stem from the different, and in some senses, rival forms of capitalism that are practised in North America, western Europe and East Asia. A second limit relates to the epistemological aspects of neo-liberal political economy. Neo-liberal thinking is weak in apprehending and theorizing the social dimensions of change, so that it has a politically perverse, and in many respects somewhat ecologically and socially myopic orientation. In conventional macroeconomic terms, the triumph of neo-liberalism over the Keynesian and state-planning perspectives also casts doubt on the idea that the G-7 could act as a collective steering agent for the transnationalization of capital and the liberalization of global and national economic structures. A third set of limits is more socio-structural in so far as existing patterns of accumulation and consumption appear to be unsustainable, both in terms of their ecological consequences, and in terms of the political and social contradictions they engender. With these issues in mind, we outline possible lessons for former communist states drawn from the Latin American and especially African examples.[3]

GLOBAL RESTRUCTURING AND THE DEBT CRISIS IN LATIN AMERICA

Between 1979–82 the most severe world recession since the 1930s occurred. It occurred in the context of cumulative economic stagnation and the specific effect of a substantial rise in oil prices following the Iranian revolution, and a swift tightening of US monetary policy in 1979. The change in monetary policy in the US triggered a massive rise in world real interest rates (see Figure 7.1 below). The 1980s saw recession in the OECD and economic depression in Latin America and Africa, as well as in many other Third World Countries. The wider backdrop for these developments were cumulative changes in the political economy of capitalism, including the growing importance of global finance in an era of increased government indebtedness and slower economic growth.

Figure 7.1   Real interest rates, 1964–91: major industrial countries and USA (in per cent a year).

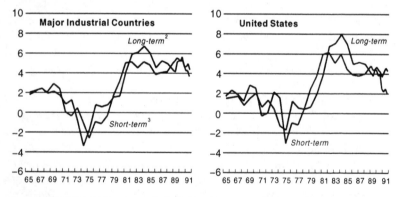

Source: IMF, *World Economic Outlook* (Washington, DC, IMF, 1992), adapted from chart 5, p.8.

Much of the financing of both OECD and Third World balance of payments deficits in the 1970s (and the 1980s) came from the immense 'offshore' financial (or Euro) that now constitute a gigantic pool of mobile capital. In the mid-1970s, these markets were used to recycle the petrodollars earned by many OPEC members unable to invest all of their economic rents because of low internal absorptive capacity, so that loans were offered to both OECD and Third World borrowers at favourable rates: indeed, in real terms, interest rates were, for a period, either zero or negative. In the early 1980s, however, US and global interest rates rose rapidly, making for much higher debt service charges, when demand in the OECD was falling with the onset of a deep recession. A combination of declining terms of trade for primary products – the staple exports of many Third World countries - and, in many cases, poor domestic investments made with borrowed funds made for financial and economic disaster.

It was in this context that the debt crisis emerged, initially in Poland in 1981 (showing how communist states had been drawn into the credit structures of world capitalism), and then, in more explosive fashion in the Mexican default of 1982, which brought the threat of collapse of a number of the biggest commercial banks in America, and indirectly, therefore, the Western financial system. This led to the IMF-organized rescue package, backed by the heretofore *laissez-faire* Reagan administration, and to a period of IMF and World Bank supervision of Mexican economic policy, with the United States Treasury also involved.

As the debt situation worsened world-wide, governments with balance of payments problems were driven to the IMF for 'assistance'. In the 1976, Britain was pressured by the IMF to shift towards market-monetarism. When IMF conditions were applied in the 1980s in the Third World, they required a more liberal and welcoming stance towards foreign private capital, a reduction in budget deficits and the size of the public sector, where possible through privatization of state assets, as well as the internal and external liberalization of markets, including labour markets. In every Latin American case where IMF conditions applied in the 1980s there was a fall in the share of wages in overall national income (Pastor, 1989).

Massive inflows of capital went to the US, much of it drawn from impoverished Third World countries: the 1980s witnessed the defunding of Latin America to the tune of annual resource transfers of around $20 billion (Feinberg, 1989), although this process began to be reversed in the early 1990s with the return of flight capital when investors in the USA could borrow funds cheaply. This process continued at least until the collapse of the Mexican peso in 1994–5, when footloose Third World capital sought a safe haven in the USA, Britain and Switzerland. More broadly, restructuring in context of the Third World debt crisis arose primarily because of effects of more stringent levels of financial discipline. Thus if there is a relative glut of capital available (for instance, during the phase of recycling petrodollars in the mid-1970s which involved very low real rates of interest; the situation in the USA in 1990–94) this may lead to lending which is made on less-than-commercial or prudential criteria. When capital is relatively scarce (when real rates of interest are high) then bankers can be more demanding in terms of the conditions they may set for a loan, or they may call in existing loans and pressure debtors for repayments of interest. The capital may 'come home' with great speed.

By 1985, it had become obvious that the debt crisis was one of solvency not just liquidity, and that it could have serious political ramifications. The debt burden of developing countries was growing and their ability to service this debt declining. Indeed, positive net transfers to the financial institutions were coming from developing countries. The response was another managed solution: the Baker Plan of October 1985. New capital was to come from the Bretton Woods agencies and increased lending by commercial banks: a concept that became known as 'involuntary' lending. The launching of the Baker Plan thus involved a move away from the 'market place magic' approach announced in Reagan's speech to the Cancun Summit of 1981, towards more internationally co-ordinated action to ensure that the creditors continued to have access to credit lines from overseas banks. The basic operative logic was simple: the debt burden will be lightened just enough to keep the system going, but not enough to remove its oppressive and distorting effects. The underlying market principles had not been abandoned, merely slightly diluted, although the private banks were unhappy at IMF and United States coercion.

The announcement of the Baker Plan was, in part, an attempt to steal the limelight in the global debt debate from radical initiatives by Latin American leaders Fidel Castro of Cuba and Alan Garcia of Peru. Whereas a key concern of western countries (particularly the USA) in the early 1980s was on how to reverse left-leaning revolutions in Africa and Central America without too much military commitment, a more important issue in the mid-1980s became how to pre-empt insurrections in the most important debt-ravaged countries and thereby save the west from a financial calamity. The 1989 Brady Plan was also triggered by the force of circumstances, in this case the riots and political instability occurring in Venezuela, a staunch US ally and a nation which had been pursuing strict austerity policies in order to service its debts. The Brady Plan was thus both financial and strategic: a political response to the fear of the rise of populist, socialist or nationalist, state capitalist governments in Latin America.[4]

THE AFRICAN DEBT CRISIS: RE-COLONIZATION BY ANOTHER NAME?

The African case highlights the lack of success in restructuring the state apparatus and solving the continent's economic and social crisis on the part of the World Bank and IMF. Africa does not have the same strategic importance to the G-7, or the opportunities for profit-making afforded by other Third World regions. Nevertheless, Africa, although in smaller numbers than Latin America, has transferred billions of dollars of hard currency to the western creditors at a time when it lacked sufficient resources to even maintain present levels of growth.

In the face of Africa's increasing debt service burden and arrears, OECD nations have implemented a number of debt relief measures, but to date these have failed to provide any substantial solution. Although much has been written on the causes of the crisis, the basic philosophy of adjustment programme have been to get indebted countries to export their way, while devoting less attention to internal production for domestic needs, scaling down the role of the state in national planning and by allowing market forces to play a greater role in national development. Unfortunately, most African countries have instead slid backwards amidst growing poverty, ecological degradation, and mounting debt. Africa's debt crisis is part of a wider development problem and it cannot be understood in isolation from the global restructuring of capital, and the strategies of development promoted by the Bretton Woods agencies in the 1980s and early 1990s.[5]

This strategy, combining both export promotion of primary products and import-substitution industries, is largely dependent on Western markets and financial and technological inputs. While benefiting local élites and some western interests in the short term, this approach has widened social inequalities and ultimately bankrupted African economies. Import-substitution strategy has run its course. Since 1980, capacity utilization levels have dropped as a result of the lack of inputs and spare parts due to the foreign exchange famine. Agriculture, the main source of foreign exchange, has suffered most as a result of years of anti-peasant government policies and recurrent droughts. With their economies extremely vulnerable to external shocks such as oil price rises, coupled with declining prices for African export commodities, very little room was left for most governments to manoeuvre. The widening gap between exports and imports has had to be filled by more and more borrowing at high interest rates (or in recent years narrowed by sharp, often detrimental, reductions in imports). The increased borrowing has, of course, boosted debt service charges, which in turn required new borrowing in the spiral that entraps much of the Third World.

African countries have tried to offset lower world prices by increasing their share of the world market. However, this simply drove down prices further – in a fallacy of composition – dozens of developing countries tried to flood the world market, for example with their coffee and cocoa, as part of an IMF or World Bank 'structural adjustment' programme to generate foreign exchange to service their external debt obligations. While a large number of African countries liberalized their trade regimes at great social, economic and political cost, the champions of free trade in the OECD raised their tariff and non-tariff barriers. Thus, to the extent that the OECD nations prevented Africans from earning their way out of debt, they themselves must take some responsibility for Africa's inability to pay its creditors.

The structure and size of African debt

African debt is dwarfed by that of Latin America but has none the less grown tremendously. Until recently, western indifference towards Africa's debt was rooted in simple figures: only one of every seven dollars owed by Third World nations is held by Africans. There is no single country on the continent that could threaten the international banking system with default (as did Mexico in 1982). Yet, by conventional economic indicators, such as debt service as percentage of export earnings, the African debt burden is considerably greater than that in Latin America. Indeed, over the last decade, over half of the IMF's austerity programme were in effect in African nations. Indebtedness has tended to crush all possibilities for development by diverting scarce foreign exchange and sizeable local resources toward debt repayment.

The second distinguishing feature is the structure of debt. While much of Latin America's debt is owed to private financial institutions, Africa's debt is owed to public institutions such as the World Bank and the IMF. Unlike commercial debts, those owed to the World Bank are not subject to rescheduling. Debt service to the Bretton Woods organizations constitutes the largest portion of payments for a number of debt-ridden low-income African countries. Moreover, non-payment can be costly since access to private sources always requires the IMF seal of approval. For many sub-Saharan African countries, debt servicing to multilateral creditors has become part of the problem, in spite of the expansion of concessional facilities. Since 1985, new disbursements from Bretton Woods agencies have not covered debt service, resulting in negative transfers of increasing magnitude.[6] This macabre situation is akin to the one satirized by Shakespeare in the *Merchant of Venice*, where the moneylender was prepared to accept payment in human flesh.

African debt and structural adjustment

In the course of the debt crisis, the IMF and the World Bank consistently offered an 'internalist' explanation, placing the blame on African governments, and coupling this with an emphasis to rely more on market forces. This was to be achieved through implementation of structural adjustment programmes, or more precisely a convergence of IMF and World Bank policies.

A typical structural adjustment programme included measures to maximize reliance upon markets in goods, capital, and labour flows; to minimize governmental expenditures and economic interventions by reducing public ownership, subsidies, and regulation; and to improve the state's efficiency in allocating and using resources. One decade later, the role of the state in Africa has been significantly curtailed, the dominance of market forces is set in place and economies have been wide open to external penetration. Yet, substantial economic turnaround has not occurred in any of the countries that submitted to them, living standards for the majority of Africans have declined and investment in the productive and social sectors of the economy have dwindled. Despite mounting evidence against the applicability of conventional SAPs in the African context, and in the face of growing popular discontent over years of austerity measures, many African governments have continued to implement them. By doing so they hope to gain access to badly needed foreign exchange, reschedule their outstanding debts, and receive a steady flow of official development assistance.

The creditor strategies

More money/more austerity

In the wake of the 1984 drought and economic collapse, the need for policy reform in Africa became the centre of national and international attention. The following year, the Organisation of African

Unity (OAU) adopted Africa's Priority Program for Economic Recovery, 1986–1990 (APPER). In May 1986, the UN convened a Special Session on Africa dramatizing the critical situation of the continent. The General Assembly adopted its Program of Action for African Economic Recovery and Development, 1986–90 (UNPAAERD).[7] It committed African governments to undertake reforms to create a climate for long-term self-sustaining economic development, and donor governments to provide sufficient resources to support and supplement the African effort. The cost of the five-year programme was estimated at $128 billion, of which $45 billion (over $9 billion per annum) was expected to come from external sources.

The Special Session underlined the crisis and the marginal role of Africa in the world economy. The adjustment called for required not only reform of African economies by opening up markets, but creation of political guarantees for the further expansion of capital. The Africans insisted that the crisis and economic collapse had come about as a result of external shocks: soaring interest rates, declining commodity prices, growing protectionism, and unsustainable levels of debt service commitments. In the end, the African governments were brought to heel and they grudgingly admitted their own mistakes and agreed to implement Structural Adjustment Programmes in return for new money.

The African nations largely kept their part of the bargain. Since 1986, over 30 African countries annually concluded arrangements with the IMF and other creditors and have been implementing policy reforms established within the frameworks mentioned above. Over four-fifth of countries surveyed by UN agencies adopted price incentives and another two-thirds have action to improve internal distribution channels. Nearly two-thirds of reporting countries achieved the target of 25 per cent of total investment allocation to agriculture. About two-thirds of the countries surveyed reduced subsidies. In its final review of progress however, the United Nations concluded that the programme has failed and that the crisis facing Africa today is worse than it was in 1986. It cited the following findings:

- Gross domestic investment, as a percentage of GDP, remained at low levels and actually declined, and gross domestic savings stagnated.
- Both the region's terms of trade and the purchasing power of exports declined markedly during the programme period.
- The performance of the agricultural sector continued to show no recovery at all. The share of agricultural production in GDP

remained virtually constant at about 24 per cent during the period. Drought, locusts and civil wars affected the food supply situation in many parts of Africa.

- GDP per capita continued to decline during the programme period at an average of 0.7 per cent. This means that the average African continued to get poorer and to suffer persistent fall in an already extremely meagre standard of living.
- 'Northern' donors on the whole did not meet their financial commitments, while many African governments continued to devote resources to military and other unproductive uses, and in some cases promoted development policies which favoured special interests (élites, urban dwellers, wage earners) at the expense of the poor, rural majority.[8]

Debt rescheduling

Both bilateral and multilateral public institutions refused rescheduling. Yet debt service owed to them was often no longer offset by new disbursements. The IMF became the first of these institutions to face the likelihood of generalized default, due to massive lending to low-income African countries have had a very high record of failure (Zulu and Nsouli, 1985). Consequently, the IMF established its Structural Adjustment Facility in 1986 and the Enhanced Structural Adjustment Facility in 1987. Both facilities provided assistance on concessional terms to refinance IMF loans to low-income countries which came due in the mid-1980s. Of the 62 countries which qualified for access to these facilities, over half (34) were in sub-Saharan Africa.[9]

The World Bank also launched the Special Program of Assistance (SPA) in 1987 and increased international development assistance (IDA) disbursements to Africa by about $1.5 billion. The increased support however, was nullified by unsustainable levels of debt-service payments from Africa to the Bretton Woods organizations. New disbursements have gone to refinance arrears in debt servicing or principal. Also, about 40 per cent of the 1988 long-term non-concessional Paris Club debt rescheduled for low-income African countries represented interest capitalized by the Paris Club.[10] Growing international recognition of Africa's inability to service its debt and fears of social upheaval resulted in a number of debt relief schemes. In 1988, the Paris Club began to extend debt reduction to some of the poorest countries. Both under Toronto and Trinidad Terms, several African countries, who had IMF/World Bank agreed adjustment programmes in place, got their debts reduced by some bilateral donors. These measures were largely palliative, failing to address the root causes of the debt crisis. The practice of rescheduling debt only postpones the day of reckoning.[11] The total value of cash savings achieved by the 15 countries qualifying for Toronto terms by the end of 1989 equalled $50 million, or only 2 per cent of actual debt service. By contrast, Poland's debt was cut in half to emancipate it from communism while Egypt got a substantial write off of its military debts as a reward for its participation in the 1991 Gulf War against Iraq.

Some bilateral creditors, such as Sweden and France, recognised the inadequacy of the Toronto Terms and put forward proposals to improve the concessional nature of debt relief.[12] By far the most promising of the new initiatives was the Trinidad Terms, proposed by the UK at the Commonwealth Finance Ministers meeting in 1990. One of its key elements was a proposal to write off two-thirds of total outstanding stock of bilateral debt, with reductions being additional to existing debt. However, when the UK tried to get agreement at the 1993 Tokyo summit for an 80 per cent write-off of the poorest countries' debt, its proposals foundered largely on opposition from Japan.

G-7 strategy after the Somalian and Rwandan crises

The 1994 G-7 Summit in Naples proposed a more radical solution to tackle the African debt crisis, in part motivated by the West's realization of the cost involved in seeking to contain civil and political crises, such as in Rwanda, which are caused on the one hand, by contagious forms of genocide and brutal violence, and, on the other, by poverty, debt and unemployment. Thus a proposal by the governments of Canada, Britain and France argued for a cut in overall debt levels in Africa. It was accepted by other G-7 countries, including Japan, that was previously been hostile to such moves. Countries with IMF reform programmes in place and a reliable record of recent debt payments, would be eligible for write-offs.[13] While writing-off debt is not entirely a bad idea, relief and rescheduling programme have been designed to satisfy creditors, and these policies may have postponed adjustment and lowered long-term growth rates in both developed and developing countries.

Disarming the poor: from debt relief to democratization

One response to the debt crisis has been popular pressure and insurgency that led to the collapse of many of the governments that had built up debt, for example in Argentina, Brazil, Peru, the Philippines, Guatemala and Haiti. In Africa, resistance to adjustment has taken many forms: food riots in Morocco, Egypt, Tunisia, Algeria, Sudan, Zambia and many others; political mobilization under the umbrella of multi-party movements; and undermining of state authority through withdrawal from the formal economy, refusing to pay taxes, and so on.

Democracy for cash or for people?

The World Bank recognized this popular challenge in its review of African economies, *Sub-Saharan Africa: From Crisis to Sustainable Growth* (1989). The Bank put its weight behind democratization and decentralization as a *sine qua non* for economic recovery and transformation. While the report stands by many of its basic messages of the Bank's earlier work, it places great emphasis on peoples' participation, meeting basic human needs, recognizing the role of women, and ensuring food security, provision of social services and creation of jobs. Nevertheless, the Bank explicitly acknowledged that the success of its structural adjustment programmes in many countries have been negligible. It recommended that Fund and Bank need less dogmatic approaches. This sentiment was expressed by the Bank's Vice President for Africa, Edward Jaycox, who told a gathering in New York that SAPs in Africa have failed.[14]

One of the key elements in the 1989 report was the recognition that Africa's economic crisis has its roots in political malaise and poor leadership. Corruption is specifically mentioned as a negative factor, as is the élitist orientation of public policy. The Bank calls for wide-ranging changes in the democratization of society within the social and economic framework as well as in development strategies and policies. This is a major departure from the Bank's early position when it released its controversial 1980 report, *Accelerated Development*. Whereas in the early 1980s the Bank consistently advocated a retreat of the state on 'efficiency' grounds, by 1989, 'shrinking the state' was advocated as a strategy for liberating civil society and empowering people. But as Beckman (1992) argued, it is the resistance to SAPs, rather than the structural adjustment process itself that can provide a source of democratization.

Bilateral donors have also jumped on the bandwagon of 'democracy' and 'good governance' following the lead of the US government and the World Bank. At the La Baule Francophone African summit in 1990, President Mitterrand said that France would in the future link its aid contribution to political democratization. A British version was also promulgated in 1990. The European Union and the Commonwealth have also adopted similar approaches, emphasizing accountability, openness and less corruption in government. However, western donors have wanted a state that will open up the economy for capitalist development, and political stability rather than participatory democracy. At best, they want a democracy imposed from the top down. This leads us to the conclusion that while in theory democracy means accountability to the governed, in reality, African governments are accountable to debt structures and the structural adjustment programmes.

Neither democracy nor economic growth has taken place in much of Africa. A first hand observation tells us that the creation of new parties has not directly involved many citizens from outside existing political élites, and particularly not on the basis of pre-existing grass-roots organizations and interest groups in rural areas. Even when there is an appearance of rural support, people have not necessarily consented to it voluntarily; they are forced to accept it or face political persecution. Thus after the general elections, President Moi of Kenya used his prerogatives to nominate back to parliament his supporters who were voted out of office by the public. Moi's action sends a clear message: your vote does not count![15]

Urban 'appeasement'

The collapse of one-party states is rarely accompanied by a substantial reorientation of power relations between urban and rural areas. Indeed, the urban-bias remains overwhelmingly strong. African governments can sit and do nothing when a rural province starves to death. While peasants die in huge numbers, the 'urban' government still survives politically, although it would not survive if basic commodities such as milk and sugar were to disappear from shops in the capital city for a week. The policy of 'urban appeasement' will remain strong even with a multi-party political system unless rural people find a way to have a leverage over policy. More than simply the modification of state forms and the recognition of parties, social movements in Africa and elsewhere have to be given time and space to breath and for non-statist movements to emerge and create an authentic democracy.

Governments have been able to establish a *modus vivendi* with the population by providing citizens with the autonomy and conditions of predictability to set their own 'rules of survival'. A crucial aspect of this is the legitimation of the informal sector, thus allowing space into which to divert personal energies and within which to develop alternative bases of social reproduction. Yet, the vibrancy of these new institutions contrasts obviously with the paucity of their power and resources. In this respect, donor mandated adjustment programmes can only be judged successful when introduced into a national policy environment that also supports and strengthens the capacities of civic groups, informal sector operators and others in civil society.

Popular resistance

Amidst collapsing economies, stratospheric debt and stringent austerity programmes imposed by the IMF, African governments have ceded sovereignty to the IMF, the World Bank and creditor nations. Simultaneously, their standing as sovereign states has been compromised in the eyes of their own people, who see them as predatory and corrupt, and servile executors of the First World's economic agenda. Despite calls for unity at conferences in Cartagena, Havana, Abuja and elsewhere, collective resistance by Third World governments to the First World remains a dream. Those who tried to challenge the prevailing norms, values and institutions of the global political economy, for example Tanzania and Peru, were quickly brought to heel through financial and trade sanctions.

After 30 years of 'maldevelopment' and a decade of austerity and structural adjustment, ordinary Africans have began to defend themselves by simply dropping out of the formal economy, thereby allowing themselves greater freedom for creative adaptation to meet their basic needs. People who are otherwise law abiding citizens are completely disregarding the law and voting with their feet. This is logical because, for peasants and the urban poor, the future is not necessarily more knowable and thus they prefer security and subsistence over uncertain progress. Although the resistance to debt at the bottom has been sporadic and unorganized, this resistance is real, and will grow because it must (Cheru, 1989: Scott, 1985).

Resistance to structural adjustment has given birth to democracy movements. The delegitimation of the state has opened up considerable room for elaboration of new civil society relations. This terrain has been occupied by civic associations, women's groups, human rights groups, pressing demand on the state in a variety of ways. Concerns of these popular protests and movements have challenged not only the policies but even the character of the regimes. Their concerns have been economic (unemployment, declining real wages), social (cuts in welfare services), and political (repression, lack of human rights): all testimony to misdirection of resources and lack of accountability. These social movements co-operate across borders and regions and are waging concerted defiance of austerity programmes and structural adjustment. In short, social movements are redefining issues in terms that address more fundamental questions of resource distribution and access, political rights and processes.

THE G-7 AND THE 'EASTERN QUESTION'

The stated goal of the G-7 nexus towards the former communist states was to transform them in a very short period into capitalist societies. Strategically, this would fundamentally change the geopolitical landscape, since prior to the collapse, 'all roads led to Moscow'. Crucial to the success of the strategy was to be the swift reconstruction of the Polish economy, since this was to be the laboratory experiment whose success would have a demonstration effect for all the others (hence the scale of debt write-offs noted above). Given the strong public support for the new Solidarity government, and its willingness to embark upon draconian 'shock therapy', it was felt that the political conditions for successful transformation from communism to capitalism existed in Poland.

The standpoint that prevailed in informing Western strategy and initiatives for the East can be called 'disciplinary neo-liberalism', with its stress on self-regulating markets and self-disciplined government. Government intervention should thus be premised upon sustaining the conditions for markets to operate with maximum freedom, which was in turn, equated rhetorically with the flowering of democracy. These sentiments gained some support among the people of the former communist countries before, during and immediately following what Timothy Gàrton Ash called the 'refolutions' of 1989–91. This neo-liberal perspective contrasts with a more gradualist state capitalist orientation that was mooted in Germany in the late 1980s (see Chapter 9). It is consistent with the strategic aim of not just the incorporation, but also the attempt to discipline the peripheral countries in a more systematic, long-term way: to 'westernise' these nations.

As noted in the introduction to this book, the models used by economists of the G-7 nexus in the former Soviet Union were developed initially in Latin America. Eastern Europe is of course much more urbanized than Africa, and, like much of Latin American industry, industrial production in the former communist states was fairly inefficient and not competitive by international standards, some evidence that productivity rates have ceased to rise in the context of general economic stagnation in the 1980s.

Disciplinary neo-liberalism

The first dimension of disciplinary neo-liberalism relates to what can be called the direct form of the structural power of capital – that is it is linked to the application of state power and the attempt to co-ordinate G-7 policy, in ways which involve both public agencies and private actors. The process has been led by the G-7, IMF and World Bank, with the OECD giving substantial support. What is remarkable here, and in contrast say with the Marshall Plan, is the speed, incisiveness and relatively low financial cost of IMF/G-7 action since 1989, (as compared, for example, with the Mexican rescue operation in early 1995 where $50 billion in loans was involved).

In time, the new EBRD will fit into this set of arrangements, but in a new way since it has expressly political conditions built into its Articles of Agreement – in contrast to the IMF, World Bank and other regional development banks. The EBRD has to consciously promote liberal democracy as well as capitalist development. So far, however, the EBRD has been notorious for its slow disbursement of loans and for the extravagant offices, salaries and perks it provides to its personnel. In its first two years of its operation it spent more on itself than it did in east European investments; it operated against the backdrop of corruption scandals which plagued key G-7 governments in the early 1990s. Its first chairman, Jacques Attali, was forced to resign and was replaced by the former governor of the Banque de France and ex-Managing Director of the IMF, Jacques de la Rosière – partly because Attali favoured a more state capitalist, planned form of reconstruction in the east.

The perspective that came to dominate the G-7 policies and devolved to the IMF, World Bank and EBRD, was a neo-liberal one. Following Hayek (1944), state intervention should be premised upon the liberalization and guardianship of markets for factors of production under the Rule of Law. For this to be possible requires a strong state apparatus and measures to assure tax collection and public order in a period of austerity. This is because economic restructuring is occurring at a time of severe fiscal crisis for most states, and any attempt to resolve such fiscal crisis requires an increase in the effective rate of tax collection, as well as a more efficient state bureaucracy. Some of the neo-liberal approach is based upon the Hungarian economist Janos Kornai's analysis of state socialism: these economies were/are characterized by 'soft budget constraints' so that the communist state provided open-ended subsidies and bail-outs to enterprises. Thus firms are not subjected to any real competitive pressures (Kornai, 1986). This was intimately linked with what Kornai – now a colleague of Jeffrey Sachs of Harvard who was an adviser to Solidarity and the first post-communist Russian government – calls the 'reproduction of shortage', partly caused by the fact that enterprises tended to hoard factors of production (labour, materials, foreign currency if possible) in order to meet production targets ('storming'), thus compounding the bottlenecks in the economic system. This aspect of communist political economy also had the effect of giving structural power to the skilled and semi-skilled working classes who had the capacity to keep machines operating and to respond to demands for surges in production.

From this perspective both Eastern European and Latin American governments and producers are seen as lacking the iron discipline of 'hard budget constraints' provided in a more demand-led, market system of risk, profit and loss, as well as a more stringent macroeconomic environment. The essence of the approach is to restore the discipline of the self-regulating market and indirectly, to subject development patterns to both the logic and power of capital, on the grounds of greater efficiency. This also means greater labour market discipline to break the structural power of the communist labour aristocracies. A prerequisite for success, is, therefore, the need to reconcile this logic with the necessity of providing sufficient capital to nurture the growth of an enterprise culture and to allow a breathing space for new enterprises and institutions to be able to function effectively in a dangerous and politically unpredictable period of transition.

Timing the transition programme

For western economists – either pure liberal 'shock therapists' or the more compensatory liberals who wanted some type of Marshall Plan style transition programme – the debate has revolved around four elements (Islam, 1993: 59–60). These are:

- The need for macroeconomic stabilization, with tight budget and monetary policies to curb inflation and lower external deficits; necessarily this means cuts in real wages in the context of other measures.
- Liberalization, meaning the freeing of prices, interest rates, and currency devaluation (until the currency is stabilized), free labour markets, with trade barriers lowered and eventually removed, in the context of World Trade Organization membership.
- Privatization, with the creation of joint stock companies; laws protecting property rights and the creation of capital and equity markets.
- Institutionalization. This means constitutional reform, the development of a new legal system, and new arrangements for political activity and association. In addition other innovations were seen as necessary, such as accounting and regulatory procedures, social insurance and 'safety nets' for those hard hit in the transition, such as pensioners who have seen their life savings liquidated by hyper-inflation since 1991.

One of the key issues is the sequencing of reforms and there are a range of positions taken. So far the G-7 response has, to a degree included all of them. Nevertheless, none of the proposals – for example from the IMF on redesigning central banking structures as well as in stabilization and education of cadres (the IMF began training programmes for officials in Russia, the Ukraine and elsewhere) – has been completely carried through. The result is that there has been hyperinflation, massive capital flight and a huge collapse of industrial production and real economic activity.

Poland: the first laboratory experiment

In the Polish case the G-7 supported substantial debt restructuring through concerted action in the Paris Club (responsible for about $30 billion of Poland's debt), and increased supplies of foreign exchange and long-term capital from the IMF and World Bank. As Jeffrey Sachs was quick to point out, the costs to the West were but a 'pittance'. The measures agreed with the IMF were designed to repair the collapse in supplies of vital consumer goods, restore price stability (inflation ranged between 5800 and 7200 per cent during 1989) and monetary discipline to the government by eliminating enormous budget deficits (which were almost entirely monetized) and devaluation of the zloty (by about two-thirds against the dollar). These measures – and others – were intended to create the conditions for an autonomous enterprise and, eventually, a private sector, to emerge and function effectively, although privatization has proven very difficult. There still remains the problem of creating a legal regime for property rights and a system of accounting in all the former communist economies.

Part of the social cost of these measures was a massive fall in production and real incomes since prices rose, subsidies have been gradually eliminated and wage increases were restrained to about one-fifth of the rate of price inflation. Nevertheless the Polish government went against IMF advice and chose a strongly-damped wage inflation rather than a wage freeze. Unemployment, unknown under communism (although there was substantial under-employment) rose rapidly. The measures eventually succeeded in stabilizing the zloty. Nevertheless, the Solidarity government fragmented, popular discontent rose and a mood of anxiety and pessimism swept the country. In late 1995 the leader of the revolution, Lech Walesa, was defeated in his bid for re-relection as President by a former communist.

In this sense, the radical 'reforms' went beyond the willingness of the populace to support them. IMF-sponsored policies of shock therapy have been subject to populist attacks both inside and outside parliament, and the former communist party reorganized and regained political support. This is partly because many of the key entrepreneurial agents of the new market system were crooks, swindlers and thieves (there have been a rash of big banking and financial scandals). IMF-backed policies were insensitive to social considerations, despite their success in curbing hyper-inflation and stabilizing the zloty. The government also had difficulty in collecting all the taxes it is owed – an ironic repercussion of the privatization strategy (collecting taxes from state enterprises was much easier). Moreover, tax evasion and other forms of passive resistance are on the rise on the part of many workers. The most aggrieved were those laid off from the former state enterprises: people who had been the staunchest supporters of Solidarity.

The strategy towards Russia

After the Russian referendum of April 1993 which showed a majority in favour of President Boris Yeltsin's reform programme, Yeltsin began moves to strengthen the powers of the President, backing the market reforms and linking them to constitutional reforms so that private property guarantees would be of 'world standards'.[16] Yeltsin also gained the support of most G-7 governments when he instructed the military to storm the parliament buildings to oust his opponents (only the Japanese government seemed to criticize the actions).

With Yeltsin apparently strengthening his power, the G-7 became more explicit about its strategy for eliminating 'hyper-inflation'. This, according to the Managing Director of the IMF, Michel Camdessus, is the principal initial goal of policy in Russia. The Fund consistently pointed the finger at the Russian central bank as being primarily responsible for hyper-inflationary forces, with its tendency to direct credits at subsidized interest rates to sustain production whilst keeping ceilings on the deposit rates of savings banks. Camdessus put it this way in an interview with the US correspondent of *Izvestia*:

> After almost fifty years of experience with so many countries in the world, we know well that hyperinflation is a disaster, because reforms cannot develop in the context of hyperinflation, because hyperinflation strikes mainly the poorest in the society, and, finally, because, at the end of the day, it is most dangerous for democracy itself... hyperinflation must be stopped at all costs.

He then emphasized what Russia needed to do in order to expect an adequate disbursement of funds from the G-7 and IMF:

> ... the strongest principle of international financial coopera-tion... is ... The stronger the policies of the country for stabiliza-tion and reform, the more effective, the more abundant, the external support [for welfare, unemployment benefits, pensions, nuclear safety, transformation of the military-industrial complex. Such sup-port]... is dependent not essentially on the generosity of the West, but on the *credibility* of your own policies... I used to say that one of the most inspiring words of [Article I] of the charter of the IMF is... 'give confidence to members,' and this means... two things. Give *confidence* to the Russians that if they do the right thing, these policies will lead, one day or another, and possibly sooner than we believe, to prosperity in your country. And simultaneously, give *confidence* to the world that if the world supports you enough at the critical moment that you adopt the right policies, this will have a pay-off in terms of prosperity for Russia and the world.[17]

This meant replacing the existing head of the central bank with a market-monetarist reformer and tightening credit to squeeze out inflation and restore financial discipline. However, this strategy requires – as in Poland – significant popular support, so that, once the process begins and the inevitable bankruptcies occur, and unemployment rises, there is less and less leeway for turning back. Nevertheless, a broad basis of political support for this strategy simply did not exist between 1992–5 and, as a result, hardly any of G-7 funds had actually been disbursed by late 1995 (for example when compared with the Mexican rescue of 1994–5). The Japanese were very reluctant to advance funds, citing the conflict over the Kurile Islands as the main reason, but the reality was that the Japanese government favoured the model of restructuring adopted by the bureaucratic-authoritarian NICs, rather than the Anglo-American 'shock therapy' approach.

Thus, the Russian stabilization programme has been, to say the least, hanging in the balance, with huge falls in output, roaring inflation and a general economic contraction of an extraordinary scale. Despite the hopes and expectations of western economists, the rate of inflation has not been mastered and might even soar further if Russia's social safety net expands to avoid further chaos and political unrest. Only if the rouble is finally stabilized will foreign investors move in larger numbers.

In 1993–4, capital flight from Russia was estimated at about $1 billion per month, and investigation into this problem was quickly shelved by Russian authorities, suggesting that key members of the state apparatus were probably involved. London has become a key centre for 'Russian flight capital of dubious legality'.[18] Indeed, Russian capitalism is associated increasingly with Mafia-like organizations openly flouting state authority. In the new spirit of international co-operation, the United States FBI now has an office in Moscow and is working with Russian criminal enforcement agencies to try to deal with organized crime.

None the less, the speed of post-Soviet economic and social decline was staggering, and many believe that the collapse was accelerated by the attempt – albeit a contradictory one – to pursue neo-liberal reforms long before the appropriate institutional and political infra-structure were in place (see Table 9.2). With its chaotic economic and social effects, the post-communist reform process was associated with growing unemployment, a massive redistribution of wealth, especially since the majority have lost their savings to inflation. This hit pensioners and others on fixed incomes particularly hard. An opinion poll, reported that 28 per cent of Russian respondents said they lived in 'intolerable poverty' whereas 1 per cent of the population believed they were 'very well off'.[19] Growing evidence of hunger and disease appeared: in the summer of 1994 it was reported that cholera and anthrax epidemics broke out in a number of major population centres in Russia. A breakdown in law and order with escalation of violent crime and murder was linked to the state losing its monopoly over weapons: its arsenals were plundered of assault weapons and, it was reported, nuclear installations of plutonium by Mafia-like criminal organizations. In all the former communist countries the death rate soared after the transition; in Russia it jumped by 20 per cent in 1992 alone. There was been an unprecedented and sharp fall in life expectancy, especially among men. Researchers have concluded that this was because of social crisis and growing violence in Russia.[20]

The gigantic depreciation of the rouble against other hard currencies in the past 5 years (from officially 1:1$ to over 4000:1) reflects a collapse in the value of the Russian economy, and in a bargain price for Russian assets. Thus it is important to note the following comments by Lawrence Summers, Under-Secretary of State for International Affairs at the United States Treasury (and the key official concerned with the G-7 and the international financial institutions). These comments indicate the way in which G-7 financial leverage over Russian reforms has increased massively, in so far as these reforms require external financing. Russia has received $12 billion in 1996 in an orthodox IMF stabilization programme after earlier receiving more modest yet concessional financing. This facility, reviewed on a monthly basis, was conditional on macroeconomic discipline being maintained. The funds were also intended to support the re-election of President Yeltsin. More fundamentally:

[The collapse in the rouble enhances western aid]...Hyper-devaluation is an opportunity for small amounts of Western support to really make a difference...so that $1 billion given to Russia has the same impact on the fiscal situation as $100 billion in the United States. (Delamaide, 1993: 78)[21]

What is rarely noted in the press is the degree to which the Bretton Woods organizations and the G-7 governments (and members of their private sectors) have co-operated in the re-training (political and economic re-education) of the former governing cadres, indeed setting up a training institute in Vienna to instruct the new managers of ministries in financial planning and in micro- and macroeconomic policy-making. This is an attempt to widen the political bases of support for reforms, as well as providing the indigenous technical capability to reshape the post-Soviet political economy towards capitalism. The World Bank has tended to concentrate much of its efforts in giving loans to new private enterprises and assisting the privatization programmes.

Nevertheless, signs of a backlash against the G-7 policies have also been apparent. President Yeltsin's rule has become more idiosyncratic and authoritarian, and elements associated with the national security complex are becoming more powerful in Moscow. The nationalist right and the former communists regrouped and from their different perspectives, oppose the liberal 'reformers' and called for a return to a more statist economic order. Miners strikes reflected the fact that many workers had not been paid for months. There was a huge build up of inter-enterprise debts, a problem that far outweighed the financial consequences of Russia's fiscal crisis as conventionally defined. President Yeltsin opposed the G-7 project to expand NATO membership to include former communist states, and declared the onset of a 'cold peace'. The Yeltsin government authorized some re-nationalization of privatized assets. Agencies of transnational civil society, such as United States foundations (for instance, the Carnegie Endowment, which like others, opened an office in Moscow) were accused of spying for the CIA; others, like the private western banks, were portrayed by some of the Yeltsin inner circle as engaged in a conspiracy to ruin the Russian economy.

CONCLUSIONS

Lessons for the former communist states

Lessons which might be drawn by the citizens of eastern Europe from Latin American, and especially African experience might include the following:

- The roots of the debt crisis lie in a global system of political economy that is profoundly unequal in terms of power and distributional consequences, and that that is continuously reproducing social marginalization and perpetuating the disadvantaged position of the poor Third World countries. Attempts by the Third World to change this system were blocked in the mid-1970s, and reversed in the 1980s, through a combination of the direct and indirect aspects of the power of capital. The intransigence of the G-7 nexus during this period must be understood by East Europeans who misguidedly look to the West and to market forces as liberators.

- The adoption of free markets is not the solution to the social and economic crisis in Eastern Europe; indeed, free-market reforms have deepened the crisis. East European states cannot export their way out of stagnation, especially when G-7 trade barriers remain high.
- The state has an important role to play in national development, and the state is not necessarily or inevitably parasitic or corrupt. Indeed, the G-7 reform process actually requires a strengthening of key aspects of the state apparatus, although the rhetoric of structural adjustment and 'systemic transformation' may suggest otherwise.
- Free markets are not necessarily synonymous with democracy, and indeed the notion of competitive free markets needs to be placed in the context of the transnational oligopolies which dominate world trade and commerce. East Europeans must recognize that markets are an outcome of social struggle, and that G-7 governments are likely to prefer order to political freedom if the alternatives involve the sacrifice of the goal of creating market societies in the east.
- Foreign aid, as it is currently defined, may well be part of the problem, not the solution, since it goes with demands for constitutional and political reforms. Foreign aid needs to be used in different ways, and less tied to market objectives, and focused more on fostering autonomous capabilities within civil society, for example in education, primary and preventative health care and appropriate technology, so that an active and democratic process of empowerment becomes more feasible.
- Even the writing off of debt by creditors, while on balance probably a good thing, would not ensure by itself the transition from debt to development for most Third World countries. The growth in the debt pyramid and the growth in the debt burden of African countries despite debt relief from donors testifies to the success of the creditor strategy, in promoting a net transfer of resources from rich to poor.
- The peoples of indebted countries in Africa, Latin America, eastern Europe and elsewhere must come up with their own initiatives rather than waiting for solutions to come from above, that is

directly or indirectly from the creditor nations. The most important step is to recognize and to reassert their own longer-term interests and identity ahead of the needs of creditors. A continuing commitment to repaying debts that cannot be realistically paid is to continue to make the problem a problem of the debtor, rather than a problem of the creditor. Instead of adjusting to external factors, indebted countries must try to tailor their external relations to the needs of internal development. One of the first steps is to gain control over flight capital and place resources at the disposal of more democratically-controlled productive interests within Third World countries.

Democratisation and resistance

The elements of the restructuring process discussed in this paper all came into play under unprecedented conditions after the collapse of communist power in Poland in 1989: a moment of the apparent triumph of popular, democratic forces. The example of Solidarity indicates that then, as today, the 'limits of the possible' are not fixed or immutable. They can be changed by collective human action, at local and at global levels of struggle.

The masses in the indebted countries paid heavily for a decade of uncertainty. Private investors, both domestic and foreign, have been reluctant to make commitments and Third World governments have been largely unable to obtain additional resources from world capital markets. Politically, these governments put themselves in the dangerous position of agreeing to the dictates of the creditors in imposing politically unpopular reform programmes. Reform became necessary to satisfy creditors, and not adequately internalized as a domestic requirement for growth. But perhaps more important, the failure to resolve the debt problem placed a balanced form of economic growth on hold; an untenable position both politically and economically in countries where poverty and growing populations are combined.

Thus, it may be that resistance to structural adjustment – not only passive, but perhaps also active – which offers the source for a more authentic democratization. The term 'democracy' is a highly elastic one, and we now live in an age where virtually every government claims it is part of a democratic system. What we have in mind is a democracy which is not only formal, but also substantive, and one which is authentic in the sense of providing for the collective possibility that all can participate politically in processes which configure or determine their life chances.

Moreover, with regard to the revolutions in Eastern Europe and elsewhere, we should note that some forms of 'democratization' may not necessarily involve the development of progressive forces. For example, in Hungary and Poland, it has gone recently with the rise in right-wing populism and a resurgence of fascist political movements. Similar trends are discernible in other parts of the former Soviet Union to say nothing of Russia itself. Whereas some forms of democratization and resistance in the Third World are intended to sustain the self-protection of the people from unfettered market forces, and can be understood as relatively progressive forms of self-empowerment, elsewhere the evidence is mixed. In parts of the Third World, resistance to the processes of commodification and western rationalisation of social life, and especially to the marginalisation this entails for the urban masses, often has given rise to religious fundamentalism, some of which has a socially repressive character. This is not incidentally, to equate either Islam or Hinduism with fundamentalism – each religious tradition is quite broad and diverse.

What is needed is the creation of a distinct (that is, non-western) form of identity within the Third World which can combine, mobilize, and democratize in both a progressive and an emancipatory manner – indeed this is part of the problematic for the achievement of authentic development. There is evidence that such developments have already begun. Indeed, forces within the OECD countries should attempt to forge links with progressive elements in, for example, the Islamic world, to strengthen a transnational social movement which can create more local and transnational political support for a new global social order – one which is more equitable and democratic. In this context, it is important to challenge the rhetorical and ideological more that equates neo-liberal 'reform' with progress, and delegitimates all alternatives as conservative or reactionary. Indeed neo-liberal restructuring is quite compatible with authoritarian government.

We may, in this context, be entering a period of struggle in global politics between the dark forces of reaction and those which are more associated with democratization and an emancipatory politics. Indeed, whilst some forms of passive resistance may be isolated instances which appear nihilistic, or may involve *anomie* or a sense of abandonment, others may be simply sporadic survival strategies. Elsewhere, passive resistance may take on the character of a broader social force and have a class and thus a political dimension. What might emerge is a form of collective action which produces structural change (as in the case of the Chinese peasantry in response to the mass starvation associated with the Great Leap Forward, which eventually forced the government to change its policies in the country-side, and to allow locally controlled agricultural markets to emerge). The key is to capitalize on the links between more progressive and culturally tolerant forces to create new forms of multilateralism.

In this context, the debt crisis is a symptom of a larger crisis of development (see Chapter 6 by Isabella Bakker and Chapter 8 by David Law on other dimensions). It raises fundamental questions of policy and institutional structure. The devastating effect of debt and financial discipline in the global political economy is forcing popular movements across the globe to reconceptualize how to struggle for their economic rights, often outside the bounds of state power. As eastern Europe and the former USSR embark on ambitious pro-grammes of economic reform, they should take note of the experiences of Africa and Latin America which gained neither meaningful devel-opment nor real, that is substantive, democracy.

We conclude therefore that there is no simple or single solution to the problems of debt, development or democratization. In the final analysis, it is up to the peoples of the Third World and the former Soviet Union and eastern and central Europe to develop their own solutions, albeit not in ways which forego the possibilities of alliances with sympathetic and progressive counter-hegemonic forces in other parts of the world. The forces that enjoy the great popular support in coming years will probably be those that can offer effective solutions to the sources of mass discontent while retaining a commitment to civil liberties and ideological pluralism and toleration of differences. While the 'local' is still the primary point of engagement for popular movements, the other main battlefield – where the rules and dynamics of the struggle are imposed – is the world economy. The latter is driven by forces which in general seek to superimpose economic and cultural homogenization and political hierarchy, principles associated with the attempt to create a global market society.

Notes

1. We would like to thank David Law, Kees van der Pijl and David Moore for comments on the first version of this chapter, and participants at the symposium in Vikersund for their reflections on the paper.

2. Stabilization aims to reduce short-term disequilibrium, especially budget deficits, inflation and balance of payments deficits (the role of the IMF). Structural adjustments are concerned with a reorientation of the structure of the economy towards greater market efficiency, aimed at restoring growth in the medium term (the role of the World Bank). In reality, however, the distinction between the two is blurred because World Bank programmes are never instituted unless an IMF programme is already in place.

3. It is worth noting here that what are often represented as 'successful' models of adjustment by the Bretton Woods organizations, namely the 'Asian Tigers', are the product of a very different era and policy mix to those urged on the African countries and nations that were members of the former Soviet Union and COMECON. The newly industrializing countries (NICs) of east Asia grew in the context of unique strategic commitments by the USA in the Cold War, which provided them with direct resource inputs as well as privileged access to American markets. The NICs never entrusted development to pure market forces: development was channelled and capital was disciplined by bureaucratic authoritarian state structures to achieve international competitiveness. When the World Bank sought to reproduce this pattern in the 1980s and encourage new and more competitive NICs, it did so with little regard for democratization, as the case of the Philippines under Marcos illustrates, and indeed its policies met with very poor economic results.

4. The Japanese government developed the first version of this plan, (involving substantial debt restructuring and forgiveness) at the Toronto summit of 1988. This was blocked by the USA which did not wish to see Japan take a leading role. When the Brady Plan emerged, however, a condition was that the Japanese supply a substantial proportion of the funds needed.

5. In the 1990s most of the GDP growth in the Third World took place in east Asia and China, with some increases in the western hemisphere. Real output in Africa was weak, and the continent's terms of trade declined by a further 6 per cent and export receipts fell, with the drought in Southern Africa having a massive impact. The crisis in the Middle East surrounding the 1991 Gulf War in effect reduced economic growth in the region virtually to zero. Although there was a small decline in debt-service ratios from 39 per cent to 32 per cent between 1986 and 1991, the total external debt of Third World countries increased by 5.25 per cent.

6. In 1980, Bretton Woods organizations accounted for 14 per cent of Africa's debt. In 1992, it was closer to 25 per cent. Sixteen African countries owed 50 per cent or more of their foreign debt to the Bretton Woods agencies, and another eight, 40 per cent or more. See Roy Laishley, 'Renewed Calls for Less Debt, More Aid', *Africa Recovery*, Vol. 6, No. 4, pp 4–5, December 1992–February 1993.

7. United Nations, *United Nations Program of Action for African Economic Recovery and Development 1986–1990*, Report of the Secretary-General, document A/42/560, New York: 1 October 1987.

8.   United Nations, *Economic Crisis in Africa*, Final Review and Appraisal of the Implementation of the United Nations Program of Action for African Economic Recovery and Development 1986–1990 (UNPAAERD), report of the UN Secretary-General, New York: United Nations, 3–13 September 1991.

9.   SAF disbursements to Africa at the end of July 1990 were $1.2 billion (or 60 per cent of total SAF disbursements) and ESAF disbursements were $970 million (or 86 per cent of total ESAF disbursements). See UN, *Economic Crisis in Africa*, Final Review and Appraisal of the Implementation of the United Nations Program of Action (UNPAAERD), Report of the Secretary-General New York: United Nations, 28 August 1991.

10.   European Campaign on Debt and Development, 'The South's External Official Debt: Trends and Key Issues', *Third World Economics*, No. 47, 16–31 August 1992, p.12.

11.   The Toronto 'menu', announced at the 1988 G7 summit, offered creditors the option to either cancel one-third of debt, extend maturities (to 25 years) or reduce interest rates. The debt relief measures were applicable only to low-income countries implementing approved structural adjustment programmes which had persistent debt service problems and poor balance of payments prospects. However, the Toronto Terms were applied sparingly. By the end of 1989, only $6 billion of the $64 billion of qualifying debt had been cancelled or converted. See UNDP, *Human Development Report 1992*, New York. United Nations, p. 46.

12.   While Sweden waived all interest charges for eight years on export–credit debt of a number of African countries, France wrote off $2.4 billion in concessional debt owed by 35 of the poorest African countries. In addition, the US announced a similar measure for $1.4 billion of concessional debt owed by 22 African countries pursuing IMF or World Bank adjustment programmes. Italy also announced in April 1990 that it would cancel about $1 billion of the ODA debt owed by the most indebted low income countries, most of which are African. United Nations, *Economic Crisis in Africa*, New York: United Nations, 28 August 1991, p.21.

13.   The proportion of debt written off will be raised from the present 50 per cent to at least 66 per cent and perhaps more. Until now, even least developed countries have only been granted reductions in payment maturities falling due over a limited period, such as 18 months.

14.   Remarks by Edward V.K. Jaycox before the African–American Institute's Annual Conference, 20 May, 1993, reported in the *Washington Post*, 'World Bank to Strengthen African Nation's Role in Aid', 21 May 1993.

15.   For brief details, see F. Cheru, 'Kenya', in J. Krieger (ed.) (1993) *The Oxford Companion to Politics of the World* (New York: Oxford University Press), pp. 502–3.

16.   *Financial Times* 15 April, 1993, p. 3. Yeltsin obtained a constitution in which Presidential power dominates all other state institutions, with the right to nominate the Prime Minister, heads of the armed forces, top judges, the central bank chair, as well as the power to issue decrees and to dissolve parliament at will. *Financial Times*, 24–5 April 1993.

17.   *IMF Survey* 1993, Vol. 22, No. 4, pp. 50; 52–3
18.   *Financial Times*, 14 February 1994.
19.   *Financial Times*, 19–20 April 1994.
20.   *Financial Times*, 14 February 1994
21.   The Fund claims that the amount of official financial assistance from the OECD countries and the international financial institutions to Russia between 1992 and 1993 was $38 billion, of which $15 billion was official debt relief. In all $55 billion was allocated – the $17 billion shortfall was blamed on the inability of the Russian government to deliver in its agreements with the international financial institutions. The Fund had announced $14 billion in loan facilities and stabilisation funds but as of 1994, only $2.5 billion was disbursed – $6 billion to stabilize the ruble was not issued because Russia failed to put the necessary policies in place. The World Bank allocated $5 billion, but only disbursed $500 million for the same reasons.

8 Global Environmental Issues and the World Bank[1]

David Law

Until quite recently, research in international political economy as an emerging field paid little attention to environmental issues. When exploitation was discussed it was with reference to labour and less developed countries rather than to the environment and natural resources. Radical as well as mainstream perspectives tended to take for granted the sustainability of economic growth. Radical writers who analyzed the structures and contradictions of global capitalism stressed inequalities, unemployment, North–South tensions and loss of legitimacy much more than cumulative environmental degradation and the way it was linked to the spread of industrialization, private enterprise and commodification. As concern over environmental issues grew, all perspectives, radical and mainstream, faced the challenge of extending their framework to integrate such issues into a truly global analysis. It became clear that the 'issue areas' of deforestation and climate change were interlinked and global in character. Further, problems of ozone depletion, acid rain, pollution of the seas and over-fishing were, like deforestation and global warming, associated with economic and population growth.

More than a narrow set of measures is at issue. Questions of 'what kind of development and for whom?' are involved. There is a struggle for hegemony in which a revamped liberal multilateralism is attempting to manage some of the contradictions of the latest transnational and global phase of capitalism. The contradictions of financial instability, the spread of weapons and drugs, the erosion of community and traditional social institutions, are linked to, and exacerbated by, various kinds of environmental abuse that threaten health, safety and material living standards, especially in the long-term.

These problems threaten not just people but the very legitimacy of neo-liberal ideas and institutions, such as the World Bank, as well as the social forces and interests that support them. These problems and

171

contradictions offer an opportunity for, and challenge to, emerging counter-hegemonic forces. Neo-liberal analysis and policies based on competitive economic liberalism with some allowance for environmental issues, such as those favoured by the World Bank, do not go far enough in exposing and dealing with the sources of pressure on the environment. Thus I use a broader political economy approach to shed light on failures of the World Bank and limits to its 'greening' as well as possibilities of and obstacles to developing a counter-hegemonic bloc in which NGOs would play a key role.

Central to analysis must be explanation of changes in international agendas and how they have been managed and affected by the 'old multilateralism', for example the IMF and the World Bank. Here I focus chiefly on the World Bank, ideas about 'sustainable development' which it now claims to promote and the role of non-governmental organizations (NGOs). How far can existing institutions be reformed? What part do NGOs play in this process? In approaching these questions we will need to examine the nature and limits of environmental discourse and the agenda of global politics in the 1980s and 1990s. Environmental issues received a deal of public attention in the 1980s: the Commission on Environment and Development's Brundtland report, *Our Common Future* (1987) marked a change in the international agenda that was confirmed in conferences and gatherings that preceded the Earth Summit in Rio in 1992. However, the attitude of President Bush of the US before and during the summit and other leaders such as Malaysia's Prime Minister, Dr Mahathir, illustrated the continuing priority accorded to growth, both of profits and living standards. Central to the rhetoric of established politicians seeking the green vote was the phrase 'sustainable development'. The very popularity of this vague and essentially contestable expression was a testimony to its political usefulness: it could be used to mean different things to different people in different places.[1]

CAPITAL MOBILITY, GROWTH AND ENVIRONMENTAL SUSTAINABILITY: A CONTRADICTION IN TERMS?

Today, social forces associated with, and supportive of, transnational capital exert growing influence over economic and social policies. Tremendous mobility of capital between countries is now truly global with the collapse of communism. Privatization, deregulation, fiscal consolidation and 'market disciplining' of the public sector have spread, almost like a global epidemic, since the early 1980s. These changes, according to their proponents, such as the World Bank, will boost economic efficiency and growth. Economic growth needs huge investments in infrastructure such as power stations – the kind of project the Bank has promoted through its loans and expertise. The Bank, like the IMF, favours countries that adopt the policies of openness to foreign investment and trade liberalization. The rapid growth of most East Asian countries in the 1980s (and 1970s in some cases) is seen as proof of the transnational liberal recipe. The Bank and its allies have faced a chorus of criticism on two counts: growing poverty and environmental degradation in much of Asia, Africa and Latin America made worse by the Bank's structural adjustment programmes.[2] In response to such criticism the Bank has sought to 'green' the development it promotes through policies, procedures and institutional changes that reflect a concern for sustainable development.

The term 'sustainable development' is probably here to stay, but its meaning and practical interpretation is a matter for contestation. Where concepts are 'essentially contestable' one needs to ask 'sustainable for whom, why and in what way?' Traditionally 'economic development' has been associated with output growth, technological change, more intensive use of resources, increased use of energy, urbanization and industrialization (amongst other things). In developing, the North has burned up (and continues to burn up) vast amounts of fossil fuels. Since such development has often gone with the growth of pollution and the depletion of natural resources it is far from clear what, if any, kind of 'development' is sustainable. Recently a discourse on sustainability and development featured in the Bank's 1992 *World Development Report, Development and the Environment*. The timing of the report before the Earth Summit was to help boost the World Bank's green credentials.

In practice, the term sustainable development is popular, partly because it seems to conjure up the possibility of combining output growth and higher living standards with sustainability. If the size of the cake cannot keep growing in the long term then very awkward political questions arise about its distribution – between groups, classes, nations and generations. Such questions are especially awkward for the 'haves', such as the industrialized countries of the 'North' and for their rich élites in particular. However, the 'South' also have rich people, whose wealth often contrasts glaringly with widespread extreme poverty. Furthermore, population growth has been much

174   *Global Environmental Issues and the World Bank*

more rapid in the South in the twentieth century than in the North. Thus their political élites have compelling reasons to prioritize growth and these are reinforced by their wish to catch-up with the North – partly with regard to relative power and status. While a concern for sustainable development could be of interest to powerful people in the South, *if* able to take a sufficiently long-term view, it is not surprising that so far the major pressures for putting environmental issues on the international political agenda have come from the North. While this owes something to the greater political impact of environmental groups in the North than the South, there are other reasons why certain kinds of global environmental issues are of growing concern to people and interests based in the North. Certain research findings, notably those on global climate trends and ozone layer depletion have cast doubt on the planetary feasibility of old-style development for *all* countries.

Chances of the 'South' reaching consumption and production patterns found in Japan and Western Europe without the latter making *sacrifices*, look far-fetched. This is even more true if comparison is with the 'petroholic' United States. In the run-up to the Rio Summit (and an American election), President Bush said 'our life-style is not negotiable'. If the North wishes to further increase living standards then the likelihood of environmental overload is even greater and development as imitation of the North, no longer plausible for most less developed countries, unless the character of development is modified. If much of the South fails to develop higher living standards and opportunities then migration from South to North will probably rise even more rapidly. If the South does develop in a conventional (unsustainable) way then the spillover effects for the North (climate change, ozone depletion, resource shortages, declining fish stocks etc.), will be large. Such a set of dilemmas gives many people in the North an interest in curbing and regulating 'development' in the South.

The slogan of the North tends to be, 'don't do as we did, do as we say!' So whilst the research findings have helped environmental groups gain more recognition and public support, they have also alerted Northern élites to the need to manage the process of economic 'greening' on an international scale for their own advantage and that of segments of big business which may profit from a 'managed transition' towards a less unsustainable development in both North and South – and in the former Soviet Bloc countries too. All this presumes that there are ways of combining prolonged economic growth and sustainability. Failing this, awkward political questions about global equity and North–South transfers are intensified, given the huge and growing mass of poverty in the South, especially in sub-Saharan Africa and South Asia.

The 'official' Northern line is that a lot of 'green growth' is possible: as the *1992 World Development Report* puts it in its title for Chapter 1: 'Development and the Environment: a false dichotomy' (*World Development Report* 1992: v). Governments of North and South go along with this as do most schools of environmental thought except the radical and deep ecologists and eco-feminists (see Merchant, 1992). Even this this leaves scope for disagreement over how development is to be made sustainable. For example, what changes in policy and institutions are needed and how are they to be financed? What of changes in life-styles and power structures? Which changes are to be given priority and which 'issues' are to top the agenda? (such as curbing deforestation and population growth or curbing fossil fuel consumption and acid rain) Since changes involve difficult 'adjustment', then who is to be made to adjust by whom?

Such questions have permeated debates on economic development for decades. Since the 1980s ideas about, and answers to, such questions were often resolved on terms favoured by, and favourable to, the North. Trade liberalization, privatization, deregulation, reduced bureaucracy, efforts to attract foreign direct investment, other sources of external funds, and boosting of primary product exports, were and are, favoured by the more powerful Northern governments and associated Northern-dominated multilateral organizations. They have helped ensure, notably through their management of the debt crisis, that the actually emerging global economic order has been a liberal capitalist one. This restructuring underlies the recent international debates on moves towards sustainable development. Thus the North has sought to ensure that the World Bank plays a key role in the management of international 'green aid' and green conditionality. The Bank runs the Global Environmental Facility (GEF), a key organization for loans and projects linked to avoiding ozone depletion and global warming.

It should be noted that these debates over policy are not just about what can and should be done but about the nature and causes of environmental decline and coming crisis. A diagnosis of *either* specific (such as market) failures *or* of deeper systemic contradictions (such as cultural ones) affects one's view about the efficacy of a 'market-friendly' reformist approach of the World Bank.

THE WIDER DEBATE

So how is the debate on the practical meaning of sustainable development being managed and contested? One aspect concerns analysis of sustainability with regard to the fashionable notion of the environment as 'natural capital'. Various schools focus on this concept and there is a spectrum of views about how far man-made capital (equipment, knowledge) can substitute for natural capital. The latter can be seen as made up of a variety of 'source and sink' resources, for example, minerals in contrast to the capacity of oceans and rivers to absorb wastes. 'Sustainable development is then defined as the *maximum* development that can be achieved without running down the capital assets of the nation' (Turner, 1993:3). (Notice the bias towards growth in the word maximum.) Just how these assets are to be valued is not just a technical matter: it involves value judgements about other species' 'usefulness' and rights (if any) and also scenery.

Four schools distinguished by Turner exclude radical and deep ecologists who would question this maximal bias towards higher consumption. He labels the others: the mainstream neo-classical school; the London School (Pearce *et al.*, 1991; the post-Keynesian school; and the thermo-dynamic school. It includes Herman Daly who was a senior economist in the World Bank's Environment Department which has existed for only a few years (see Daly and Cobb, 1989). What Turner calls the 'neo-classical' school waxes optimistic about substituting man-made for natural capital implying that a substantial further rundown of the latter is sustainable. The 'London school' is a form of neo-classical economics that specializes on the environment and allows for limits to substitutability due to problems of complex interdependence between species and eco-systems and the risk of irreversibility. The loss of flora and fauna from the rain forests is an example of the latter. At the other end of the spectrum is the steady state system sustainability advocated by Daly and others. It stresses global scale constraints that are ultimately thermo-dynamic in nature. These relate to limited solar energy input to the earth and the limits to recycling because of a natural tendency to entropy – the second law of thermo-dynamics. Here 'zero economic growth and zero population growth are required for a zero increase in the scale of the economy' (Turner, 1993:4). The usual implication drawn is that the growth of scale must come to an end sometime in the next century. Then a more modest form of qualitative development is all that will be possible in the steady state economy.

Thus these schools hold different views about the nature and severity of trade-offs between man-made and natural capital. Most of these schools (except perhaps optimistic versions of the neo-classical) accept some notion of 'critical natural capital', that is, certain resources and processes are of special systemic importance. The more widely this category is interpreted the greater the stress on conservation. The 1992 *World Development Report* sounded a cautiously optimistic note about conservation and relief of poverty (World Bank, 1993: 4, 42–3).

However, it is the poor who are least able to buy their way out of environmental difficulties (e.g. switching fuels, water sources and dwelling area). It is at this point that some recognition is given by the World Bank to social and political aspects of sustainable development. Indeed earlier the report notes that 'raising living standards and improving education, health and equality of opportunity are all essential components of economic development. Ensuring political and civil rights is a broader development goal' (World Bank, 1993: 34). The report seems not to make much of scale issues and it does see great scope for efficient substitution. As for minerals it takes an easy going optimistic line on the basis of price trends in the twentieth century. Thus on balance the report takes a position akin to that of the London School – a modified neo-classical line that allows for critical natural capital. This is particularly marked by its stress on 'getting prices right' so that they reflect environmental costs and benefits, for example for water, forests and energy.

However, the valuation of environmental impacts is difficult. For example, valuation of road projects has not allowed for the increased need to escort or drive children to school which is an added burden on parents and the transport system. Instead it has concentrated on time saved for motorists. Above all, the values we place on nature are socially shaped, reflecting a combination of priorities, information, experience and understanding, rather than some objective value of nature itself. In practice the schools of thought differ on more than supposedly 'technical' questions of substitution and scale. Both the neo-classical and London schools are somewhat technocratic and focus on monetary valuations and modified market mechanisms – as has the World Bank, so far. Wider systemic perspectives on sustainable development have queried the mainstream economics focus on the self-interested individual and consumer sovereignty arguing that the role of the individual as a citizen and the maintenance of community are worthy of attention.

One view that has been emerging is that *needs* should be distinguished from individual wants – a view adopted by the Brundtland report. In the early 1970s the Bank did take on board some of the ideas associated with the 'basic needs' approach but this fell from favour in the 1980s as American influence branded such ideas as socialistic. In the Bank's recent report a high priority is given to reducing water and air pollution on the grounds that it would benefit large numbers of poor people. Climate change and ozone depletion are not given pride of place in the way they often are in the statements of governments of the North. Indeed, this has led Lance Taylor to suggest that this report 'represents a step away from neo-liberalism and back towards the Bank's attitude of the 1960s' (Taylor, 1993: 869). He also notes the report's concern for local consultation and drawing on local knowledge – in order to avoid mistakes in project design and implementation. The desirability of protecting indigenous peoples and their environmental knowledge also receives a brief mention. Such references come close to a recognition of 'cultural capital' as a category that needs to be included within a wider systemic analysis of sustainability. For example, community integration may be weakened by extreme reliance on motor vehicles if this curbs social, especially local interaction and facilitates a more distanced and commuter-based way of life. What is not made clear in the report is that 'market forces', greed and business lobbying (the road building lobby in this example) can have a systematic tendency to erode cultural and social capital.

The Bank report does have a section on the 'political economy of environmental degradation' (1993: 83–5). However, while acknowledging the domestic abuse of power and wealth it is rather weak on changing institutions and empowerment, both at the local and national levels (let alone the international). Thus land reform is neglected though security of tenure is recognized as important. Perhaps as an organization that is constantly dealing with national governments either as clients (South) or as its patrons (North) it is bound to be diplomatic. Also as a large bureaucracy it has a vested interest in maintaining its activities and contacts in a wide range of countries.

At this stage it should be noted that a technocratic tendency to de-emphasize or even ignore some structural sources of pressure on the environment, especially those embedded in the international state system and the global economy, has characterized much writing as far back as the *Limits to Growth* report (Meadows *et al.*, 1972) Global modelling has persisted in this to a large extent, one notable exception being the GLOBUS model (Bremner, 1989). Thus 'empowering' environmental discourse leaves much to be desired. In this context the Bretton Woods organizations' recent and critical interest in military expenditure in the Third World might be seen as a small advance (Hewitt, 1991; McNamara, 1991). However, in so far as the Bank's position points to needed structural and institutional changes they are 'domestic' within the less developed countries. The earlier quotation referring to the 'rich and influential' and to political and civil rights makes this explicit. Domestic political and social stability are now seen as preconditions for development and a good business climate. In contrast the international structures that encourage patterns of unsustainable development – and in which the Bank is deeply implicated – are neglected. Compared to the discourse of the early 1980s the Bank's position now is 'greener', albeit in a somewhat limited and self-serving way.

NEO-LIBERALISM, SOCIAL FORCES AND ENVIRONMENTAL STRUGGLE

Social forces associated with neo-liberal ideas and policies are transnational in character featuring transnational business, some international organizations, notably the World Bank, élites of both North and South and highly skilled labour that is often internationally mobile. Amongst those in opposition to such forces are unions in developed countries, some segments of 'national' small business, threatened indigenous peoples (such as those of the rain forests) and many environmental groups. The contrast drawn here is rather over-simplified since some highly affluent people in developed countries have become concerned about localized environmental issues such as conservation, air and water quality. However, once environmental consciousness is raised it may not stop at local issues. Thus the trend to deregulation in the economy may be reversed in some areas. Long-term concerns of developed countries explained earlier, allied to the growing strength of environmental groups, combine to promote some selective re-regulation. Governments in the North need to maintain legitimacy.

Concern over high unemployment in the 1990s has demoted environmental issues on the political agenda. Greater environmental regulation is sometimes seen as threatening jobs. Unemployment in an age of increased global competition for both export markets and foreign investment is no longer seen in mainly macroeconomic terms. High wages, taxes and environmental regulations have become a growing concern with some developed countries fearing 'social dumping' in which less regulated countries gain jobs and investment at the expense of more regulated ones. It has even been suggested that less developed countries have a comparative advantage in 'dirty' industries.

One response in the OECD has been to call for fair trade and a more level playing field with less developed countries being pressured (and occasionally helped by economic aid) to raise their standards. The United States successfully brought environmental regulations into the North American Free Trade Agreement (NAFTA) and Mexico has had to modify its behaviour. North–South tensions are a source of contradiction here with the South taking the more liberal, deregulationist stance. It is worth noting that some big business based in the North has expertise in coping with environmental regulation that smaller firms in less developed countries lack. The interests of 'capital' are not always in favour of deregulation. Such tensions can also arise between developed countries: for example within the European Union where German business (notably equipment firms) are better placed to cope with strict regulations. The above tensions and divisions have been evident in international negotiations over global environmental issues.

The 1992 Earth Summit marked a new high in attempts at a multilateral approach to environmental issues. About 30 000 people are thought to have gone to Rio, including over 100 government leaders and thousands of conference participants, many from NGOs. This was in contrast to the much more modest scale of proceedings in Stockholm in 1972 which led to the establishment of UNEP (the United Nations Environmental Programme). Thousands of journalists at Rio ensured enormous publicity. Over 300 scientists were involved in the Intergovernmental Panel on Climate Change set up in 1988 by the General Assembly so as to offer expert advice to world leaders. At the summit two conventions were negotiated, on Climate Change and Bio-diversity. In addition various principles were agreed and more specific areas elaborated in the Agenda 21 action plan. A new UN body, the Sustainable Development Commission, was to oversee the follow-up of Agenda 21 and co-ordinate the efforts of various UN bodies and related multilateral organizations (Johnson, 1993).

Results were long on words and short on practical commitments, such as targets for reducing particular greenhouse gases. The statement on Forest Principles fell well short of the convention sought by many Northern states but it was resisted by some from the South, notably timber-exporters. Funding commitments by the North were very modest. By October 1992 there were reports that the $5 billion 'sustainable development fund' to be administered by the World Bank's International Development Association was unlikely to be received in full (Watkins, 1992). Some critics thought there should have been conventions on population growth, agri-business, automobiles, international debts, and trade. Hopes of a new and more enlightened multilateralism were disappointed.

An examination of the powerful social forces in the global political economy makes hopes of a *rapid* move towards realizing equitable and sustainable development seem unrealistic. The transnational interests of big business and finance and their political allies, especially in the North, demonstrated their strength in the 1980s. The collapse of Communism reinforced their position and ideology. Hopes attached to the Earth Summit were sometimes compared to the 1970s demands by the South for a New International Economic Order. Instead of the oil weapon there was now the 'green weapon'. Hence the bargaining situation of the South had improved after the disastrous 1980s. The South could hope to win major financial concessions albeit with 'green' strings attached. Yet such an approach is oversimplified. The 'South' is even more divided than twenty years ago. Economic contrasts between East Asia, South Asia, Africa and Latin America have grown. Competition between these countries (and those of the North) for foreign investment has risen, while access to commercial bank loans has not fully recovered from the debt crisis. Africa remains in crisis and continues to experience a net capital drain. Interests of oil-exporting countries diverge from other less developed countries that import fossil fuels. OPEC interests were more congruent with those of the transnational oil companies and their allies in the North (the road building lobby, motorists).

Where policies of Southern governments damage the environment it is people of the South who are the main victims of flooding, disease, desertification and poverty. Global warming and a rise in ocean levels is a more serious threat (if it occurs) to low-lying less developed countries such as Bangladesh, Egypt (the delta) and small island states, than to wealthy Northern states (countries like Holland have made huge investments in flood-protection). On the other hand, China and India with large coal reserves, vast interior and huge populations have reason to be very reluctant to restrain their growing use of fossil fuels.

None the less some Southern solidarity was demonstrated at Rio, particularly over bio-diversity where they gained recognition for their sovereignty over natural resources opening up the possibility of future compensation for access to their genetic riches (only in so far as these are not already in the gene banks of the North). However, the convention accepts patents in the area of living resources and excluded the question of rights over gene banks. Vandana Shiva (1993) has written on these flaws. Also the North–South fault line showed in the question of population control, which was played down. Northern representatives knew that suggestions that the South should restrain their population growth would be countered by suggestions that the North restrain its consumption!

The limited progress at Rio may reflect, an unholy alliance between the growth-starved élites of the South and the growth fatalists of the North. Both are ready to sacrifice hope for an ecological conversion on the altar of development. The South attempts to 'catch-up' at whatever cost, while the North self-righteously invokes the inexorable forces of market competition' (Sachs, 1993). Robert Cox (1987), has warned of the tendencies towards a transnational historic bloc that cuts across both class and North–South lines. Hence, those who wish to combat 'unholy alliances' might consider links between environmental groups of both North and South.

Negotiations in the mid-1990s over the future of the Global Environment Facility have shown that the North–South divide continues and that the South can show a significant degree of co-ordination and solidarity on some issues. The facility set up in the early 1990s disbursed funds to developing countries for projects related to climate change, loss of bio-diversity, ozone depletion and pollution of international waters. However, it was dominated by the World Bank. Many of its projects were related to existing ones involving the Bank – with a view to making them less environmentally damaging. The countries of the South sought a bigger say in the future of the GEF. In the end a compromise was reached between the 87 countries who participate in the Facility. The voting system agreed gives both North and South a veto. Of the 32 seats on the governing council 16 go to developing countries, 14 to industrialized countries and 2 to former communist countries.

One feature of the summit and, hopefully, the follow-up to Agenda 21, is the greater recognition given to the growing numbers of NGOs, that were recognized as potentially very important in the Brundtland report which recommended that they receive more funding (World

Commission on Environment and Development, 1987: 329) Some NGOs are better placed to contribute widely than others but all can be significant in terms of public participation, and they 'sometimes reach target groups that public agencies cannot' (Brundtland, 1987: 328). NGO criticism of the multilateral development banks did much to push these institutions into signing the 1980 Declaration of Environmental Policies and Procedures relating to Economic Development. NGO lobbying before and during the Earth Summit was intense and they were able to play a formal and informal part in the Conference. However, governments are to exclude NGOs when they choose, as was shown in Rio.

Nevertheless, the Commission on Sustainable Development (CSD) is required to encourage the participation of NGOs, particularly women's groups (Johnson, 1993: 493). In theory the CSD should critically monitor the activities of the World Bank, but will it be any more able to do this than UNEP was? The role of UNEP might even be weakened by the establishment of the CSD, for example if energies and resources are diverted to it. The CSD's co-ordinating role is subordinate to the Administrative Committee on Co-ordination headed by the UN Secretary General. Mark Imber is of the opinion that: 'the larger system, including the specialised agencies, the World Bank and other multilateral development banks can only be transformed through the entirely separate decision-making processes of these organisations' (Imber, 1993: 70.). So while NGOs may be pleased at the CSD, they would do well to continue efforts at 'greening' institutions like the World Bank. The latter is mainly responsive to major donors. Without their support there will be no change in the Bank's Articles of Agreement to give the UN some regular influence in its management. In this case if the North–South divide is to be overcome it may need a change in ideas, interests and institutions in the North.

Just as governments of North and South often have different priorities, so do NGOs. NGOs that have been most involved in debates about global warming have been based in the North, for instance, the World Resources Institute, and Greenpeace. The concerns of some Southern NGOs were more local and 'down-to-earth', for example the Chipko movement in India that sought to protect forests. Some Southern NGOs are wary of Northern counterparts since they fear the latter will try and impose their definitions and practice of sustainable development. A more differentiated analysis is needed such as that of Norman Uphoff who distinguishes between grass-roots organizations (GROs) and NGOs in rural development (Uphoff, 1993; see also Brett, 1993). NGOs may not be very democratic in their decision-making – an accusation levelled at Greenpeace.

At Rio, journalists noted contrasts between large, well funded (mainly Northern) NGOs and the 'shoe-string' NGOs: the poor relation. NGOs may see themselves in a competitive relationship – for funds, publicity, contacts and influence. The problems they face in co-operating bear comparison with those facing labour organizations. At Rio there was the further complication that some, often transnational, business interests were accredited as NGOs: for example the (very influential) Business Council for Sustainable Development, the Global Climate Coalition, the Association of Coal Producers of the European Community, the Asbestos Institute of Canada and the Petroleum Association of Japan. This makes one wonder how far such 'NGOs' will forge links to the CSD. That transnational business interests can go far in 'capturing' a UN body is shown by the Codex Alimentarius Commission, a UN food standards body run jointly by the FAO and the World Health Organization (WHO). Their recommendations are likely to take on added significance given the completion of the GATT Uruguay trade round which makes these recommendations mandatory: for example in the case of trade in pesticides.

One area in which co-operation between NGOs would be beneficial is in monitoring how far governments abide by the Conventions and any commitments that may emerge from the Agenda 21 process. Already they have used the courts, mainly in a national context, to challenge governments to comply with their previous commitments for example, over water standards. One disappointing feature of Rio was that it did little to enhance international legal opportunities for 'watchdog' NGOs. However, they can contribute to the process of checking implementation. In future negotiations they could press for stricter non-compliance procedures with the possibility of arbitration panels in the new World Trade Organization and even sanctions such as are now envisaged under the Montreal Protocol (amended in November 1992).

The question of trade sanctions is controversial, particularly since the relationship between trade and the environment was a major omission from the Rio conventions and from the Uruguay Round negotiations. Environmental groups, particularly in the US, campaigned hard against a multilateral trade organization that would subsume GATT and proposed sister bodies on intellectual property and trade in services. The World Wide Fund for Nature argued for a

World Trade Organization, that would include environmental protection and the eradication of poverty as explicit objectives and give NGOs rights of consultation. A 'green' WTO would have a trade and sustainable development council. Ideas of this kind have extended to other UN-related bodies, even to suggesting that 'environmental security' should be on the agenda of the Security Council itself (Imber, 1993: 67–8).

THE WORLD BANK

The sheer scale of resources linked to the Bank make it a giant among international organizations. In 1993 the Bank's total 'callable' capital was $165.59 *billion*, of which only $10.53 billion was paid-in. (Rich, 1994: 8) This contrasts with the programme budget for UNEP in 1990–1 of $68 *million*! The Bank lent $18 *billion* in the year to end June 1993, with a sharp fall in loans to Africa more than offset by higher lending to former communist countries in Eastern Europe and Central Asia (*Economist*, 10 July 1993).

In the 1990s the spotlight for reforms is on the World Bank group. It runs the Global Environmental Facility, handled through the International Development Association, a branch of the Bank. The Bank has admitted past mistakes – projects that have damaged the environment. It claims to have 'greened' its operations, for example in '*The World Bank and the Environment – A Progress Report*' (1991) where the Bank makes a case that its projects are being redesigned to reduce adverse effects on the environment and on people from resettlement in a number of selected cases. Even the International Finance Corporation (IFC) branch of the Bank group, that focuses on the private sector, includes environmental considerations in project appraisal and has dropped several projects due to environmental problems. The Bank has taken a lead in researching environmental accounting, developing expertise and alternatives to the current system of national accounting based on GNP.

However, when one probes beneath the surface, a rather less flattering story emerges. In none of three cases (Thailand, Ivory Coast and Mexico) examined did the Bank give explicit consideration to the effect of the restructuring on the countries' natural resource base (Reed, 1992). While in a complex and changing situation it was found difficult to quantify the effects of either indebtedness or structural adjustment loans there was no doubt that, 'disproportionate cutbacks in health and education services in many developing countries will potentially constrain future growth potential. Likewise, the short-sighted cutbacks in environmental investments will certainly engender constraints to further development possibilities' (Reed, 1992: 151). In judging what are the 'right' prices, the Bank is criticized for its reliance on international border prices. Here the Bank's stress on boosting primary product exports has served to further depress world prices. One of its 'star pupils', Ghana, did this by an unsustainable rise in logging. Indeed, the internal (unpublished but leaked) Wapenhans report of 1992 put the Bank very much on the defensive. It shows that the proportion of projects with poor results has increased and that some of these failures go with adverse environmental effects. Borrowers see the Bank as pursuing its own concerns without much regard to local realities.

Even worse, half of the 1992 adjustment loans failed to include specific poverty reduction measures. To add to the embarrassment, a memo by the then chief economist of the World Bank, Lawrence Summers, was leaked (Summers subsequently became United States Under-Secretary of Treasury for International Affairs). The memo advocated shifting polluting industries to the Third World on grounds that this was in line with their comparative advantage in capacity to absorb pollution (as if human life is 'cheaper' there!). To cap it all there was the massive mounting scandal of the Narmada dam(s): projects in India to generate more electricity, but flood vast areas of land and displace large numbers of poor people. The Bank approved this project in 1985 (it would take many years). Most of the $450 million loan had been spent by the time the Bank ceased support. This occurred in 1993 when the Indian government's repeated neglect of the environmental and resettlement guidelines made it difficult to resist world-wide calls for the Bank to withdraw. The whole saga cast doubt on the Bank's capacity to monitor large or complex projects. The prominent role in the Narmada (or Sardar Sarovar) affair of the late World Bank President, Lewis Preston, led to calls for his resignation. Given the Indian government's ruthless enthusiasm for the dam project, it is not so surprising that the Bank was inclined to support the project.

In response to such revelations the Bank's shareholder countries agreed, in July 1993 a programme called 'Next Steps', to encourage a shift from the quantity (expansion) of the loan portfolio to its quality. What makes for 'quality' is now the subject of debate, with NGOs fearing insufficient attention will be paid to poverty reduction and environmental costs and benefits. Another idea that was under discussion was that of an (internal) appeals commission which could examine complaints from local citizens and environmental and human rights groups. This has now materialized in the form of the Inspection Panel, although it is too soon to know if this will be effective. More action is likely because the Bank is anxious to continue to get further funding from the US Congress (for the IDA) and American NGOs are vocal. Pressure from within leading shareholder countries is crucial given the Bank's dependence on them for infusions of capital that help maintain its triple-A credit rating (this is especially so for the International Development Association). A change in the Bank's Articles of Agreement requires three-fifths of its members, with 85 per cent of the voting power, to agree. Hence democratization of the Bank is very unlikely. Borrowing countries have 43 per cent of the votes but some of their governments would not welcome public scrutiny of projects they are undertaking jointly with the World Bank.

None the less, there are signs of progress within the Bank, which does employ a growing number of people who are concerned about the environment albeit in marginal positions. There are now over 200 environmentalists employed compared to only five in the mid-1980s. A small group of agriculturists in the World Bank's Asia division have been extolling the virtues of vetiver (a tropical grass) as a means of combating soil erosion. A more far-reaching change concerns the Bank's encouragement of National Environmental Action Plans (NEAPs). In 1987 the Bank offered its help to countries wishing to develop a plan of their own. Madagascar was the first country to take up this offer (Larson, 1994). Many African counties have followed suit. International NGOs have also become involved, although local NGOs have at times been suspicious of the government and foreign NGOs. The more participatory the Plan, both in design and implementation, the less risk is there that it will be manipulated by short-termist politicians and an over-mighty World Bank. However, in Africa the growth of local NGOs has been inhibited by lack of democracy and civil rights. The shortage of skilled and educated people is another problem that creates dangers of external dependence.

In so far as local NGOs can draw on, and build up, their knowledge and skills (including those of mobilization) then they may gain power *vis-à-vis* financially hard-pressed governments that are short of human capital (within the bureaucracy) and legitimacy, as well as money. NGOs, including co-operatives like the Spanish Montagnon group, self-help community-based movements like Sarvodaya Shramadana (Meadows, 1991) and people's banks like the Grameen Bank in Bangladesh, might make people and governments less dependent on big business and capital markets. This would serve to limit the 'structural power' of capital both economically and ideologically as it institutionalizes and exemplifies an alternative to total reliance on markets and profit-seeking enterprises. A true greening of the Bank would be one supportive of democratization and the development of civil society, where the latter is much more than the private business sector. Falloux and Talbot (both connected with the Bank) point out:

> national NGOs in African countries often can strengthen their positions and effectiveness by federating, by joining some types of NGO associations or networks, and in some cases, by associating with their international cousins. This was done...in Burkina Faso and Madagascar. We should re-emphasise the importance of women's associations in Africa. Particularly in view of the predominant role of African women in the management of environmental resources in rural areas. In addition to providing opportunities for women to contribute to the NEAP process, such associations can influence public opinion and the government in ways which may help improve the situation. (Falloux and Talbot, 1993: 282)

Given the proliferation of NEAPs in the 1990s their record by the year 2000 will be of major interest not just for assessing whether the World Bank can change its 'culture' but for the possibilities of, and prospects for, a more locally-based and self-reliant form of development such as advocated by the Other Economic Summits, held at the same times and in the same locations as the G-7 leaders' summits (Schroyer, 1992). Taken together, the publicized plight of Africa, the scope for increased out-migration and environmental damage and the political and economic constraints on Northern aid and funding for the World Bank (and the African Development Bank) give the North an interest (largely selfish) in *economical* ways of alleviating the situation. It was therefore rational for the Bank to shift some of its focus to smaller projects (such as micro-enterprises), an advisory role with more local participation, up to a point. (The Bank now has a small branch concerned to foster micro-enterprises on the model of the Grameen Bank.) The sustainability of its projects after their completion is a major problem unless local participation is increased. On the other hand, the fear of critics of the Bank is that increased links to NGOs, not least women's organisations – a trend of the 1990s – will enable the Bank to extend its influence so further developing its transnational 'empire' or 'galaxy' (a term sometimes used to refer to dependent networks of sub-contractors associated with a transnational corporation).

The Bank as an institution is dominated by the North and with Articles that privilege the private sector (its loans and advice are to be complementary and supportive to business). Thus, it is bound to be biased towards 'development' that maintains the supply of primary product exports and enhances the opportunities for business. Its institutional interests are geared more to sustaining global capitalism than to sustaining the environment. This is not to suggest it is totally lacking in accountability but it is the G-7 countries (who dominate the board of the Bank) that count and who the Bank relies on for regular replenishment of its branch for subsidized interest loans – the International Development Association. Of key importance is the Bank's need to sustain its reputation in the financial markets (its triple-A credit rating, and so on) to raise the funds to sustain its activities. Except for its IDA branch it has to go for a fully commercial rate of return when it makes loans. Because of their unique 'seniority' status, World Bank loans are almost certain to be repaid (everyone else has to wait until the Bank is paid first – even the IMF is not as privileged in practice, given the frequency of arrears to the IMF). Because of the World Bank's privileged position, therefore, the Bank has a degree of autonomy from financial market discipline. It faces less pressure to make a commercial success of its projects (except those of the IFC) than is the case for a private company: even when projects perform badly it is usually paid on time. Indeed, the historic bias to bigger projects can partly be explained by economic logic (it economizes on overhead costs). Despite the 'Next Steps' proposals, as yet convincing action is lacking.

Nevertheless, within the Bank a growing number of social scientists (mainly sociologists and social anthropologists) have sought to increase monitoring and attention to poverty and resettlement effects of projects. Often adverse environmental and poverty effects of projects go together. An example is the impact on tribal peoples when a dam is built and local flora and fauna as well as agricultural land are lost. All too often inadequate provisions are made for displaced people. Such in-house groups within the Bank may succeed in changing guidelines for project design in some cases (Kardam, 1994). With regard to its 'framework of thought' the World Bank is economically liberal. In this it reflects the ideology of transnational business with which it has so many links and working relationships (projects, joint ventures, consultancy). However, in the 1970s the president of the Bank, Robert McNamara, seemed to adopt some of the 'basic needs' approach favoured by left-wing social scientists. This kind of concern faded in the 1980s partly due to pressure from the Reagan Administration. As excesses of neo-liberal policies have become more obvious and the environmental lobby has grown in influence, notably in the US, there are signs that a more social/welfare kind of liberalism is reviving – at least at the level of rhetoric.

In liberal thought great stress is laid on efficiency and the social advantages of self-seeking individual behaviour in markets. In so far as environmental externalities need correction then there is a role for the state and also NGOs, that is state and civil society. Increasingly the Bank has shown an interest since the later 1980s in good governance and developing a particular kind of civil society – one which is modernizing, conducive to efficiency and sustained economic growth led by private enterprise. In this vision some NGOs are more suitable than others. Certain traditional organizations based on ethnic, clan and religious ties are not favoured unless they fit the model. Thus in so far as the Bank has a philosophy that is more than purely economic it is still one which is geared to economic growth as the top priority (Williams and Young, 1994).

THE NEW MULTILATERALISM: CONCLUSION AND A RESEARCH AGENDA

The World Bank reflects contradictions of neo-liberalism in which sustainability of the environment and the stability of political and civil society are put at risk. During the 1980s the Bank and liberal academics came to realize that structural adjustment policies were not working as well as expected, especially in Africa. Poverty, inequality and environmental decay were interrelated and inadequate governmental institutions were in danger of being weakened in terms of their efficiency and administrative capability. Thus the Bank's attempts at greening should be seen as part of a wider attempt to 'stretch' the liberal framework. This is not to deny that in some respects the Bank, given its expertise, has an interest and ability to promote some important policy changes needed for sustainable development, for instance, more economic pricing of water, energy and wood, the use of environmental accounting, projects concerning clean water supply, and so on. Continued efforts by environmental NGOs to monitor and criticize the Bank are necessary and useful. However, such efforts are bound to be of limited value unless international economic and political structures are modified.

A neo-liberal reform of the Bank would involve breaking it into parts with perhaps the IBRD losing seniority status so making it more dependent on the capital markets and private credit rating agencies. It can plausibly be argued that the private sector, compared to fifty years ago, is much more able to channel funds (bond, equity as well as bank finance) to less developed countries; also to provide them economic advice and give them a business 'rating'. There is pressure from some OECD governments to concentrate expansion on the IFC rather than on the 'aid' section of the Bank, the IDA. The IFC lacks a government guarantee when it raises funds in the international capital markets so that it is under greater commercial pressure to maintain its triple-A credit rating.

Perhaps the role of the Bank was originally meant to be for a transitional era in which the market mechanism was held in check and international economic integration was limited, that is both the IMF and the World Bank were gradually to promote liberalization and globalization. This 'modernizing mission' of the Bank is by no means completed. The 'disciplinary' role of the World Bank, often in tandem with the IMF, should not be forgotten. The Bank in the 1980s came to put increasing stress on conditionality, a significant change in its brand of multilateralism. When (if) it becomes greener it may mean *more*, not less, conditionality. At the moment green conditionality is not strictly enforced. Thus while a reformed Bank – in accordance with changes proposed at the 1995 G-7 Summit in Halifax, Nova Scotia – might be greener, it might also be leaner and meaner – in large part to sustain its credit rating and to work more assiduously in promoting the private sector. Thus reform of the Bank is more likely to stress efficiency (reduced bureaucracy) and empowering private business than the empowering of non-profit-making NGOs and local people. Lewis Preston suggested that a leaner Bank would mean fewer staff and that the Bank would charge fees for advisory services while denying there need be any conflict between development and the environment although there had been in the past for Bank projects (Prowse, 1994).

Just as there is a struggle to shape the global environmental agenda, so there is a struggle over the size, mission and methods of international organizations. At the Earth Summit it was organizations like the Business Council for Sustainable Development (a forum for top transnational firms) and people like the co-ordinator Maurice Strong (Chairman of Ontario Hydro and a member of the Trilateral Commission) who did much to shape the agenda. The role of such 'business NGOs' is a topic for further research. As for environmental NGOs and also grass roots organizations concerned with local environmental issues, their influence and abilities varies. Their outlook and interests differ. The way the Bank and governments co-operate with NGOs needs researching given that a purely critical and opposition role is inadequate and risks of co-optation and dependence are significant. Attempts by NGOs to form regional and transnational networks were encouraged by the Rio Summit experience: what are the factors affecting the extent and usefulness of such networking? Here it should be noted that NGOs as well as the World Bank can be bureaucratic and empire building! Perhaps the Bank will choose 'allies' of its own kind? Also there is the question of how far NGOs can contribute to the growth of a non-profit sector that alleviates market dependence and the structural power of capital. One recent study notes that NGO projects too often neglect questions of land distribution, gender or class relations and/or control over resources (Vivian, 1994).

In trying to move towards a more equitable, democratic and 'greener' kind of multilateralism there is a strong case for encouraging reform in terms of existing institutions (GATT, World Bank, IMF, FAO, and so on). However, this faces limits reflected in power structures, including forms of discourse. These need to be changed to foster democratization and accountability. High-level lobbying cannot be a substitute for grass roots activity – involving GROs rather than just large international NGOs with their technocratic temptations. More generally there are problems in firstly, getting NGOs to work together, and secondly, in handling 'co-optation' by governments and multilateral institutions. This is true for aid charities in the North but it could become even more so for NGOs in the poorer South. They need to build up their own discourse and counter-culture in the face of those new efforts centred in the North that seek to go beyond neo-liberalism to a new kind of competitive liberal welfarism with some green credentials. Both big business (in some but not all cases) and the Bank see opportunities for profits and/or bureaucratic empire-building in contributing to *one* version of 'sustainable development'. However, in some cases, such as the promotion of environmental accounting, Bank self-interest may involve disclosure of information that can be useful to environmentalists as they try to raise public consciousness and win policy changes. Above all, GROs and NGOs need to build up sources of structural power including knowledge defined broadly to include local environmental expertise and skills in networking. Perhaps then, especially with a deepening environmental crisis in the future, multilateral institutions like the World Bank, will have to engage in some radical 'structural adjustment' themselves.

Notes

1. I would like to thank Stephen Gill for his suggestions and help in reworking this chapter.
2. Structural adjustment programmes have been criticized for their adverse effects on education and health and on other kinds of investment as well as for the disproportionate burden of adjustment borne by the poor. The dismal performance of Sub-Saharan Africa is especially embarrassing for the Bank given the great influence it has wielded. Environmental degradation has been substantial in Africa and many Bank projects have damaged the environment. On the evaluation of structural adjustment programmes see Mosely *et al.* (1991).

9 Atlantic Rivalries and the Collapse of the USSR[1]

Kees van der Pijl

The aim of this chapter is to provide a framework for understanding the policies of different Atlantic states and social forces in the circumstances that accompanied the demise of the Soviet bloc. It is an argument of this chapter that ultimately, the collapse of the USSR and the defeat of the rapprochement between important segments of West German capital (and implicitly, segments of organized labour) and the tottering Soviet giant, may be seen as part of a single process.

The collapse of the USSR has been celebrated in the West as the consummation of a civilizing mission of the capitalist system, to which state socialism has finally succumbed. In Fukuyama's rendition (1989), this event brought out the innate superiority of the system of free enterprise and representative democracy. Such triumphalism overlooks the way that the Cold War limited the ways that mutual differences between Western states could be expressed politically. Indeed, such differences assumed a new acuteness in the final stages of the East–West conflict. For example, a Pentagon planning document, *Defence Planning Guidance*, made public in early 1992 revealed that United States policy planners considered the integration of West Germany and Japan into the US-led 'system of collective security' as having been contingent on the Cold War, and warned against the ambitions of potential global rivals. The document recommended that the United States:

> must show the leadership necessary to establish and protect a new order that holds the promise of convincing potential competitors that they need not aspire to a greater role or pursue a more aggressive posture to protect their legitimate interests... We must account sufficiently for the interests of the advanced industrial nations to discourage them from challenging our leadership or seeking to overturn the established political and economic order.[2]

This line of thinking is consistent with the struggles over a common policy that have characterized the responses of the capitalist world to the construction of state socialism in the USSR ever since 1917. All along, different segments or *fractions* of the Atlantic ruling class have been engaged in fierce struggles over how to deal with the Soviet challenge. After the USSR adopted its *perestroika* policy of political renewal, struggles intensified, in this case over how to deal with the implications of this transformation. Thus in West Germany, under the 'Grand Coalition' and especially, under Willy Brandt's Social Democratic (SDP) majority government, by the late 1960s, the government had charted a course away from the Cold War: the *Ostpolitik*. By the mid-1980s, powerful economic forces in Germany sought to capitalize on links established under this policy to work out new agreements with Gorbachev, in effect attempting to outflank the aggressive Cold War policies pursued by Britain and the United States under Thatcher and Reagan. However, the strongest political force behind *Ostpolitik*, the German SPD, were in opposition, while the economic forces most actively behind it failed to build a sufficiently broad coalition to carry the day.

In this chapter then, I will first present an overview of the different social forces and economic structures which underlay the rival approaches towards the USSR pursued by US and various European governments. I then investigate the activity of transnational policy planning networks and élite multilateralism and their role in the process of formulating strategy. Many questions relating to the issues discussed in this paper still remain unanswerable, and any conclusions are tentative. Although information is scarce and often intentionally distorted, the world-historical event that was the collapse of the USSR has to be saved from the self-congratulatory incantations of the advocates of liberal capitalism. Their high-handed moralism should at least be contrasted with what we already know about the actual chain of events, as it has been well documented in the quality press, in journals and a number of recently published books.

STRUCTURES AND AGENTS OF ATLANTIC CAPITALISM

Global hegemony is not a matter of single states taking turns as the 'hegemon', but of transnational coalitions of social forces committed to a particular *concept of control* (Van der Pijl, 1984, 1989a). Such a concept expresses the power of a concrete configuration of economic and political forces, while leading other forces in the absence of a viable alternative. One or several states will perform certain key functions in the military or monetary fields, but the primary source of the hegemony resides in a 'recipe' for handling challenges in national and international arenas that emanates from a specific class configuration interacting with, but not expressing state power.

In this sense, the *Pax Britannica* may be seen as the era of hegemony of the class configuration committed to freeing the labour market, industrial production, and overseas trade from state and other social controls. The small-scale textile and early machinery industries were still heavily concentrated in a few countries as late as 1860 (Britain, followed at a distance by Switzerland and Belgium: Senghaas, 1982: 32, Table 2). Such industrial products, shipped all over the world by the preponderant British merchant navy, constituted the economic backbone of this orientation. But the compelling logic of this form of liberal internationalism was evident to most other national bourgeoisies as well.

When a new generation of industries emerged, notably iron and steel, with coal mining, and, after the turn of the century, chemicals and electrical engineering, British liberal internationalism was challenged. Cartelization and protective state intervention fostered the crystallization of a new concept of control, tending towards state monopolism. One reason for this was its coincidence with what we have called the 'paradigmatic scale of operation' – the optimal economic scale of ascendant industries in a given nation state (Overbeek and Van der Pijl, 1993: 7). The era of classical imperialism can be viewed as a period in which rival concepts, both of liberal internationalism and of state-monopoly, vied for supremacy. Thus such contemporary authors as the liberal Hobson, and the Marxists Hilferding or Bukharin, could analyze imperialism respectively as either an aberration from 'normal' liberalism, or a logical transition to socialism.

Germany was the state most clearly identified with the new state monopolism, which combined cartelization, protectionism, and state intervention in the labour market to regulate the vast manpower requirements of large scale heavy industry (such as coal and steel, heavy equipment). With such developments in mind, in *The Road to Serfdom* written in 1944, F.A. von Hayek argued that by 1870, after two hundred years of eastward spread of liberal, English ideas, the trend was reversed and German ideas about state intervention, socialist or otherwise, were ascendant for the next sixty years, also in

Britain itself. It was the meteoric rise of Germany and the aspirations of its ruling class for world power (Fischer, 1984) that forced the English-speaking states to draw together again after a centrifugal phase coinciding with the heyday of liberal internationalism. In 1911, the United States and the United Kingdom concluded the Arbitration Treaty outlawing war between them as a mode of conflict resolution; in the same year, the establishment of the British Commonwealth reinforced Britain's ties with the self-governing colonies. With Britain's longest-standing rival, France, drawn to their side on account of its fears of German expansion, this English-speaking bloc emerged triumphant from the eventual clash with Germany in the First World War. In temporary alliance with the Soviet Union, it defeated the fascist challenge in the Second World War.

Whereas on the European continent, wartime state intervention and socialism stifled liberalism, in the English-speaking world a synthesis was achieved in the course of the same period. A new concept of control, which we have called corporate liberalism, rose to hegemony with the growth of a domestic market for consumer durables pioneered by Henry Ford. It reflected the class compromises of Fordist mass production, for which the basis was laid in the American New Deal. It also prescribed a regulative, 'Keynesian' state role in sustaining effective demand, severely restricting the profit opportunities of the typical 'private investor', the *rentier*.

The state for a time substituted for the role of the *haute finance* of private investment banks, the stock exchange, and so on. The first steps in this direction were taken with the establishment of the United States Federal Reserve system in 1913, a year before the role of the world's banker was transferred from London to New York. The establishment of the liberal Bretton Woods system of international monetary regulation in 1944-5, on the other hand, shifted the relative weight of productive and liberal-financial considerations away from New Deal state intervention again. Despite serious disagreement between cash-strapped Britain and the US, the 'special relationship' and Commonwealth ties deeply rooted in a common political culture allowed the transition to proceed. Thus corporate liberalism was inscribed in a structure of integration long cherished by British imperialists such as Cecil Rhodes (Shoup and Minter, 1977: 12–13). Already in the late 1930s, E.H. Carr had written that most Englishmen compensated for their country's declining stature with:

the dream that British supremacy, instead of passing altogether away, would be transmuted into the higher and more effective form of an ascendancy of the English-speaking peoples.... The *pax Britannica* will be put into commission and become a *pax Anglo-Saxonica*, under which the British Dominions, standing half-way between the mother country and the United States, will be cunningly woven into a fabric of Anglo-American co-operation. (Carr, 1964: 232)

The Marshall Plan extended the New Deal corporate liberal model to Western European reconstruction. Moreover, the Occupation and subsequent reconstruction occurred in ways which severely circumscribed the 'socialist' potential of various national class compromises by the simultaneous turn to Cold War. However, in the course of the 1960s and early 1970s, the post-war structure of Atlantic welfare states integrated against communism began to crumble as the United States was losing control of the arenas of decolonization where Western interests had to be defended by force (Indo-China, Portuguese Africa), while Arab oil-producing countries and the Soviet bloc were able to lead the Third World into a more militant posture against the West, on account of rising energy prices.

Parallel to this, several Western European countries began to take their distance from the Atlantic Cold War posture. Partly in response to labour militancy at home, the governments of Georges Pompidou (France) and Willy Brandt, Edward Heath (UK), Aldo Moro (Italy) and Olof Palme (Sweden), each in its own way sought to accommodate the forces of reform, both at home and abroad, by exploiting opportunities offered by *détente* and Third World industrialization. Each leader hoped to save domestic class compromise from the impact of rising oil prices and other factors threatening the Atlantic welfare states with fiscal crisis.

As in the late nineteenth century, by 1970 German capital had begun to pose a challenge to Anglo-American supremacy (as did Japanese capital). The key to medium-term economic primacy, industrial labour productivity, rose by 72 per cent in France and 70 per cent in West Germany, against 27 per cent in both Britain and the USA between 1967 and 1977, while the Japanese figure was 107 per cent.[3] Across the range of industrial production, export growth, and currency parities, the improvement of the continental European *vis-à-vis* the British and American positions was translated into a growing control over resources. The Anglo-Americans also suffered a decline of relative financial power. The UK/US share in the stock of foreign direct investment declined from two-thirds of the total in 1960–70, to 56 per cent in 1980 and 49 per cent in 1988. Germany and Japan meanwhile climbed from a 1 per cent share each in 1960 to a 9–10 per cent share each in 1988 (Stopford and Strange, 1991: 17). More important was the eventual reversal of the roles of capital exporters and importers (international creditors/debtors) between the US on the one hand, and Germany and Japan on the other. From 1979–81 to 1985–8, the US outflow of capital of $2 billion became a $129 billion inflow; whereas for Germany and Japan, the figures went from $8 billion inflow to $40 billion outflow, and $5 billion inflow to $75 billion outflow, respectively, over the same period.[4]

By 1978–9, both in the United States and Britain a political orientation emerged committed to a return to full-fledged liberalism. Hayek's Nobel Prize for Economics of 1974 was part of the resurfacing of the notion that society should be organized around the self-regulating market, with state interference reduced to a minimum. Concretely, Hayek's neo-liberal concept envisaged removing all those regulative structures which impeded the free movement of capital. The class compromise with organized labour especially became the target of attack of the incoming Thatcher and Reagan governments in Britain and the US (Overbeek, 1990).

The driving forces behind the neo-liberal offensive against corporate liberalism were to be found among the financial market operators catering to the resurrected *rentier*, the new high-tech industries of the 1980s, and arms industries suffering from the budgetary constraints of corporate liberalism in crisis. There were also what might be termed assorted 'auxiliary' forces ranged, for various reasons, against the welfare state and the international political environment which was taking shape in the context of a crisis of Cold War Atlanticism. The rise to power of neo-liberal leaders in Britain and the US created the semblance of a rift between them and continental Europe. Thus Michel Albert (1992) contrasts what he terms a 'Rhineland' model of capitalism corresponding roughly to our corporate liberalism, with the 'neo-American' model (our neo-liberalism). In reality, a struggle between transnational coalitions of social forces committed to conflicting concepts of control was set in motion, not unlike the one operative in the era of classical imperialism. This struggle, which on the surface may have looked like a conflict between states, was more fundamentally a fight between two interpretations of 'normalcy' and between the class configurations and economic interests supporting them. This fight was taking place within each state, as well as between them. As Lenin had put it:

> the epoch of the latest stage of capitalism shows us that certain relations between capitalist associations grow up, based on the economic division of the world; while parallel to and in connection with it, certain relations grow up between political alliances, between states, on the basis of the territorial division of the world, of the struggle for colonies, of the 'struggle for spheres of influence'. (Lenin, *Works*, Vol. 22: 253)

The articulation of economic interests into a broader concept claiming to express the general interest, can be understood as a process of coalition building in which 'organic intellectuals' function as the organizers of the general consensus. The material substance of the coalition is constituted by particular fractions of capital: blocs of firms active in one or more particular sectors, sharing a common perspective, and dependent on specific patterns of profit and income distribution (Van der Pijl, 1984: 277–87). If private planning councils often provide the environment in which the various, 'fractional' viewpoints are synthesized into a consensus and the 'intellectual' function is most pronounced, *financial groups* constitute the nodal points for capital fractions at the level of the economy.

A financial group, according to Menshikov (1973: 201), consists of formally independent companies whose more general and longer-term problems are dealt with at a level superior to firm management. Co-ordination of company policies is achieved through interlocking boards and councils composed of bankers, owner family members, personalities linked to the overall government and state structures, or 'network specialists' – multiple outside directors with no management functions (Fennema, 1982: 209). The centre of a financial group is not necessarily a single firm, but often the main bank in a group comes closest to it. Up to the early 1970s, Morgan Guaranty Trust formed the centre of the most powerful financial group in the Atlantic economy. Historically, J.P. Morgan had been the channel through which most of the British portfolio investment flowed to the United States, and the famous US trusts of the turn of the century, attracting such investment, were often of Morgan's making. In Britain, a subsidiary was set up for which J.P. Morgan in 1901 solicited the partnership of one of the leading figures in the British Empire, Lord Milner. When he declined, E.C. Grenfell lent his name to the investment bank.

Morgan led the financing of Britain's and France's war effort against the Central Powers in the First World War.

If we confine ourselves to only the biggest corporations, Morgan in 1970 was directly linked to General Electric, Procter & Gamble, General Motors, as well as International Nickel of Canada. The first two firms were controlled largely by Morgan. Control of GM was shared with other groups (Fennema, 1982: 128; Menshikov, 1973: 254–5). Of these, Morgan, GE, and International Nickel were also among the most centrally located corporations in an international network of interlocking directorates in 1970 – along with Chemical Bank, Chase Manhattan Bank, Royal Dutch/Shell, Deutsche Bank, and the Dutch chemical concern AKZO (Fennema, 1982: 117). Centrality is understood here as constituting a key channel to assess and influence information flows circulating through boards of directors within and in between financial groups, on which non-corporate planning groups may feed in turn.

Chase Manhattan Bank, Morgan's rival, was the centre of a financial group historically associated with the Rockefeller family and their oil interests (reflected in its control of Standard Oil, N.J., today's Exxon, among others – Menshikov, 1973: 273). However, the international dimension is essential. Chase Manhattan came to be the very centre of the Atlantic network of joint directorates by 1976 (Fennema, 1982: 191). Since the 1920s, the Chase financial group followed a course which had been much more accommodating to German interests – when compared with the Morgan group. Chase's German interests were becoming stronger in the mid-1970s. This brings us to the German side and we seek merely to identify a segment of the German bourgeoisie allied with counterparts in the United States and Britain, and another segment embodying a less deferential attitude and willing, if need be, to confront the Anglo-Saxon ruling class on an issue like the relationship with the Soviet Union.

One view, propounded by Kuczynski, sees German capital divided between a reactionary bloc of coal and steel interests, prone to repression and war; versus an 'enlightened' coalition of, notably, the chemical and electrical engineering industries, opting for a conciliatory posture *vis-à-vis* the working class and foreign powers. This view has been rightly criticized for not including the bank/financial group dimension (see Gossweiler, 1975: 11–24; Pfeiffer, 1993: 48–9). The issue, of enduring interest if only in light of the question 'who helped Hitler to power' has produced a wealth of literature (Czichon, 1989; Sohn-Rethel, 1975; Stegmann, 1976; Abraham, 1981 – to name only some of the most salient authors). Gossweiler's analysis of German capital in the inter-war years has offered both a sophisticated theory of German financial groups and of the international dimension of their strategies. German capital was divided into industrial groupings (coal and steel versus chemical/electrical and automobile); but this division was cut across by the overarching division into financial groups named after the biggest general banks, the Deutsche Bank (with the Discontogesellschaft absorbed by it); and the Dresdner Bank (with the likewise absorbed Danat Bank). The constellation in its entirety would then revolve around particular key investment bank houses with the decisive political connections, notably the Cologne investment bank of J.H. Stein, and the New York–London–Hamburg chain of Schröder banks (Gossweiler, 1975:344; see also Van der Pijl, 1984: 45).[5]

In this complex picture, the Dresdner Bank was the nodal point of the dependent group. It was still as an equal partner that it concluded a business agreement with Morgan in 1905, but after the First World War, this turned into a dependent position (Gossweiler, 1975:42–3). Its links were, in heavy industry, Thyssen (part of the Vestag steel trust dependent on foreign capital), Krupp, and the Flick group; in the newer industries, it was connected to the (partly) foreign-owned AEG [1929, GE] and Opel [1927, GM].

The Deutsche Bank was the big bank in the combination representing the independent fraction of German capital. It was always stronger than Dresdner Bank, and its allies in industry were often the more innovative and independent corporations. Mannesmann, Hoesch, Haniel and Klöckner in the steel industry; the chemical trust IG Farben established in 1925; the car firms Daimler-Benz and BMW; and Siemens (Gossweiler, 1975: 329, 344). While there were many links with American capital (Deutsche Bank with Rockefeller since 1913, Mannesmann with Bethlehem Steel, Siemens with Westinghouse, and so on), none of these implied the dependence characteristic of the links of the Dresdner Bank group.

The American military occupation authorities at the end of the Second World War also investigated the structure of German capital around the two banks (OMGUS 1985, 1986). For the more recent period, we have data from Ziegler et al. (1985) for 1976, and Pfeiffer (1993) for 1983. In Table 9.1, we have brought together the pertinent connections to show their stability over time. As can be seen, the Deutsche Bank group is clearly the most stable and salient of the two (the third bank, Commerzbank, has no comparable network; its profile otherwise is comparable to the Dresdner bank in terms of international orientation).

Table 9.1   Financial group structure of the Deutsche and Dresdner Bank groups between c.1930–83 (firms listed in two sources or more)

	Nazi era: 'special relationships'	*1976: greatest number of links within overall core*	*1983: 'core' of each*
Deutsche Bank	Daimler-Benz	Daimler-Benz	Daimler-Benz
	Mannesmann	Mannesmann	Mannesmann
	Siemens	Siemens	Siemens
	Hoesch		Hoesch
		Allianz	Allianz
		RWE	RWE
		VEBA	VEBA
	HAPAG		
	BMW		
	Reemtsma		
Shared Influence	RWE		
		HAPAG	
		Thyssen	Thyssen*
Dresdner Bank	Krupp	Krupp	Krupp
	AEG		AEG
			BMW
			Reemtsma

*Thyssen industrial belongs to the core of the Deutsche Bank, Thyssen trade to the core of the Dresdner Bank.
Sources: (Nazi era) OMGUS, 1985: 103–32; OMGUS, 1986: 33ff; (1976) Ziegler *et al.*, 1985: 99, Table 5.1; (1983) Pfeiffer, 1993: 239–40, Tables II/ IV; 243–5, Tables II/IV.

Of course any attempt to give a listing by formal criteria falls short of a concrete analysis, for which, among others, the indispensable economic journalism of Kurt Pritzkoleit would have to be consulted. Even with the present sources, there are problems. OMGUS uses a different methodology in the two volumes; Ziegler *et al.* deny the existence of groups, and so on. We should also bear in mind that we are speaking of financial groups, not of bank empires; the question who is controlling whom is secondary here. With such caveats, how-ever, Table 9.1 can nevertheless serve as a background to our analysis of the prominent role of the Deutsche Bank in pursuing a *rapproche-ment* with the USSR independent from Britain and the United States.

Meanwhile the terrain of competition was transformed in the 1980s. In countries with a strong state-interventionist legacy, like Japan, Germany, and France, *banks* remained the privileged vehicles for financial activities, and remained strongly interlocked with industrial groups. In the Anglo-Saxon countries, the *stock exchange* and markets for financial derivatives like options and swaps became more prominent: thus in line with the brand of neo-liberal economic philosophy which draws inspiration from the perspective of the financier and speculator, banks were often forced to hunt for quick profits. This sometimes meant banks divested themselves of industrial assets to obtain liquidity, intensifying competition for other asset 'bargains'. American banks, carrying heavy debt loads since the credit boom of the 1970s, lost their stake in industrial capital (in 1970, 80 per cent of US corporations' capital needs were covered by bank credits; in 1990, only 20 per cent) and turned to short-term, often risky transactions and new financial instruments to uphold profitability (Albert, 1992: 65). US institutions therefore gradually disappeared from lists of the world's most powerful banks (when ranked by assets), to be replaced by Japanese banks (one in top 10 of 1970; eight of the top 10 banks ranked by assets in 1993), with Crédit Lyonnais of France and the Deutsche Bank following at some distance (Fennema and Van der Pijl, 1987: 31).[6]

As US and British financial market structures become more and more deregulated and fragile, the power of non-Anglo-Saxon banks, with their stable group affiliations to commerce and industry, allowed them to penetrate the Anglo-Saxon banking structures which – in common with others around the world (for example in the Nordic countries) have experienced severe crisis in the 1980s and 1990s. Between 1973 and 1986, foreign ownership of US banks increased nearly fourteen-fold, bringing 17 per cent of US banking assets into foreign hands in 1986 as compared to only 3.8 per cent in 1973 (Tolchin and Tolchin, 1989: 120). In 1990, Japanese owners ranked first with 55.3 per cent of foreign-held US bank assets.[7]

Deutsche Bank advanced to the second most central institution in the Atlantic interlock network behind Chase Manhattan by the mid-seventies (it was number 5 in 1970). In 1979 it opened a US branch just in time to avoid the impact of new legislation meant to subject foreign banks to the same laws as their American competitors. Noteworthy here is the fact that German banks are 'universal' banks entitled to all types of banking activity, and this gave the Deutsche Bank an advantage over US competitors in their own market – United States competitors who were effectively barred from similarly diversified activity. The position of bank capital in the economy is of course a strategic one, and the direct presence of major foreign banks raised concern in the host countries. As a member of the US House Banking Committee commented, foreign banks in particular 'give unfriendly foreign powers a window into things they ought not to see' (quoted in Tolchin and Tolchin, 1989: 140).

But the axis along which German capital was deploying was not only the Atlantic one. The Deutsche Bank group, in particular, was active also on the new markets opened up by the *Ostpolitik* of Willy Brandt. The bank was chief negotiator of credits awarded to the Soviet Union (Sörgel, 1985: 1236), while Mannesmann (with Deutsche Bank director F. Wilhelm Christians as its Chairman), invariably was the key industrial supplier in the equipment-for-energy deals with the USSR. In 1980, the famous 10 billion DM contract to contruct a gas pipeline from Urengoi in North Siberia to Bavaria was signed by a consortium headed by the Deutsche Bank, awarded to Mannesmann with assistance from AEG and Salzgitter.[8] This contract led to grave concern in the USA. Even disregarding alarmist visions of the USSR obtaining a control panel on German affairs, a basis for a convergence of interest between the German bourgeoisie and the Soviet leadership was set in place, contradicting the Reagan Administration's new hard line. Administration members such as Under-Secretary of Defense Richard Perle pressed for 'a well designed program of economic sanctions' to 'damage the Soviet economy' (quoted in Van der Pijl, 1989b: 76). A director of AEG, on the other hand, argued that there was a growing German interest in raising the productivity and enhancing the efficiency of the Soviet economy to ensure the envisaged Soviet export surplus by which debt service was to be covered.[9] After a short interval, the Polish crisis allowed the hard-liners to triumph in this matter. This forced the USSR to lay the entire pipeline itself at a record pace and we may assume, great cost as well (Aganbegjan, 1989: 300; on the US domestic conflict, Van der Pijl, 1989b: 76). By 1984, the German Confederation of Industries (BDI) in its annual report had to acknowledge that uncertainties created by the US-instigated embargoes were a key reason why East–West trade was losing steam (BDI, 1984: 173–4).

Meanwhile the advance of the German banks (and even more so, of their Japanese counterparts) continued. The Deutsche Bank in 1984 purchased a 4.9 per cent interest in Morgan Grenfell in London. In 1986 it acquired the Banca d'America e Italia, Italian subsidiary of the Bank of America; in the same year, the Dresdner Bank acquired ABD Securities in the US. In 1989, Deutsche Bank, at a stroke, established itself as a leader in the European merger and acquisition field by purchasing the remainder of Morgan Grenfell for $1.5 billion. Meanwhile, Deutsche Bank's investment banking subsidiaries in other English-speaking countries included McLean McCarthy in Canada and 50 per cent of Bain & Co of Australia. 'By the late 1980s, Deutsche Bank was actively pursuing the goal of becoming a global investment bank and a European-wide universal bank, offering corporate and consumer services as well as mutual funds and asset management. To do so, the bank, led by Alfred Herrhausen as a sole Sprecher (rather than the usual co-spokesmen arrangement), was trying to change its traditionally conservative corporate culture into something more aggressive' (Mattera, 1992: 202).

This should be seen in the perspective of a parallel growth of the Deutsche Bank financial group in the same period: Daimler-Benz in 1985 acquired aircraft companies MTU and Dornier, as well as AEG; in 1989, following an abortive attempt by Franz Josef Strauss's Bavarian government, the Dresdner Bank, and BMW, to constitute a rival conglomerate to Daimler, the latter snatched away MBB, the aircraft company that was to have been part of the 'Bavarian' complex.[10] Also, in 1986, Deutsche Bank acquired the Libyan participation in FIAT, making it the second shareholder behind the Agnelli founder family.[11] To deal with the manifold policy implications of its economic advance, Herrhausen created a special working group on strategy within the Deutsche Bank (Wisnewski *et al.*, 1993: 148). Two issues of strategic importance facing the bank at this point were the question of global debt, and the future of Eastern Europe and the USSR, especially once perestroika opened new perspectives on economic co-operation and penetration. To understand how these two issues were entangled with high politics, we must turn our attention to the activities of transnational planning councils.

TRANSNATIONAL PLANNING COUNCILS AND THE GORBACHEV CHALLENGE

The role of transnational private planning councils was characterized by Gramsci (discussing Freemasonry and comparable networks), as one of 'mediating the extremes, of "socialising" the technical discoveries which provide the impetus for all activities of leadership, of devising compromises between, and ways out of, extreme solutions' (Gramsci, 1971: 182 n).

In struggles between corporate liberalism and neo-liberalism, the Atlantic orientation and a narrower European one, and in conflicts over how to deal with the challenge posed by Gorbachev's USSR, planning councils have served as a relay for synthesizing different currents of opinion, but also, as we will see, of isolating particular options deemed detrimental to longer-term Western interests. While their nature often varies (for instance, whether there is a common policy orientation or not, whether the scope of problems dealt with is sectoral or comprehensive, and so on), the transnational planning councils can be seen to have reflected in part the political restructuring of the capitalist world (see the overview in Gill, 1990: 123 ff.).

The most salient North Atlantic planning council, the Bilderberg Conferences (which began in 1954) by the mid-1970s according to a participant in the twenty-third Bilderberg Meeting at Megève (France) in 1974, 'had seemed to lose its sense of direction' (quoted in Eringer, 1980: 31). In late 1975, the Church Committee hearings in the US Senate exposed Bilderberg's chairman, Holland's Prince Bernhard, and other Bilderberg luminaries such as Franz Josef Strauss, to have been part of a bribery network for the sales of US aeroplanes in Europe, using the World Wildlife Fund (set up by the Prince in 1961) as a cover (Sampson, 1978: 271 ff.).

A few years before, Chase Manhattan chairman David Rockefeller at a Bilderberg meeting had proposed to broaden the consultation to include Japan. The Trilateral Commission (TC) that resulted from this proposal adopted a more sophisticated, Gramscian 'intellectual' posture contrasting with the secrecy of Bilderberg. At least for the period coinciding with the Carter Administration (1977–81) when its US membership was strongly represented in government, the TC remained committed to the corporate liberal consensus. Within this broad formula the Carter Administration sought to recapture the initiative lost in the crisis of the Cold War and Vietnam, by a moral crusade under the banner of 'human rights' aimed particularly at putting the Soviet bloc states on the defensive. Bilderberg, continuing separately but overlapping in membership with the TC, reflected the shift in economic power in the Atlantic area when in 1979 it appointed Alfred Herrhausen, of Deutsche Bank to its steering committee; while Walter Scheel, Brandt's Free Democrat Secretary of Foreign Affairs, replaced Alec Douglas Home as chairman.[12]

Propagation of a hard line against the left and *détente* was taken up by a different body, launched by an original Bilderberg member, former French Prime Minister, Antoine Pinay. In 1969, he set up a group designated as either the Pinay Circle, or the Cercle Violet (after Jean Violet, a lawyer connected with the French secret service, SDECE). Among its founders was Archduke Otto von Habsburg, heir to the Austrian throne and head of several extreme right-wing organizations for the promotion of European unity under a Roman Catholic aegis (Teacher, 1993: 9). In 1982, *Der Spiegel* magazine made public an internal German security service document exposing an unsuccessful campaign sponsored by the Pinay Circle to bring Franz Jozef Strauss to power in Germany through manipulating fears of left-wing terrorism (translated in *Lobster* 17, November 1988: 14–15). Other activities of the Pinay Circle showed that it functioned as a meeting place for European conservatives with key representatives of the ascendant neo-liberal *rentier* concept such as Paul Volcker, former chairman of the United States Federal Reserve Bank (and ex-Chase Manhattan banker and now North American Chairman of the Trilateral Commission in succession to David Rockefeller); Ed Feulner, of the Heritage Foundation, one of the think-tanks behind the 'Reagan revolution'; West-German European Commissioner K-H. Narjes (also a TC member); and William Colby, the former CIA chief and organizer of the Gladio undercover network in Europe. Each participated in the Pinay Circle conference in December 1979 in Washington.[13]

Herrhausen's appearance on the Bilderberg steering committee would seem to contradict the traditional prominence of Dresdner Bank in such planning bodies. Indeed, German corporate leaders on the TC in this period (1973–80) were typically from the Dresdner Bank group, from Thyssen, and trade and private investment banking (Van der Pijl, 1994: 181; see Table 9.1 above). In the early 1980s, however, the Deutsche Bank group became as active as Dresdner in Atlantic planning bodies. For example the 1982 membership list of the Atlantik-Brücke ('Atlantic bridge'), the German sister organization of the American Council on Germany set up in the 1950s, shows Chancellor Schmidt next to Free Democrat Minister of Economic Affairs Count Lambsdorff, and directors of Dresdner Bank group firms like BMW next to directors from the Deutsche Bank group.[14] Also members were Manfred Wörner (later to become the head of NATO) and the former chief of the German intelligence service BND (Wisnewski *et al.*, 1993: 76–7).

Germany's role in pursuing *détente* with the Soviet bloc had of course been a matter of intense debate in these planning councils. The 1979 NATO missile deployment decision was made, in part, to undermine the growing economic interdependence between Western Europe and the Soviet bloc. In a 1983 interview in *Trialogue*, the TC journal, Zbigniew Brzezinski, the first Director of the TC, and President Carter's National Security Adviser (1977–81), stated that the deployment of INF missiles in Europe first of all was necessary to prevent Western Europe from turning to the East to overcome its current economic malaise. However, at the April 1984 TC Conference in Rome, Austrian Social Democrat leader Bruno Kreisky and West-German President Richard von Weiszäcker continued to defend East–West trade.[15] Weiszäcker in 1983 had declared that 'basket two', economic co-operation, was the most important element in the Helsinki Agreements of 1975 (Garton Ash, 1992: 264), whereas in the English-speaking world, from Carter on, 'basket three', human rights and free movement, had been declared central.

Responding to pressures on the part of a powerful combination of arms-industrial and intelligence interests organized in the Committee on the Present Danger, the Reagan Administration stepped up the arms race to force the USSR into bankruptcy. Richard Pipes, Reagan's Soviet specialist on the National Security Council and a prominent CPD member, estimated in 1982 that intensified US pressure would force the Soviet Union to shift resources to light industry, away from the military sector.[16] The launching of the 'Star Wars' project (SDI) in 1983, highly contested by technical specialists from the beginning, was meant to achieve just that. Gorbachev's intention, made clear soon after taking power in 1985, to opt out of the arms race, could not alter this course. Preparing Ronald Reagan's first meeting with Mikhail Gorbachev in November, 1985, the President's Chief of Staff, former Merrill Lynch banker Donald Regan, analyzed the US position entirely in terms of the economic implications of SDI:

> The Soviets [Regan wrote in his memoirs] could not spend more on arms without running the risk of bankrupting the state ... I urged the President to stay strong in dealing with Gorbachev .... Faced with the choice between bankruptcy and a fall from power that would deliver the U.S.S.R. back into the hands of the faction that had all but ruined her economically, [Gorbachev] would have no choice ... The key was SDI. To match it, Gorbachev would have to mortgage the whole future of communism. (Regan, 1988: 296–7, 298–9)

At the same time, Under-Secretary of Defense and CPD member Fred Ikle chose a visit to Munich to exhort the West European allies to abandon the 'principle of stability between East and West' and instead bring the West's 'technological and economic superiority' to bear on relations with the USSR.[17] However, West-German interests moved to capitalize on privileged relations with the Soviet Union that developed in the *Ostpolitik* period. Big corporations prominent in that policy, such as Mannesmann, as well as Krupp, Salzgitter, and Ruhrgas, immediately began cultivating the new leadership. Christians (Mannesmann/Deutsche Bank), the architect of the gas pipeline deal, stated that China and the Soviet Union were the markets of the future, but that the USSR was the more promising 'since relations are very close as a result of longer cooperation'.[18] At a meeting in Moscow in 1987, dedicated by Soviet leader Gorbachev to 'a world without nuclear arms, and to the survival of mankind', Christians, a personal friend of the Gorbachevs, was a member of a powerful West German delegation (the most prestigious one from abroad) which came to try and work out the economic implications of such a development.

The second issue on which the Deutsche Bank group took a position contradicting the neo-liberalism of the English-speaking world, was the debt crisis. Herrhausen and the Deutsche Bank director for North America, Werner Blessing, were convinced that US banks' credit strategies and the deficit spending policies of the American governments were the main cause of the debt crisis. The Deutsche Bank had also participated in the credit spree, but in Latin America (where after the 1982 Mexican crisis and Castro's calls for a debtors' cartel, repayment was becoming uncertain), German banks had only a 6 per cent share of the outstanding debt of the eight most indebted countries against the 35 per cent for the United States' commercial banks. Also, the Deutsche Bank covered doubtful debts for around 50 per cent by extra reserves against a rate of 20 to 30 per cent for most of the large American banks (Bank of America and Manufacturers Hanover had even poorer coverage).[19] Citicorp, the biggest US bank, with $14.9 billion Third World debt on its books by the mid-eighties (against total reserves of $4.9 billion), failed to secure reinsurance of its non-performing loans.[20]

By 1985, however, Blessing and Herrhausen were in effect advocating a debt pardon for Third World countries: a policy especially detrimental to the American banks. The two were at a meeting of the Heinrich Dräger Stiftung, a German private planning group, in November of that year, dedicated to discussing the debt crisis in this light. Other speakers included Hans Tietmeyer, Deputy German Gov-

ernor at the World Bank (later President of the Bundesbank). Tietmeyer was linked to the Deutsche Bank group by his directorship of
VEBA. In late 1987 Herrhausen repeated his proposals in Washington
and was met with intense hostility. Such hostility was echoed in
Germany by the head of the Commerzbank (Wisnewski *et al.*,
1993: 154, 162). Nevertheless in late 1988, a majority of US bankers
also came round to a conditional debt pardon or at least some debt
forgiveness; with only Manufacturers Hanover rejecting it and Citicorp making reservations.[21]

In an attempt to work out a common position on the challenge of
the new Soviet posture, the Trilateral Commission met in April 1989 in
Paris. The Commission discussed a report by former French President
Giscard d'Estaing, former United States Secretary of State Kissinger,
and former Japanese Prime Minister Nakasone. This report advised
recapturing the initiative from Gorbachev by developing a strategy of
long-term, conditional reconciliation, a mixture of 'cooperation and
confrontation'. The authors sought to strike a balance between different positions by proposing to give the USSR observer status in
GATT and the IMF, so that it might be able to get acquainted with
the rules of the game. (Membership of these organizations was
rejected by the United States). Other suggestions included joint ventures in *light industry* and the creation of a monitoring institution for
aid to the former Soviet bloc.[22] The European Bank for Reconstruction and Development (EBRD) that came out of these deliberations
remained handicapped by this failure to choose between an EC or
OECD orientation. Qualified by *Le Monde* as 'one-third EC, one
third World Bank, and one-third Banque Lazard or J.P. Morgan', it
became the target of a sustained smear campaign against its head,
Mitterrand intimate Jacques Attali, for his eventual refusal to apply a
neo-liberal recipe on the defunct USSR.[23]

In 1989, a month after the Paris TC meeting, the thirty-seventh
Bilderberg meeting took place in La Toja, Spain. German economic
statesmen were conspicuously absent (except for veteran Atlanticist
Otto Wolff von Amerongen, a stalwart from Deutsche Bank group
and advocate of East–West trade), although the topic of the meeting
was the future of Eastern Europe. At the meeting, the new *Ostpolitik*
was criticized by Oxford academic Timothy Garton Ash, foreign
editor of the conservative British magazine *The Spectator*.[24] Garton
Ash addressed a prestigious gathering of European royalty, a cross-
section of Atlantic power holders, opinion-makers, NATO commanders, and heads of Anglo-Saxon banks potentially or actually harmed

by the Deutsche Bank strategy, such as (the chairmen of) Chase Manhattan, S.G. Warburg, and Drexel Burnham Lambert. Garton Ash advocated a forward Western strategy that would make Soviet concessions to areas breaking away from the USSR irreversible. He emphatically warned against premature deals that might compromise a complete 'westernisation' of Eastern Europe. Ash declared himself in favour of an active role of the US and Canada in the transformation process to ensure that it be guided by 'Western values' (Bilderberg, 1989).

It seemed at this point, at least for some, as if Germany rather than the USSR was the problem, as reflected in the March, 1990, meeting of 'experts on Germany' convened at Mrs Thatcher's request (notes of the meeting were subsequently published in *The Spectator*). German overtures to Gorbachev, in the perspective of German reunification, were causing grave concern among its Western allies. For example, in 1988, Christians had proposed to turn the Kaliningrad area, the Russian enclave between Lithuania and Poland (formerly part of German East Prussia), into a special economic zone where ethnic Germans from the USSR should be resettled (Garton Ash, 1993: 405). Apart from conferring directly with Gorbachev, Deutsche Bank group corporations like Siemens, Daimler-Benz, and Robert Bosch, as well as Thyssen, were represented in the European Round Table of Industrialists (ERT) set up in 1983. This private body, originally composed of 17 European industry leaders, was launched to deal with the deteriorating competitive position of the European Union economy. It proposed a strategy of regeneration which included large-scale infrastructure projects. In the second half of the 1980s, ERT proposals began to reflect a more protectionist orientation which, at the political level, was welcomed by the Socialist French government but rejected by the Thatcher and Kohl governments. At this point, key British and Anglo-Dutch corporations such as Royal Dutch/Shell, ICI and Unilever, left the ERT, only to return in 1991 (Van Tulder and Junne, 1988: 215; Holman, 1992).

The first ERT project proposal (of 1984), a continent-wide high-speed train network, was elaborated on in a comprehensive 10-points programme for German and European economic unity announced by Chancellor Kohl on 28 November 1989, nineteen days after the opening of the Berlin Wall had given a new quality to German-Soviet relations. A Paris–Berlin–Moscow extension of the envisaged high-speed train network was part of these 10 Points.[25] Herrhausen had co-authored the 10 Points programme and did not subscribe to the protectionist orientation that temporarily got the upper hand in the ERT. He was, however, a pronounced advocate of an integrated, constructive approach to Eastern Europe and favoured a *separate* European bank to prevent the area's economy and infrastructure from falling victim to IMF conditionality or GATT trade liberalism.[26] Two days after the presentation of the 10 Points, however (and three days after the Deutsche Bank take-over of Morgan Grenfell), Herrhausen's armoured Mercedes was blown up in the open street, killing the banker but not his driver. This high tech assassination (ascribed, falsely to the extreme left terror organization of the 1970s, the Red Army Faction, RAF), was the first of several assassinations of prominent figures from the Deutsche Bank group.

Several months after the assassination of Herrhausen, the GDR parliament set up the Treuhand privatization trust as part of the transition to a capitalist economy – the biggest industrial trust in the world. In August 1990, the month when the GDR parliament declared its wish to accede to the Federal Republic, Detlev Rohwedder was appointed to head the Treuhand. Rohwedder combined two qualities which associated him with greater economic interdependence and political compromise with the USSR: first he was chairman of the board of Hoesch, a steel firm long part of the Deutsche Bank orbit (see Table 9.1), and second, he was a member of the SPD, the opposition party developing a non-governmental 'Second *Ostpolitik*' angering many Atlanticist policy intellectuals (see Garton Ash, 1993).

Rohwedder considered making use of the industrial assets of the former GDR economy. These would be used to sustain the East German and wider East European economy. Whilst Rohwedder judged all-out privatization to be an illusion, others on the Treuhand Board thought differently. Most vocal among Rohwedder's critics was Birgit Breuel, a member of the Atlantik-Brücke and daughter of Alwin Münchmeyer (see note 4). Breuel had made her name as Christian Democratic Union (CDU) Economics Minister in Lower Saxony. There, in tandem with the Finance Minister and chairman of the Atlantik-Brücke, W.L. Kiep, she implemented a programme of radical privatization (Wisnewski *et al.*, 1993: 260–2). Rohwedder was also criticized from abroad, especially by British and American financial circles. Among complaints concerning the privatization conditions was that conditions concerning ecological regulation and employment protection put in place by Rohwedder were keeping out non-German investors as well as not allowing privatization to be handled by private investment banks (Wisnewski *et al.* 1993: 236–38). On 1 April 1991, Rohwedder was killed by a professional assassin. The murder was again ascribed to the RAF. Rohwedder was succeeded by Breuel and thereafter east German privatization accelerated. Investment firms such as Goldman Sachs, S.G. Warburg, Crédit Suisse First Boston, Price Waterhouse, J.P. Morgan, and Merrill Lynch were allowed to move in as brokers for major deals. Only Morgan Grenfell was largely left out of this business, for which its connection with the Deutsche Bank was held responsible.[27]

Table 9.2 Eastern Europe: development of Gross Domestic Product, 1988–92 (per cent change compared with previous year)

	1988	1989	1990	1991	1992
Bulgaria	+2.6	−1.9	− 9.1	−11.7	− 7.7
Czech Rep.		+1.5	− 2.0	−14.0	− 7.1
Hungary	−0.1	−0.2	− 3.3	−11.9	− 4.6
Poland	+4.1	+0.2	−11.6	− 7.6	+1.0
Romania	−0.5	−5.8	− 7.4	−13.7	−15.4
Russia*				− 9.0	−19.0
Slovakia				−16.4	− 8.7
Slovenia	−1.9	−2.7	− 3.4	− 9.3	− 6.5
Ukraine*				−11.2	−15.0 to −18.0

*Russia, Ukraine: Gross National Product.
Source: Wiener Institut für Internationale Wirtschaftsvergleiche. Reprinted in *Manifest*, 1 July 1993.

As Gramsci wrote, transnational private planning councils serve, among other things, as channels for 'devising compromises between, and ways out of, extreme solutions' (1971: 182n). Obviously, the Deutsche Bank group failed to win enough support for its strategy in these planning networks. Historically, it was the Dresdner Bank group which was most prominently represented on them, and supporters of the neo-liberal concept were ascendant in them all through the 1980s and early 1990s. When personalities and corporations belonging to the Deutsche Bank group persisted in compromising with Gorbachev and retaining and expanding the infrastructure of the former Soviet bloc, some 'extreme solutions', one might infer, were no longer to be avoided. Of course this is only part of the picture, since a wide range of influences were at work and the Soviet model was exhausted. But the real collapse of the East European economies began when the social protection and infrastructure continuity was buried with its key protagonist, Herrhausen, in November, 1989. Table 9.2 gives an indication of this acceleration of the general economic collapse that developed between 1989 and 1992 in the context of the strategy of neo-liberal shock therapy that was adopted to promote the transition from state socialism.

The smear campaign against Attali begun by the London *Financial Times* and which resulted in his resignation in 1993, prompted former French foreign minister Roland Dumas to ascribe the bringing down of the EBRD head as the work of 'the Anglo-Saxon establishment'.[28] The resentment felt on the part of the French that they were out-manoeuvred in the developments leading up to German reunification was understandable. Mitterrand's last minute state visit to the GDR in December 1989 was a vain gesture, unable to stem the tide that was leading to the country's re-incorporation into the Federal Republic. But the Germans' own attempt to make reunification part of a wider process of trans-European integration, remained under fire as well. As long as the Germans co-operated with Gorbachev, they faced opposing forces in the English-speaking countries committed to the dismemberment of the USSR and the application of a neo-liberal recipe of reform in the East.

On the eve of the Yanayev coup of 1991 that triggered the break-up of the USSR, a *Newsweek* editorial, written by Fred Coleman, reiterated reasons why the Atlantic world should press on with its strategy of political dismemberment and destroying state socialism. Even at this point, the Western consensus was not secure and a warning had to be issued against potential support for Gorbachev on the part of other countries – presumably France and Germany:

> Some Western leaders [the comment went] believe that the world would be a safer place if the Soviet Union survives in its present form. They believe that dealing with a president in Moscow whom they consider a known quantity is a greater guarantee of stability than having to deal with the unknown leaders of 15 or more newly independent...countries if the Soviet Union were to break up. They also believe that in Mikhail Gorbachev they have a reliable partner for building a constructive new world order. They err on all counts.[29]

And after explaining a preference for the 'peaceful collapse of the Soviet Union' for long-term political reasons including the reduction of 'the threat of totalitarianism throughout the world', Coleman continued:

> the West can fund Gorbachev...[who] would use the help only in order to buy time, to postpone essential reforms and prop up the present Soviet system. Giving aid directly to Yeltsin and other leaders in the republics would accomplish far more...there is no better way to serve the world community.[30]

This was written at a time when the Bush Administration had knowledge of an impending coup attempt against Gorbachev and was assisting Yeltsin to use that opportunity to move to centre-stage.

In early 1991, the CIA and the US National Security Agency (NSA) discovered that a plot was in the making. When the Yanayev coup came in August, with Gorbachev confined in his Presidential dacha on the Black Sea, Bush ordered US intelligence intercepts to be given to Yeltsin in Moscow, while a US embassy communications specialist went to Yeltsin to help him establish contact with military commanders. At that juncture, 'the Bush Administration...turned to Yeltsin as a possible alternative leader', assigning CIA and NSA resources to Yeltsin to provide personal and communications security (Hersh, 1994: 84–6). This marked the beginning of the end of the Soviet Union – consummated when Gorbachev had to step down as president of the USSR in December 1991. It also terminated the attempt by a segment of the German capitalist class, in tandem with Socialists in their own country and France, to seek a rapprochement that would have improved the European Union's economic perspectives while saving the East European economies from collapse.

Notes

1. I owe a debt to Stephen Gill, the editor of this collection, for his detailed suggestions for a reorganisation of the original paper; and to my colleague in Amsterdam, Cees Wiebes, as well as participants at the August 1993 MUNS meeting in Vikersund, Norway (in particular Magnus Ryner), for critical comments. None of those mentioned are in any way responsible for the contents of this chapter.
2. *New York Times*, 8 March 1992.
3. *International Herald Tribune*, 1 August 1978.
4. *The Economist*, 19 September 1992.

5. Of the Schröder bank it is often said that it 'brought Hitler to power' (for example, recently, *De Volkskrant*, 26 May 1994). Baron Kurt von Schröder was indeed a critical figure in this process. The Schröder bank has remained a nodal point in the Atlantic ruling class. Allan Dulles, later head of the CIA, was a director in the New York branch of the London-based J.H. Schröder bank, J. Henry Schroeder Corp., set up in 1923 (Gossweiler, 1975: 353). In the early 1970s, the board of directors of the London Schröder bank (cf. *Jane's* 1971) included two key architects of the new Cold War launched later in the decade: Paul Nitze, one of the animators of the key pressure group in this respect, the Committee on the Present Danger; and Harold Brown (a founder member of the Trilateral Commission and Secretary of Defense in the Carter Administration). In 1969, Alwin Münchmeyer, later head of the West-German trade and bankers' organizations merged his Hamburg bank (taken over from Jewish émigrés in the 1930s), with the Schröder bank in Hamburg, to form Schröder, Münchmeyer, Hengst & Co. Münchmeyer is also a member of the Trilateral Commission.

6. See *Business Week*, 24 May 1993.

7. *Newsweek*, 28 May 1979; *Newsweek*, 30 September 1991.

8. *NRC-Handelsblad*, 17 November 1980.

9. *Frankfurter Allgemeine*, 2 May 1978.

10. *NRC-Handelsblad* 13 November 1985; *Newsweek* 11 December 1989.

11. F. Clairmonte, *Le Monde Diplomatique*, April 1990, p. 15.

12. *NRC-Handelsblad*, 27 October 1979.

13. *Lobster* 17, November 1988, pp. 14–15; Teacher, 1993.

14. The Free Democrats brought down the Schmidt government by crossing the floor to the Christian Democrats in 1982. Lambsdorff was a member of the Executive Committee of the Trilateral Commission.

15. G.-A. Astre in *Le Monde Diplomatique*, June 1984, p. 16.

16. *Neue Zürcher Zeitung*, 10 November 1982.

17. *NRC-Handelsblad*, 3 March 1986.

18. *Der Spiegel*, September 1987.

19. *Newsweek* 1 June 1987; Wisnewski *et al.* 1993, pp. 158–61.

20. Ph. Norel in *Le Monde Diplomatique* March 1985, p. 9; *Newsweek* 1 June 1987.

21. *Volkskrant*, 9 September 1988.

22. *Le Monde*, 12 April 1989.

23. *Le Monde*, 24 April 1991.

24. Garton Ash was the author of a book on *Ostpolitik* (Garton Ash, 1993) and on the Czech overthrow of communist rule, having had close access to Vaclav Havel.

25. *Blätter für deutsche und internationale Politik*, January 1990, pp. 119–21.

26. *Het Parool*, 10 April 1993.

27. *Frankfurter Allgemeine*, 3 April 1992, quoted in Wisnewski *et al.*, 1993: 277; *Het Parool*, 10 March 1993.

28. *Financial Times*, 26–7 June 1993.

29. *Newsweek*, 24 June 1991.

30. Ibid.

10 Civil Society and Political Economy in South and Southern Africa

Fantu Cheru

For a worker living in 'deep' Soweto, the sprawling township outside Johannesburg, the world economy of today has many parallels with the apartheid system which was in place until April 1994. Indeed, South Africa is in many ways a microcosm of the world (Makhijani, 1992). Besides issues of race, language, power, urbanization, and politics, the income gap between the races is similar to that in the world as a whole, and creates similar dangers. While the blacks toiled to keep the wheels of this economy moving, the whites enjoyed the fruits. The adoption of a neo-liberal economic strategy by the first multi-racial government of Nelson Mandela is unlikely to help eradicate the dualistic structure of South African society and the region for the foreseeable future. If anything, neo-liberalism as a development strategy is likely to result in a decisive change in the productive powers and balance of social forces within South Africa, the region, and in the relationship of Southern Africa with the major powers in the world economy (Gill, 1991a).

Similarly, the relationship of South Africa with its neighbours resembles the world economy's core-periphery structure, particularly the North–South dichotomy. For decades, South Africa has been a sub-imperial power dominating the region. Even during the decade of international sanctions, South Africa consistently enjoyed a positive and growing trade balance with the neighbouring Southern African Development Community (SADC) countries.[1] SADC's priority objective of reducing dependence on South Africa has not been fulfilled. In this context, this paper examines steps southern African states must take to ensure equitable and sustainable regional development. Southern African governments will be pressed from above (that is, by forces of neo-liberal global restructuring in the world economy) and from below (by social movements resisting). Therefore, the study of South Africa and Southern Africa can teach us a great deal about the disintegrating tendencies of globalization and various forms of resistance and alternative visions coming from below (Martin, 1991).

A BRAVE NEW WORLD OR MORE OF THE SAME? SOUTH AFRICA AND THE REGION

With the end of the Cold War and the dismantling of apartheid in South Africa, the political atmosphere in southern Africa has changed drastically. Expectations have been raised of peaceful regional integration. There exists great concern across the continent that the major capitalist powers are losing interest in much of Africa as they move to greener pastures in Eastern Europe and the former Soviet Union. They fear that increasing flows of foreign investment and aid will be diverted to Eastern Europe as those countries have a better infrastructure and human capital required for expanded investment and trade relations with the West than Africa does. These concerns have forced governments in Southern Africa to adopt a framework of economic co-operation in order to become serious players in the new world order.[2]

Nevertheless, talk of regional consensus and integration comes from three sources: South African business interests who see enormous opportunities in a more tightly integrated regional market; pragmatic regional governments who see regional integration as a possibility for greater national leverage *vis-à-vis* both South Africa and protection from a hostile international trade environment; and visionaries who view a new form of regional integration as a means to begin addressing some of the enormous historical inequalities within and between the states of southern Africa.[3] In realizing these goals, African leaders often pin their hope on the new South Africa, which they expect to serve as the locomotive of growth for the whole region.

Interestingly, the renewed interest in regional Southern Africa integration has also been welcomed by the World Bank, an institution long opposed to such an idea. The two existing regional associations are the Preferential Trade Area for Eastern and Southern Africa (PTA) and the Southern African Development Community (SADC), and the World Bank has singled these out for financial and technical support despite the stagnation of intra-regional trade.[4] As Martin (1991) has argued, the purpose of such support is to facilitate the operation of the free market and competitiveness, and the strengthening of bilateral relationships with core areas. While time and space do not allow me to enumerate the reasons for the lack of progress in intra-PTA and intra-SADC trade, a more pertinent question that this paper will explore is: why do governments and citizens in the sub-region pin so much hope with a revamped regional integration effort under the leadership of a democratic South Africa?

SOUTHERN AFRICA AFTER APARTHEID

A widely held view in black Africa, and South Africa itself (especially among white élites), and at the World Bank and the African Development Bank, is that the South African economy is going to act as a continental locomotive for other African economies. As such they believe that South Africa's membership in the PTA and SADC is crucial. By applying the managerial, institutional, and financial capacity of South Africa, along with the resources of the IMF, the World Bank and bilateral donors, it is believed that market integration in the sub-region can be moved forward.

This assessment fails to take into account many contradictions of the region. First, while South Africa could play a meaningful role in the region's development, the internal development problems of the country will consume the bulk of local energies and resources. In fact, South Africa may even pursue policies that would be counterproductive to some of its neighbours – for reasons discussed below. Furthermore, it is doubtful whether South African business can conceive of the region as a potential industrializing market, as opposed merely to a hinterland from which to draw raw materials and migrant labour. Second, the strength of the South African economy should not be exaggerated. Although South Africa is a regional core power and surrounded by weak states, in world-systems terminology it would still be classified as a 'semi-peripheral' state – that is, it remains dependent on the core states and market structures of the global economy. Like its neighbours, South Africa is still dependent on primary and semi-processed exports, against which the terms of trade have turned and most of its products are uncompetitive on international markets. While there will be a post-apartheid dividend in the short-term, these savings will be inadequate to finance its ambitious Reconstruction and Development Plan (RDP), let alone to contribute to the development and growth of the rest of the region. The new government of President Mandela faced enormous pressures for greater public expenditure on education, housing, and health in order to meet the expectations of the new electorate. Consequently, the direction of South African foreign policy was likely to be determined principally by internal economic factors (Tjonneland, 1992: 97–105). The new government might therefore be obliged to act in ways which will not necessarily make South Africa a better neighbour than it has been in the past. For example, to reduce unemployment at home, South Africa might discourage migrant labour, which would have disastrous consequences for countries dependent on their remittances to shore up their foreign exchange earnings. In 1994 alone, South African immigration authorities deported an estimated 125 000 Africans who crossed the border to the Republic. Thus, despite assurances from President Mandela that 'the integration of the South African economy into the regional economy should scrupulously avoid the domination by the South African economy of the regional economy', South Africa's membership in the PTA or SADC is unlikely to lead to the equalization of economic relations between member states.[5]

Long before the ANC took power, the Johannesburg mining corporations appeared to be operating with a different agenda. De Beers sought diamonds in Angola and Zimbabwe, Genmin was after Mozambican coal and Angolan oil. In construction, the huge Murray & Roberts conglomerate signed deals with Angolan officials to construct prefabricated schools, hospitals, houses, roads and harbours, and even mining and agricultural ventures. Several South African banks moved into Zimbabwe, buying up assets cheapened through rapid devaluation of the local currency.[6] South African parastatals such as Transnet, Portnet and Eskom reached an agreement with several governments in the region in 1993 to extend their railway and electricity network throughout the region, fulfilling Cecil Rhodes' 'Cape to Cairo' dream of economic and transportation links almost a hundred years after his death. Nevertheless, most of South Africa's business élites still preferred to treat the region as a hinterland from which to draw raw materials and migrant labour, and as a dumping ground for manufactured goods from South Africa. These forces see no long term benefit in establishing an equitable regional development strategy with South Africa's neighbours. Instead, they believe that the future for South Africa's trade lies in Europe, North America and the Far East. To reach this objective, an agreement was reached between South Africa and the General Agreement on Tariffs and Trade (GATT) in 1993.

More recently, in October 1995, South Africa concluded a free trade agreement with the European Union. This was intended to give South

African exporters better access to the European market, but it also meant that South Africa would have to drop its barriers against imports from the European Union. This is likely to have a negative impact on South Africa's textile, car and transport sectors faced with stiff competition from Europe.[7] The outcome of the new accord with the European Union is a shift away from redistributive or compensatory trade arrangements between Africa and Western Europe – towards free trade. South Africa had originally asked for trade links with the EU to be covered by the Lomé Convention, the trade, aid and co-operation accord between the EU and 70 developing countries, including all South Africa's neighbours. This would have allowed South Africa to receive trade concessions from Europe without having to make similar concessions, and would have allowed for a more co-operative and less competitive regional economic strategy to evolve. Now, however, there are firm opponents of a balanced form of regional co-operation inside the new government and in the business sector. Left to the market and to the present bureaucracy in Pretoria, South Africa's contribution to regional development will have more continuities with the apartheid era than not. But one other feature of the present conjuncture bears a brief discussion: the role of neo-liberalism in breaking down state barriers and reconfiguring trade, financial and investment flows. On the one hand this will integrate Southern Africa globally by virtue of a relatively homogenous economic approach. But on the other hand, there is danger of tremendous economic and social disintegration. We will briefly consider this issue, using the strongest regional economy – that of South Africa – as an illustration.

SOUTH AFRICA: DEMOCRACY AND THE TRIUMPH OF NEO-LIBERALISM

South Africa remains a land of extreme economic and social inequalities. Average black incomes are just one ninth of those of whites, while black unemployment exceeds 45 per cent. Millions of rural blacks have no land or too little on which to survive, while in 1988 some 80 per cent of agricultural land was owned by fewer than 60 000 white farming families (Wilson and Ramphele, 1989), a situation that has so far changed little since the end of apartheid. With the end of apartheid, however, high popular expectations have exerted considerable pressure on the government for more social expenditure on education, health, and housing. Unfortunately, almost two years into the new order, delivery of goods and services has been negligible in deprived rural and urban areas, and the left's hopes for transfers of resources have been largely dashed.

What explains the gap between the ANC's pre-election promises and its post-election performance? The answer can be found in the pre-emptive actions of the De Klerk government to keep the economy in the hands of whites before an ANC dominated government took power and, in the events leading to the constitutional negotiations of 1992 and 1993 whereby the ANC was forced to surrender on the economic policy front. These two sets of events explain why the ANC government has not been able to deliver: the economic levers remain in the hands of exceptionally conservative forces associated with the National Party (led by F.W. de Klerk) and the Inkatha Freedom Party (led by Mangosothu Buthelezi). There have also been various degrees of sabotage of new initiatives by the overwhelmingly white, Afrikaner civil service.

In the 1980s, South Africa went through two states of emergency, massive labour strikes and international sanctions which brought the economy to a grinding halt. Thus, when de Klerk assumed the Presidency, he had two important challenges: how to revive the economy, and how to proceed with a political settlement that would enfranchise blacks. Important voices in South African financial circles had lobbied the government to support aggressive growth policies, attractive to foreign investors, and an export drive that would require capital-intensive investment. It was argued that a political settlement would result in a rapid inflow of foreign investment necessary, and a redistribution of benefits through trickle-down. This approach became popularly known as 'redistribution from growth' (Morris, 1991: 57).

De Klerk introduced a comprehensive programme to restructure both state and market. Taxes were raised, the currency was devalued, the budget slashed and privatization of state owned enterprises effected. Strategic industries such as the Armaments Corporation of South Africa were privatized. Tariffs were cut in line with GATT requirements, export processing zones were established, and a General Export Incentive Scheme (GEIS) was created in April 1990.[8] On the political front, the language of the newly transformed National Party became non-racialism, democracy, minority rights and elimination of ethnicity and race as the basis of group protection, and so on. De Klerk's actions caught the Mass Democratic Movement and his own conservative constituency off balance. His historic speech in parliament on 2 February 1990, 'unbanning' the ANC and the South African Communist Party (SACP), was to change the course of South African history dramatically – along with the release of Nelson Mandela.

The National Economic Forum (NEF) played a key role in bringing the protagonists together – labour, business and government – to hammer out a new compromise. While the ANC and its allies, initially held their guns to the policy of 'growth from redistribution' and to basic tenets of the 'Freedom Charter', government and its business allies proposed a strategy of 'redistribution from growth', along with a vague reference to alleviating poverty via spending on housing and infrastructure.[9] By the end of 1993, however, one could observe a considerable narrowing of the ideological gap between the ANC and the National Party – the two main negotiating partners in the constitutional negotiations. Both parties agreed on a neo-liberal – or market-monetarist – strategy as the model for tackling poverty and underdevelopment in the new South Africa. Thus the new Mandela government expanded the scope of state intervention to stimulate exports, whilst its first two budgets gave tax breaks and export incentive packages directed at the private sector. At the same time, high interest rates and tough spending controls have been instituted.

The shift in the ANC's economic policy began long before it assumed national leadership in 1994. During the pre-election negotiations, the ANC made extraordinary concessions to white power both in the formal inter-party negotiations near Johannesburg and in smoke-filled rooms at exclusive British, Swiss and South African lodges, culminating in the 'blosberaad' – bush-consultations – of early 1993 that set out the terms of the crucial interim constitution. Keynesians were marginalized within the ANC Department of Economic Planning as neo-liberalism took hold. Since April 1994 the ANC has been the leading party in the Government of National Unity with two conservative partners (the National Party and Inkatha). Neo-liberals were able to present themselves as champions of the poor by agreeing to support massive housing and public works projects to give a kick start to the economy.[10] Through this type of market intervention, so they claimed, a redistribution of income would take place. The reality has been the opposite. The late Joe Slovo, for example, had promised that in his first year as housing minister, 90 000 low-cost houses would be built using a market-oriented financing system; the eight months he served plus the preceding four yielded fewer than 5000. Failure to deliver, even at this extreme scale, was more the rule than the exception.

The main industrial component of economic strategy is believed to be an outward-looking export strategy characteristic of the Asian model.[11] This export-led drive began during previous government F.W. de Klerk, and was aimed at reversing the poor performance of the South African economy which began to worsen in the mid-1970s. Now an acceleration in liberalization and integration to world markets is taking place.

The second reason why a neo-liberal agenda became the centrepiece has to do with the decision by key players in the political scene – the representatives of labour and capital – to embrace the corporate state with a mixture of enthusiasm and relief. Since 1990, government, business and the unions came together to form the National Economic Forum (NEF) responsible for securing consensus in negotiations over the Uruguay Round. They agreed to lower tariffs radically over the next five years. Different stakeholders in the economy, in housing, health and education, sat around the table in an effort to sink their differences and work out compromises.[12]

The Reconstruction and Development Plan (RDP) and a neo-liberal agenda

Parallel to its export-led strategy, the ANC has responded to the economic and social challenge by unveiling the RDP, a grand blueprint to transform South African society, to reform government and redefine patterns of ownership, influence and power. The total cost of the Plan is estimated at R90 billion ($25 billion) over a five year period. Its priorities include the meeting of basic needs; developing human resources; building the economy; democratizing the state and society; and implementing the programme itself.[13] The goal is to reinvent South Africa and create a brave new non-racial and non-sexist world where the main institutions of society are no longer dominated by whites (Republic of South Africa, 1994). The RDP also envisioned a new regional co-operation arrangement.

The success of the Plan, of course, will depend on the willingness of the private sector, both domestic and foreign, to contribute towards implementation. The challenge facing the government is of reconciling competing interests of this sector and with those of the deprived majority population. For example, the export-led, capital intensive strategy goes against the whole purpose of generating employment. In addition, successful implementation will depend on the creation of a more efficient and responsive civil service, and provincial governments which can effectively deliver. In order to diminish white bureau-cratic opposition, the ANC guaranteed that whites who served the apartheid system will receive their pensions upon retirement. Such a promise appears not to have persuaded the white civil servants to become effective players during the transition.

Fragile coalitions: corporatism in the first year

When President Mandela addressed the parliament after 100 days in office, the mood was sombre. Confronted by a weak economy and a large budget deficit, it had become obvious that much of the fate of the nation was to be decided by foreign investors, bankers and fund managers. In this context, South African corporatism has been shaken by disputes over appropriate development strategy.[14] While ANC economists initially proposed radical measures to pump-prime the economy via spending on infrastructure, education and housing, white opposition led by the conservative South African Reserve Bank and the Ministry of Finance, backed by the IMF and the influential white press, convinced Mr Mandela that reducing the country's budget deficit and containing inflation must be the top priority.[15] The ascend-ance of neo-liberal thinking can also be partly attributed to the marginalization, disunity and disintegration of the Mass Democratic Movement, accentuated by the loss of its leadership to high-paid government jobs plus the loss of government and external funding to the NGO sector. This forced NGOs and social movements to go into partnership with businesses and corporate-oriented services for the sake of paying their bills. As a result, the strategic vision of the civic movement has been compromised. Disunity is also fuelled by ethnicity, race, gender, urban versus rural interests, and personal rivalries.[16]

Thus in the first Mandela budget, Finance Minister Derek Keys proposed a strategy of export-led growth, backed by restructuring of the domestic economy. Keys proposed high interest rates and tough spending controls, and to enact wealth, capital gains and land taxes to generate revenue. Public sector spending is under control and inflation has been brought down to single digit levels. At the same time, the government has refrained from increasing taxes on the rich to finance its social programmes. By contrast, the government's track record on social justice has fallen far short of public expectations. Keys' budget, for example, allocated only a little more than 6 per cent of what was promised over a five-year period for the ANC's reconstruction and development programme. It will be financed by cuts in other government spending and a small one-time levy on the well-to-do. Critics charge that the government is cosying up to business interests. Indeed, the government could have gone further by asking prosperous whites to carry more of the burden since the white middle class was ready for some redistribution of income before the elections. The dramatic shift in ANC economic policy put the government on a collision course with its principal supporters, mainly the poor and the unemployed. Consequently, a wave of wage disputes and strikes have been seen as symptomatic of a spreading discontent.

However, for the moment, the relationship between government and business appears rock solid, although organized labour seems to be suspicious of ANC policies. In fact, there is little prospect of a compact with labour if export-led growth translates into major job losses. The mining sector is also in crisis. Indeed, the reduction of tariffs has major consequences for uncompetitive local manufacturers, such as in the textile industry. In the first half of 1994 alone, some 1.2 million working days were lost to strike action, the country's worst industrial relations performance for several years.[17] Labour, which played a crucial role in bringing down apartheid, will continue to push hard for an immediate and substantial liberation dividend. Other issues are causing conflict, for example the questions of land and housing.

The land question

Perhaps the biggest issue affecting employment and income generation is the question of land. As noted, fewer than 60 000 white farmers own 87 per cent of the best land, approximately 107 million hectares. In contrast, some 1.2 million black farmers occupy 17 million hectares of overcrowded and often substandard land.[18] Given their precarious existence in the so-called 'homelands', many black farmers had to accept exploitative arrangements as tenant farmers on land designated for whites to obtain rights to stay or return to the land of their ancestors. Under the usual arrangement, a tenant farmer worked six months for the white farmer and six for himself.

Mandela intends to redistribute 30 per cent of the country's farmland within the next five years. Instead of giving the landless some of the thousands of acres owned by the state to start with, the government's new draft legislation would give many black tenant farmers the right to buy the field they have farmed for generations. Land claims are expected to be handled by a cumbersome system of tribunals. Even if agreement can be reached between tenant farmers and white farmers, few black farmers can afford to buy land on the free market. To pre-empt the law, white farmers have begun evicting tenant farmers in large numbers. Land policy is complicated further by the fact that the previous government of F.W. de Klerk had allowed white farmers to buy disputed farms under a special bill rushed through parliament in 1992, undercutting Africans from claiming land which was taken away from them as recently as 1977.

The World Bank has taken a unique position on the land debate. Drawing largely from the experience of Zimbabwe, the Bank councils the government not to tinker with the land issue at the periphery. It recommends instead a mix of market and non-market mechanisms that will both encourage current owners to invest more and to enable small-farmers to boost their incomes. The Bank also recommends a speedy redistribution process as a means of discouraging the landless from resorting to land invasions as well as for the removal of distortions, such as subsidies on rural credit in the commercial farm sector, which act as a bias against small-scale black farmers.[19]

The housing crisis

The second pressing issue for the Mandela administration is how to tackle the backlog on urban housing. The government hammered out a social compact that lays the foundation for a rapid acceleration in housing construction. The aim is to entice banks and developers into providing low-cost housing for blacks, through subsidies and mortgage guarantees. Developers have demanded assurance from the government that land rights will be protected, and that bankers can repossess a house if the buyer defaults on a mortgage.

However, large scale delivery of housing has not occurred because the policy is market-driven, not people-driven, and is co-ordinated by bankers. The late Housing Minister Joe Slovo and his entirely white advisers completely bypassed the civic movement that had gained considerable experience from the 'affordable housing for all' campaigns going back to the apartheid years. Slow delivery has bothered developers and contractors, fostering a lack of confidence in the housing policy. The Department of Housing has been criticized for using a only small fraction of its budget. What passes now as housing policy is simply 'toilets-in-the-bush' – part of a site-and-services programme, in addition to government subsidy and loan guarantee schemes. Considering the limits of the current housing policy, the government needs to invest directly in a public sector housing programme, focusing on the poor without having to rely on financial institutions. This can be achieved only if the government enters the lower end of the market as a developer and provides rental stock for the marginalized sector. This would involve provision of rental stock with an option to take ownership by repayment of a loan portion; loans directly through the housing budget and/or indirectly through the National Housing Finance Corporation; or by increasing the amounts available for people in lower income brackets and decrease the allowance for those in the higher income brackets. Unfortunately, the Department of Housing is not currently inclined to consider these and other similar propositions.

Public dissatisfaction with the new government's inability to deliver basic services is mounting. A wave of uncontrollable illegal squatting and take-over of low-cost housing projects by desperate citizens has presented Mandela's government with a dilemma and threatens to kill the new compact. If it looks the other way on squatting, it sends the wrong message to the bankers, developers and community groups it is relying on to build those new houses. If it evicts people, it evokes bad memories of the bully-boy past. Caught between populism and the marketplace, the government has not yet formulated a squatter policy. In the hiatus, some local municipal officials, holdovers from the apartheid era, have moved to evict squatters, while some provincial and national officials, who came to power in the country's first all-race elections, have tried to protect them.

Thus Mr Mandela is caught between a rock and a hard place. He is one person who understands very well the impatience of blacks for sweeping change while numerous former upholders of apartheid remain in the police, military and civil administration. He understands very well that no political democracy and reconciliation will succeed when the masses live in abject poverty. On the other hand, he has to send the right signals to beef up business confidence and to get the white civil service on his side so that they can effectively deliver development. This requires a difficult balancing act which sometimes forces the government to take unpopular decisions.

CAN SOUTH AFRICA REPLICATE THE EXPERIENCES OF THE 'ASIAN TIGERS'?

Some western commentators believe that South Africa could become the next Taiwan or Korea in Africa. It has the best infrastructure in

Africa, including ports and railways, telecommunications system and financial markets. Its industrial base is centred on mining of diamonds, gold, uranium and coal, as well as arms manufacturing and agricultural processing. Although the country does not have oil resources, it invested heavily in the energy industry to limit its reliance on organic fuels. These facts, however, mask many problems in the South African economy, and raise questions as to its potential.

First, much of South Africa's post-war economic boom depended largely on favourable international prices for agricultural commodities and minerals, on credit financed import-substitution industrialization, centralized state management of the economy, sheltered markets, guaranteed labour supplies and unequal income distribution (McCarthy, 1991). The limits to this type of strategy were clearly illustrated by the end of the sixties when the country started to experience severe balance-of-payments problems, low growth rates and labour unrest. This is in contrast to the Asian NICs who based their success on the development of skills, indigenous technical capacity, land reform, the creation of an enabling environment for national and international competition for production, and innovation and quality through deregulation and de-concentration of ownership (Cheru, 1994; Leysens and Thompson, 1994).

Second, the South African economy has consistently performed poorly since 1976 despite enormous government support and protection from outside competition. Only once in the 1980s has the GDP grown by more than 5 per cent, the minimum required to keep a ceiling on its dismally high unemployment figures (and to absorb more than 300 000 new workers coming onto the labour market every year). At the beginning of the 1970s, unemployment was about 19 per cent. In 1995, the figure was well over 45 per cent. Were it not for the informal sector which has grown rapidly over the past three years, the unemployment figure would have been much higher. The South African economy even did badly compared to the neighbouring countries to say nothing of competitors from other regions (see Table 10.1).

South Africa's most disappointing performance is recorded in the manufacturing sector which accounts for 25 per cent of GDP. Low quality standards, high production costs, the lack of indigenous technological innovation capabilities, exacerbated by sanctions, are some of the reasons why its products are not competitive in the world market (Natrass, 1989; McCarthy, 1988). Part of the problem origin-

Table 10.1   South Africa's average annual growth
performance, 1965–88

Country	1965–80	1980–88
Korea	9.6	9.9
Thailand	7.2	6.0
Malaysia	7.3	4.6
Singapore	10.1	5.7
Hong Kong	8.6	7.3
Mexico	6.5	0.5
Brazil	8.8	2.9
South Africa	*3.8*	*1.3*
Botswana	14.2	11.4
Lesotho	5.7	2.9
Malawi	5.6	2.6
Zimbabwe	5.0	2.7

Source: World Bank, *World Development Report 1990*
(Washington, World Bank).

ated in the focus on heavy industry for self reliance rather than on
an effort to diversify the manufacturing base in order to become
internationally competitive. Sanctions on investment stopped the
inflow of much needed technology and led to an even greater emphasis on import substitution in strategic, chemical, metal and engineering
industries (McCarthy, 1991: 10). Attempts to conceal the origin
of South African goods in order to get entry to European markets
also became expensive. In its present state, the South African
economy has little chance of replicating the strategy of the
Asian Tigers. The economy lacks the skills, with technical know-how
restricted to a small minority. Massive training and retraining
programmes among the majority are needed, or else skilled
labour would need to be attracted from the rest of Africa, a
process which began during the heyday of apartheid. But this will
only intensify the core-periphery relations between South Africa and
its neighbours.

Third, South Africa is still dependent on primary commodity
exports. Until recently, favourable prices for gold, metals and agricultural goods contributed to higher levels of GDP growth. Such
mining revenues financed imports of capital goods for the manufac-

turing sector. However, a slump in the world price for metals and gold, main source of foreign exchange, is unlikely to be reversed in the near future. This will mean more dependence on external sources of finance, conditioned on implementation of neo-liberal economic policies. According to one estimate, South Africa would require an annual inflow of foreign capital amounting to $10 billion between 1990 and 1999 in order to maintain a growth rate of 5.5 per cent, the minimum required to absorb the more than 300 000 people entering the labour market each year. Half of this amount would have to come from direct foreign investment.[20]

Fourth, economic power in South Africa is even more concentrated among whites than income. About 42 per cent of South Africa's GDP is generated by the 810 Johannesburg Stock Exchange (JSE) listed companies and their subsidiaries, which number over 20 000. The four largest conglomerates control 81 per cent of the listed companies. In terms of capitalization, percentage of control is as follows: Anglo American Corporation (43.6 per cent), Rembrandt group (14.3 per cent), Sanlam (13.9 per cent) and SA Mutual (9.2 per cent) (see Table 10.2).[21] A single firm owns almost half of all corporate stock in South Africa! Because of their monopoly power, these corporations have spawned many layers of management, inefficiency is endemic and innovation lacking. The ANC is committed to push through parliament anti-trust legislation to break the dominance of large conglomerates in the economy and to a more active competition. Yet, the most recent two budgets presented by the Mandela administration provide tax breaks to these huge corporations, thus subsidizing their investments.

Table 10.2   Corporate concentration in South Africa, by ownership of shares, 1992

Company/conglomerate	Share of total stocks listed in the JSE
SA Mutual	10.2%
Sanlam	13.2%
Rembrandt	13.6%
Anglo-American Corporation	44.2%
All Others	18.8%

Source: Congress of South African Trade Unions, 1992.

The other economic giant in South Africa is the government itself, which owns nearly half of all fixed economic assets, such as power plants, ports and harbours, etc. State companies and agencies dominate such key enterprises as transportation and communication, electric power generation and gas and water supply. To prevent the Mandela government from using its state assets and regulatory power to restructure the economy to redress the legacies of apartheid, the de Klerk government began selling off government-owned factories, power stations, transportation and communications facilities and reduced state authority over the economy. Through this 'privatisation' strategy, white business and political leaders were able to ensure white monopoly of wealth and economic power. Put differently, public white monopolies became private white monopolies.

The fifth factor deals with future prospects. Table 10.1 shows a comparative analysis of the growth performance of NICs, some southern African states, and Brazil and Mexico: two countries often said to be in the same economic league as South Africa. The latter two outperformed South Africa despite their heavy debt burden – five times greater than that of South Africa. Whether South Africa will graduate from low technology to high technology production largely depends on the availability of investment to remove capacity constraints in the economy. Ratios of fixed investment to GDP declined from a high of 30 per cent in 1974 to a low of 10 per cent in 1990.[22] The sharpest adjustments were in the public sector. Manufacturing led the collapse in investment spending, but then also led the recovery in 1987–90. Performance of this sector is central to how South Africa fares in the 1990s and beyond.

South Africa's ability to move into high technology production will also depend on how the conflict between output and employment objectives is resolved by the new government when setting up an industrial strategy. The trend toward capital intensity has been underway in South Africa for over a decade. The demands of up-market, mainly white consumers, for expensive, durable products and the policy of import-substitution to thwart the effects of international sanctions, had dictated industrial strategy. The export-led strategy, which the ANC dominated government has embraced faithfully, is likely to further entrench the past pattern of production and distribution, thus giving scant attention to the development of the basic-needs economy. Based on current political trends on the ground, this approach cannot be tolerated in an environment of high unemployment and mass poverty. As Nelson Mandela himself has put it succinctly, 'Democracy cannot be sustained in an environment of abject poverty.'

REGIONAL INTEGRATION IN THE POST-APARTHEID ERA

New regional arrangements that benefit all member states will depend on the outcome of the struggle within South Africa. Two different visions and blocs of interest exist: one articulated by the Reconstruction and Development Plan; the other coming from the business community, the influential white press, and the conservative Reserve Bank. The Plan's vision of regionalism is fundamentally different from the market-led integration proposed by the apologists of neo-liberalism. We shall examine both of them.

The Reconstruction and Development Plan: new regionalism

In addition to restructuring South African society, the Plan aims to break down apartheid and colonial geography, and open up new economic potential in the areas of production and tourism. Such co-operation entails a regional bloc to develop effective strategies for all Southern African countries, and to strengthen the region in its relations with emerging global trading blocs. Harmonisation of infrastructure, legal and operational aspects of regional Southern African transport, food security, joint action on water resource development, energy and telecommunications are all envisaged. In addition, the RDP's mining section suggests the new government to uses South African expertise in mineral exploration and exploitation to rehabilitate, develop and invest in the mineral potential of the region. RDP notes severe imbalances between South Africa and its neighbours and calls for policies in consultation with neighbours to ensure more balanced trade. In addition, the Plan called for minimum standards with regards to rights of workers to organise across the region as a whole so that a process of greater integration becomes one of levelling up rights and conditions of workers rather than of levelling them down to the lowest prevailing standards. Other key issues of regional co-operation identified in the Plan are as follows:

Food security

Because of demographic and ecological factors, South Africa will become a net importer of food in the future. Countries such as Zimbabwe, Malawi, Zambia (even Mozambique) might under certain conditions become exporters of food to South Africa. In return, South Africa can provide agricultural technology, expertise, and inputs.

Opportunities exist for joint programmes ensuring significant increases in agricultural production, especially food processing for domestic consumption and cereals for intra-regional trade.

Industrial and agro-processing strategy

A common platform is suggested for restructuring and strengthening industrial production and manufacturing capacities, especially the reduction or elimination of excess plant capacity, as well as the production of agricultural inputs, such as fertilizers, pesticides, vaccines and sprays.

Energy development strategy

Opportunities also exist for joint production of new and renewable forms of energy and up-grading existing capacities as well as trade in energy. For example, it would be in the interest of Angola to supply South Africa with oil in exchange for consumer goods and manufactures and *vice versa*. Already, a high level contact between the two countries is taking place. In addition, Angola, Lesotho, Malawi, Zambia and Mozambique are richly endowed with surface water, thus providing opportunities for cross border water and hydro-power supply schemes.

Co-ordination of trade and finance policy

Restrictive banking procedures and inadequate trade financing facilities are some of the constraints on intra-regional trade in Southern Africa, meaning the need for appropriate trade financing institutions such as an export/import bank and insurance facility. The PTA Trade and Development Bank and the Development Bank of Southern Africa can play a major role in facilitating trade in the sub-region. Closer co-operation with chambers of commerce, regional trade promotion councils, financial institutions and business and professional associations should be actively encouraged.

Human resource development

The skills gap in the region is viewed as an important constraint to intra-regional trade and production. There are many universities and training institutions in Southern Africa (25 universities, technical colleges and research institutions). Given the resource constraint in the region, ways to rationalize existing facilities and harmonization of human resource development policies must be found. Priority should be given to the adaptation of science and technology, especially for upgrading technical skills and managerial capabilities, as well as in the management of domestic and external resources for integration and co-operation.

Natural resource management

There is also a real need for integrated strategies for the protection of the environment and natural resource base, joint use of water resources and river basins and common programmes for drought management, soil erosion and desertification control. The 1992 agreement between South Africa, Mozambique and Swaziland to exploit the waters of the Nkomati River, and the joint South Africa–Mozambique accord to extend the boundaries of the Kruger National Park and its joint management, are prime examples of the types of activities which need to be pursued. There are also plans to transfer water from Zambezi and the Okavango system via canals or pipelines to the Transvaal.

Promotion of tourism

2.5 million tourists visit East Africa each year. With the end of political turmoil in Southern Africa, the region's natural beauty can make it a rival to East Africa. The entire sub-region would benefit if governments, regional airlines, chambers of commerce and tour operators co-ordinated their activities. The growth of tourism can generate billions of dollars in hard currency, employ thousands of people, and provide income to farmers, hotel and transport operators, and many more.

In translating the optimistic vision of the RDP into hard economic reality, South Africa can contribute in many ways. Monetary harmonization is one such example. The lack of common currency has been a major impediment to intra-regional trade in Southern Africa. In terms of institutional capacity, there should be little difficulty with the harmonization of monetary policies in the Common Monetary Area. A second contribution would be in the area of customs administration. As the architect of the longest running customs union, it has a wealth of experience and this can be used to strengthen the capacities of member countries in customs administration. A third contribution is in the field of domestic resource mobilization. South Africa has well developed capital market institutions (that is, issuing houses, share underwriters, security markets) and it can assist the neighbouring countries in developing similar institutions. Once similar capital markets are established, they will be able to provide long term loans for development purposes at national and regional levels. In sum, regional integration efforts in Southern Africa should go beyond a simple market integration approach and instead revive and then link production capabilities of member states, as outlined in the RDP. While trade expansion among the countries of the region is very important, it does constitute a significant barrier to self-sustained regional growth. As Martin (1990: 129) succinctly put it, 'attempts to promote wider economic exchanges based on the notion of comparative advantage immediately exacerbate uneven patterns of accumulation, and thus trigger struggles between nationally-based dominant classes. It is precisely these pressures that have torn apart regional bodies elsewhere in Africa.' This is a course that Southern Africa should avoid at any cost.

However, two years after the April 1994 election, it is clear that foreign policy is not being made with RDP promises in mind. Co-operative regionalism has taken a back seat to bilateralism, and more emphasis is put on strengthening ties with Europe and other emerging markets as opposed to the regional economy. If the visions of indigenous regional development articulated in the RDP fail to materialize, neo-liberal forces will force a different form of integration on the region – one that will entail a disintegration of other form of regional linkages and co-operative and equitable political relationships.

Maintenance of regional economic domination by South Africa

Indeed, the outcome preferred by South Africa business community is a market-integration model, with South African capital dominating, and serving the interests of local élites in the SADCC region. This might also involve a resuscitation of past patterns of accumulation, this time with the support of transnational firms and the Bretton Woods organizations.[23]

Business antagonism towards establishing an equitable regional development consistent with the vision of the RDP is based on two main factors. First, and as noted above, strong forces inside the government and business believe that the future for South Africa's trade lies in Europe, North America and the Far East. They want to see the government spend its resources to develop these lucrative markets and spead less on developing the African market. Indeed, exports to

Europe constituted 52 per cent of South Africa's R60 billion exports in 1990. This was followed by the Far East (25 per cent), the US (10 per cent), Africa (10 per cent) and South America and Australia (3 per cent).[24] The second factor relates to the defeat of the progressive agenda of the democratic forces in South Africa and the fact that its opponents claim, with some justification that Africa north of the Limpopo River is financially broke and politically unstable, and it will take a long time before weak governments in the region can establish an enabling political and economic environment for investment and trade. Many states are contested territorially and administratively weak.

With respect to the internal struggle in South Africa, the place of neo-liberalism has been secured and the white bureaucracy and big capital will continue to have monopoly power over national economic policy. The free trade-based strategy of the business community has its external and regional supporters. With access to foreign sources of capital drying up, local élites in the region are prepared to endorse the neo-liberal strategy as long as the policies facilitate their personal economic enrichment. These leaders look to South Africa as a potential ally capable of facilitating bilateral ties between them and Northern governments and their private sectors.

This fits the project of the World Bank and other donors who would like to see South Africa take the leading role to facilitate collective economic liberalization across the region by improving conditions for a more active role by private agents. South Africa will obviously be the main beneficiary although the strategy will do little to foster intra-regional trade. The United States government, for example, announced in May 1994 a $700 million 'Aid, Trade and Investment Package for South Africa' as part of the US export strategy. It included programmes targeted at social investment as well as increasing trade and business investment between the two countries. Specifically, the Overseas Private Investment Corporation's (OPIC) guarantee programmes, USAID's Micro Enterprise Development Program, the Export-Import Bank's trade finance facilities, and the Commerce Department's trade development programmes are aimed at promoting a strong private sector in South Africa. Japan and France have also put in place similar programmes. The Japanese plan to extend $1.2 billion dollars in both loans and credit to the new government in South Africa.[25] During Mr Mandela's visit to Washington in October 1994, President Clinton announced an additional $100 million economic development fund for Southern Africa and a bi-national commission to promote energy, education and development projects in South Africa. About half of the $100 million fund will go to South Africa in the belief that it will drive economic growth among its less-developed neighbours. Such packages remain a vital source of support for South Africa to restructure its economy and help to reinforce the neo-liberal strategy.

CONCLUSION

Whether southern Africa would successfully avoid embracing the narrowly defined form of market integration and opt for a development integration approach will depend on the capacity of the forces of civil society to gain sufficient influence to qualify as a genuine 'counter project' rather than merely a societal tendency confined to the margins of policy. In the current political environment in South Africa, the threat of co-optation and demoralization is very high. It may not be easy to organize against neo-liberalism when there is no clearly identifiable common enemy, particularly one with the viciousness of the former South African regime. Indeed, whilst the racist legacy is being replaced by formal democratization and, at last, the right of all citizens to vote has been established, racial conflicts are giving way to class-based contradictions in the years since Nelson Mandela was released from prison. Substantive democratization based upon a rough equality of condition and life-chances is a long way off. Despite recent setbacks, the original political project of the Mass Democratic Movement (MDM) remains valid, although this essays shows that it has been de-radicalized to some extent.

None the less, if civic associations such as the South African National Civic Organization and the labour unions in the MDM hold firm and reassert control, it will produce a very different trajectory inside South Africa and the region as a whole. Domestically, a social contract politics that is consistent with neo-liberal restructuring will be replaced by people-driven planning aimed at empowering people locally and nationally, eradicating poverty, protecting the environment and instituting substantive democracy. Specifically, this would entail developing the 'basic needs' economy to generate jobs and social services for the masses, and switching from gradually depleting a commodity base to higher value-added goods in selected export niches for which South Africa and the region can earn far more money.[26] Regionally, such an approach would be in the democratic interests of South Africa since it would help to create the conditions for less polarized economic development and a more democratic political environment throughout the region. If the whole region fails economically, these problems will grow to threaten social order and social services within the South African Republic, as well as the security of states and communities within the region. Electrified fences and panoptic surveillance techniques, which failed to halt mass movements of people to the Republic under apartheid, will not be the answer to poverty-induced migration from countries north of the Limpopo.

In the final analysis, the economic stagnation associated with the legacy of apartheid is likely to prove much harder to shake off than most would like to believe. With the exception of perhaps half a dozen African countries, the majority of African states cannot even dream of getting back to the level of development they achieved in the late 1960s. Therefore, if economies can no longer be pulled along primarily by external growth, stronger internal buying power must be generated. In the case of Southern Africa (and Sub-Saharan Africa in general), almost all the countries in the region remain predominantly agricultural societies; hence the starting point of internal demand-led development must be in farming. Rural people in Africa are, on the whole, poor tenant farmers or agricultural workers who earn only subsistence wages. Central to increasing buying power in the countryside is redistribution of wealth and productive assets. Land reform is at the centre of this redistribution – as it was, for example in South Korea or earlier in Japan. Raising productivity requires upgrading infrastructure – from irrigation and roads to credit and marketing channels. However, unless Southern African governments restructure their economies and politics to include the majority of people in a meaningful way, the chances that these countries will be able to escape the anti-democratic and restrictive forces of the world economy are virtually nil.

Notes

1. In 1989, African countries imported Rands 3 billion worth of goods from South Africa. Following the political reform of 2 February 1990 by F.W. de Klerk, exports to Africa soared to R6 billion. South African Chamber of Commerce, *SACOB Review*, 1st Quarter, 1991.
2. SADC, *Treaty of the Southern African Development Community*, adopted and signed at the SADC Summit, Windhoek, 17 August 1992.

3.   Gerhard de Kock (1989) 'Economic Cooperation in Sub-Saharan Africa', *Mining Survey*, No. 2; Rob Davis (1991) 'South Africa Joining SADC or SADC Joining South Africa?: Emerging Perspectives on Regional Economic Cooperation After Apartheid', in Nieuwkerk and Staden (ed.), *Southern Africa at the Crossroads*, South African Institute of International Affairs, Special Studies Report. Johannesburg, October, pp. 235–44.

4.   SADC was established in 1980 to promote regional development among the countries of southern Africa, and to reduce dependence on South Africa. All the members of SADC (Angola, Botswana, Lesotho, Malawi, Mozambique, Namibia, Swaziland, Tanzania, South Africa, Zambia and Zimbabwe), except for Botswana, have joined the PTA (whose other members are Burundi, Comoros, Djibouti, Eritrea, Ethiopia, Kenya, Mauritius, Rwanda, Seychelles, Somalia and Uganda). Leaving out South Africa, which has a GDP of $78 billion, the rest of SADC has a GDP of $17 billion (but its population of 65 million is almost twice as much that of South Africa, with 34 million). Although SADC has achieved some success in mobilising and co-ordinating aid flow to the region, it has had limited success in promoting intra-SADC trade, which stands at some 5 per cent of total trade (Tjonneland, 1992: 70). In addition, a decade of trade liberalisation *vis-à-vis* the outside world, initiated by adjustment programmes, has contributed to the stagnation of intra-regional trade, opening up the SADC market to cheap supplies from outside the region. The PTA, on the other hand, was established in 1981 to promote the development of its member states by creating a single internal market, undertaking regional development projects and programmes, and encouraging co-operation in all fields of economic activity. Sixteen of twenty eligible Eastern and Southern African countries have joined. The group has a GDP of $33 billion and a population of 146 million. Like SADC, the PTA has achieved limited success with regard to the promotion of intra-PTA trade (Tjonneland, 1992).

5.   An ANC discussion document on *Regional Cooperation and Integration in Southern Africa after Apartheid* released in September 1990 by the ANC Department of Economic Planning advocated the promotion of greater regional economic interaction along new lines which would not be exploitative.

6.   In the first half of 1993, South African exports to Kenya were worth $45 million as opposed to imports of $5.8 million. Further liberalization of the Kenyan economy was expected to dramatically increase South Africa's exports to Kenya (Cheru, 1994).

7.   John Fraser (1995) 'South Africa concedes to free trade with EU', *The Star*, Johannesburg, 5 October p. 20.

8.   *Sunday Times*, 'Business Times', 7 June 1992.

9.   Japie Jacob (1991) 'Financing of socio-economic programmes – alternatives and challenges', *South Africa International*, Vol. 22, No. 1 (July), 11–13.

10. South African Chamber of Commerce, *Economic Options for South Africa* (September 1990); Lesley Boyd (1992) 'Wealth Creation Beats

Charity', *The Citizen*, 19 February, p. 25, summary of speech delivered at the Annual Frankel, Max, Pollak, Vinderline Investment Conference in Johannesburg.

11. South African Chamber of Commerce (1990) *Economic Options for South Africa*. September, pp. 10–36.

12. Antony Leysens (1993) *The Politics of Economic Restructuring: The International and Domestic Constraints on Policy Formulation in South Africa*, paper presented at the Biennial Conference of the South African Political Studies Association, Bloemfontein, 20–2 October.

13. The major priority of the RDP is meeting basic needs: 1 million new houses; electrifying 2.5 million homes, 19,000 black schools (86 per cent of the total) and some 4,000 clinics; redistributing 30 per cent of the land, bringing clean water for 12 million people; creating 300–500,000 non-farm jobs each year, the creation of a national health system focused on primary health care by 1999. The plan includes phasing in a 10-year compulsory education system; limiting class sizes to no more than 40 by the end of the decade; the launch of adult education programme and the revamping of tertiary education (Republic of South Africa, Draft Report, 1994).

14. Tony Hawkins (1994) 'Corporatism: love-in that may not last', *Financial Times* 18 July.

15. IMF, *Economic Policies for a New South Africa* Washington, DC, January 1992; Abdel Senhadji and Michael Walton, *South Africa: Macroeconomic Issues for the Transition* Washington. World Bank, 23 October 1991, draft.

16. Patrick Bond (1995) 'Some South African lessons for developing resistance and resisting "development"', unpublished monograph, Johannesburg.

17. 'Labour unrest worries Mandela's government', *Daily Nation*, Nairobi (1 August 1994), p. 8.

18. Ernest Harsch (1994) 'New era dawns in South Africa', *African Farmer*, No. 12 (July), pp. 22–3.

19. World Bank (1992) *Aide Memoire: Agriculture Sector Mission for South Africa*, 11 March.

20. S. Terreblanche (1991) *The Need for a Transformation Period towards a Post-apartheid South Africa*, Economic Papers 3, Centre for Contextual Hermeneutics, Stellenbosch: University of Stellenbosch, p. 6.

21. McGregor's *Who Owns Whom*, Johannesburg, 1992.

22. World Bank (1991) *South Africa: Macroeconomic Issues for the Transition*, Draft, Washington, 23 October, p. 9.

23. RWK Parsons (1991) 'South Africa and Southern Africa: A New Era?', Address to Scandinavian-South African Business Association Conference, Oslo, Norway. 29 August.

24. Gerhard Erasmus (1990) 'Export and Trade Services', *Financial Mail Survey*, 14 September, p. 17.

25. United States Department of the Treasury, Statement by Under-Secretary Lawrence H. Summers for the USIA Conference, 'Investing in

People: US-South Africa Conference on Democracy and the Market Economy', 4 June 1994, reprinted in *Treasury News*.

26. On the 'basic needs' economy, see Patrick Bond (1991) *Commanding Heights and Community Control: New Economics for a New South Africa* Johannesburg, Raven Press; on export-orientation, see Reg Rumney (1991) 'The Path to Post-Apartheid Growth', *Weekly Mail* (May 17–23), p. 19.

11 Some Reflections on the Oslo Symposium

Robert W. Cox

There can be no question of drawing consensual conclusions from such a wide-ranging discussion, covering so many aspects of world political economy, as occurred in the course of the symposium held within the framework of the MUNS programme at Vikersund near Oslo in August 1993. It is, however, possible to point to a certain basic approach, common to most of the participants and, indeed, characterizing the MUNS programme itself as it has developed. The elements of this common approach can be discussed under the three headings of epistemology, ontology, and strategy. The first is a conscious questioning of the nature of knowledge, a critical examination of its foundations. The second is an effort to identify the significant factors in world political economy. The third is a concern with how to move world affairs from its present condition towards the normative goals enunciated in the MUNS programme.

EPISTEMOLOGY

There was a shared assumption that there is no such thing as a 'scientific' theory immune to radical critique. There is always a relationship between knowledge and power. Dominant forms of knowledge are nourished by dominant power. Dominant power orients the development of knowledge as an instrument for maintaining dominance, whether in the organization of production or in the control of deviance, whether in reinforcing the effectiveness of the state or of private capital. By the same token, the production of knowledge is inherent in challenging dominant power. Critical knowledge begins with exposing the claim to universality and exclusivity of the dominant knowledge, by demonstrating how dominant knowledge arises out of and serves to sustain dominant power.

A number of instances of such demystification arose in the discussions. The conventional economic wisdom affirms that there is no alternative to the structural adjustment programmes promoted by the IMF acting as the collective agency of globalizing capital. The effect of these programmes in placing the burden of adjustment upon the weakest and most vulnerable is represented as a virtually unquestionable law of nature. Further, many aspects of public policy, which in their formal expression appear as gender neutral, are revealed by critical analysis to have a decided gender bias against women.

Yet again, many of the concepts commonly used in social and political analysis are derived from western (and often Anglo-Saxon) historical experience. Such concepts may indeed have potentially universal application but their use may also have the implication of denying the validity of the historical experience of non-western peoples. There is a need to explore their relevance to non-western traditions and at the same time to broaden the conceptual vocabulary in order to create what Giambattista Vico called a 'mental vocabulary common to all the various articulate languages living and dead'.[1]

This is no appeal to indulge in what has been called 'politically correct' language. 'Politically correct' substitutes bland euphemism for biting analysis. What is intended, rather, is enquiry into the intersubjectivities that have evolved historically among different peoples. Intersubjective meanings are the conceptual vocabulary that defines the nature of the world for different peoples in different historical eras, the concepts through which they understand and interpret their world and formulate strategies of action. Intersubjective meanings are the 'common sense' that prevails for a certain people during a phase of their history, and through which they not only understand reality but reproduce reality. Intersubjective meanings, in other words, generate ontologies with a certain durability in time and place. Some aspects of these distinct ontologies may attain a degree of universality that enables them to be translated into one another.[2]

Those whom Gramsci called 'organic intellectuals' play a significant role in the production of knowledge critical of dominant power and its attendant hegemonic knowledge. The organic intellectual is only by chance a professional intellectual. In principle, any thinking person can perform the function of organic intellectual. You don't have to be a professor or a graduate student. The function consists of generalizing experience from struggles against dominant power so as both to disestablish the claims to irrefutability of hegemonic knowledge and to serve as an orientation to the politics of contestation. Knowledge grows out of the movement of contestation. But who are the movement? To answer this question, we have to move from epistemology to ontology, to an appraisal of the nature of the world as revealed by a questioning of dominant knowledge and power.

ONTOLOGY

The symposium began with discussion of a paper by Stephen Gill, the project co-ordinator, on the 'global panopticon'. This paper was about the mechanisms of power in general but with special reference to the global political economy. It took as its metaphor the concept of a perfect prison, conceived first by Jeremy Bentham in the nineteenth century and revived by Michel Foucault in the 1970s (Foucault, 1979). In the panopticon everything is observable from the centre (the warder); and the prisoners in segmented cells in the periphery can neither observe the centre nor communicate with one another. The metaphor is applicable to present-day global economy insofar as detailed information concerning private individuals and organizations is amassed by public and private powers, from banks to state taxation and intelligence services. The use to which this panopticon is put discriminates between more and less advantaged (for example, in the granting of credit); it rewards the conformist and penalizes the eccentric. It becomes an instrument for centralized control in the two meanings of 'control': surveillance and manipulation.

While the ideal type of the panopticon is all-pervasive, in practice it has flaws that limit its potential for full control. For one thing, it may cover only those integrated into the global economy, the taxpayers and the credit-card holders for example. (The mass of humankind may be divided into those who have credit cards, those who do not have credit cards but would like to have one, and those who do not know what a credit card is – the latter being the vast majority.) The panopticon needs willing victims. For another thing, there is the limitation in the centre's capacity to interpret what it can observe. The warder only sees what he is conditioned to see. One need only think of the failures of US intelligence to understand events in Iran or, most recently, in Somalia. The marginalized and excluded remain a world of mystery because they do not seem to participate in the 'rationality' of the centre.

Thus, the first vision of the world is of a hierarchical structure in which the centre controls the periphery; but on a second look, there are limitations to the centre's control, some of which arise from its own myopia (the limitations of its epistemology), and some from the degree of autonomy or of resistance that marginal and peripheral forces may attain either in countering the control mechanisms within the panopticon or by avoiding incorporation into the panopticon. (On the transition from an archetypal panopticist society, see the chapter by Fantu Cheru on post-apartheid South Africa).

Economic globalization has separated those peoples and social groups that have become structured hierarchically into the global economy (and its corollary, the global panopticon) from those that have become marginalized and excluded, either because they are 'useless' (that is, do not contribute to the making of profits in a global economy perspective) or because they seek their own survival apart from the oppression of global economic relations. The term 'global apartheid' was used by some participants to characterize this phenomenon, but challenged by others who pointed out that apartheid is in fact a system for including a subordinated group within the organization of global production. All, however, agreed on the substance of the phenomenon of a division between the included and the excluded in global economic relations, together with a hierarchy of dominance and subordination of those included within.

How that hierarchy is to be described has become an important matter for reflection. The nineteenth and early twentieth century reliance on the concept of social class as the basic differentiation in hierarchy seems less adequate today when the factors of gender, ethnicity, religion, language and nationality all play significant roles. The relationships among all these factors have become essential to the understanding of contemporary social structures.

A model of the global (or world, or international) political economy is an important starting point for analysis of any specific phenomenon – global finance, migration, ecology, or the potential for a specific national socio-political structure such as social democracy. National and local situations have to be related to such a concept of global system, not necessarily as subordinate to the global system but as interacting with it.

This includes problematizing the classic Westphalian conception of the state as the exclusive unit of world affairs, and especially of world economic, social, and cultural affairs. With the collapse of 'real socialism', the notion of a struggle between two rival economic, social and political systems that has dominated thinking in the four decades of the Cold War has lost its relevance. Emerging cleavages may define rival forms of capitalism, each competing for legitimacy on the world scale or having a territorial base in different world regions.

The search for ontology cannot be limited to the definition of the entities of an emerging global structure of power. It should include a consideration of process. In this regard, Karl Polanyi's theme (1957) of a 'double movement' was recurrent in the symposium discussions. Polanyi derived this idea from his reflections on the industrial revolution during the nineteenth and early twentieth centuries. The first phase of movement was an attempt to put into practice the notion of a self-regulating market, with the consequence of social polarization and the disintegrating of social bonds. The second phase was society's response, attempting to tame and control the market so as to reassert some form of social control over market processes.

At the present time, the global political economy is going through the first phase of the double movement. One may look for signs that it is reaching the limits of social tolerance. What form the response may take is perhaps the most critical issue of political economy today. Polanyi saw the second phase not only leading to a democratic welfare state but also to authoritarian forms of socialism and fascism. A clear understanding of the underlying reasons for the double movement, together with a strategy for guiding responsive movements within the norms of democracy and social equity, is the nub of the present dilemma.

The development of such a strategy takes place against the background of two phenomena which are both universal and unevenly spread. The first is the condition of the biosphere and the way in which it limits the potential for human activity. In this regard, there is an ecological power structure which enables some dominant elements of humanity to maximize their life opportunities at the expense of other subordinate elements of humanity. Ecological imperialism enables the powerful to clean up their immediate environment by exporting polluting activities to the dominated. Yet the whole of humanity ultimately shares the same fate. The metaphor of shuffling the deck chairs on the 'Titanic' fits here. The short time frame of politics tends to obscure the somewhat longer (but not perhaps very much longer) time frame of biospheric crisis. The position of President George Bush before the UN Environmental Summit in Rio in 1992, that 'our [rich country] lifestyle is not negotiable' becomes untenable in the longer perspective. Thus the issue of modes of consumption, which in turn feeds back into modes of production and finance, lies at the heart of any thinking about the future.

The second background phenomenon is the loss of legitimacy of political authority and the decomposition and recomposition of civil societies. In the richer countries, political classes have been exposed as incompetent or corrupt. In some of the poorest countries, where politics never attained much legitimacy, politics has become the activity of armed gangs. The unevenness of this phenomenon ranges from widespread electoral non-participation, through corruption scandals such as have beset Japanese and Italian or Brazilian and Nigerian politics, to the power struggles in Russia and the Caucasus (which leave people in suffering alienation from politics), and the 'black holes' of Somalia, Liberia, and Haiti.

The decline of political legitimacy and authority is accompanied (also unevenly) by a decomposition of the bonds of pre-existing forms of society. The term 'chaos' has been applied to this phenomenon especially in the Third World context where rural poverty becomes transmuted into urban squalor (Vieille, 1988). It is symptomatic of the extent of this damage to the cohesion of human groups that some of the more promising signs are the deliberate withdrawal of groups of people from both state and formal economy to seek their own survival apart from these entities which are experienced as both alien and predatory. Any reversal of this fall into decadence would have to include, beyond the rejection of opting out, a recreation of political authority and some form of state responsive to the needs of a reconstituted civil society.

STRATEGY

This suggests that the strategy for reconstituting civil and political society should be one that works from the bottom up. This, at any rate, was the approach taken in the symposium discussions. Top-down initiatives may respond to the frequently heard demand for 'leadership' but, given the erosion of deference to authority just noted, it incurs risks of disbelief and illegitimacy. A bottom-up strategy, on the other hand, presents different problems. It requires a careful building of self-confidence among initiating groups, the building of popular alliances, and the development of coherent alternatives to the dominant order.

Three words play a role in mobilizing thinking to this end: globalization, regionalization, and democratization. Each of these words evokes contradictory meanings. Globalization expresses the ideology of neo-liberalism, of the first phase of the Polanyian double movement which is to be transcended. It also signifies the interrelatedness of all life in the biosphere which, along with the principles of social equity and self-governance, would counteract this first phase. Regionalization exists in a 'top-down' form whereby decisions affecting people are removed to more distant centres, over which they have less control. A 'new regionalism' (the term put forward by Björn Hettne), on the other hand, emanates from the base of society upward, legitimizing regional structures that represent new foci of loyalty responding to society's basic needs. 'Democratization' has often been appropriated in an ideology of domination, signifying the opening of societies to penetration and manipulation by powerful external forces (finance, media, political organization). It also expresses the fundamental aim to base new political authority, civil society, and multilateralism on popular will.

This kind of contradiction arises in virtually every aspect of movement for change, which underlines the imperative need for critical thinking at all stages. There has been much emphasis, for instance, on the 'new social movements' as bearers of social and political change; but this notion itself requires critical evaluation with a view to discriminating between one kind of change and another. Contemporary social movements include some of a fascist type populism, some of exclusionary religious fundamentalisms, some that lend themselves to co-optation by dominant forces, and some that become corporatist pressures for special interests within the existing system. New social movements can become authentic autonomous voices for component elements of complex social formations; but one must distinguish critically those that adopt a strategy of openness towards an inclusive society based on the principle of equity and those that would close off this possibility through ideologies of exclusionary segmentation. To romanticize 'new social movements' in general would court serious risks.

Social change is a complex process and the movement of social forces involves careful assessment of risks for those vulnerable groups involved. Marx was brought to reflect upon this point with the disaster wreaked upon the small urban proletariat of Paris during the revolutionary upheaval of 1848. In the discussion of gender politics in this symposium, a similar point was made. Women in a vulnerable subordinate social position have to weigh carefully the risks inherent in breaking existing social bonds which could increase their vulnerability, against the potentials for empowerment. Only those directly involved are in a position to pursue their own empowerment responsibly.

Hitherto, struggles for social change have been situated primarily in the arena of production, the arena of class struggle. While production remains the activity through which societies are created and recreated, social action now is increasingly directed towards consumption. At issue is the consumption model that will define the character of the future society. Awareness of the constraints imposed by the biosphere define the limits of sustainability of consumption models. This will require a medium to long term shift in habits, especially in the more affluent areas of the world. A major obstacle in present times is that unsustainable habits of consumption by the affluent have inspired revolutionary aspirations among deprived social forces. The desire to emulate the bad habits of the rich generates a false criterion of equality among the revolutionary poor. The result is generally greater polarization between rich and poor on a global scale, together with a growth pattern which in the longer term is destructive of the life-chances of all. To attack the issue of consumption models could lead to more humane – and equitable – modes of production.

Notes

1. *The New Science of Giambattista Vico* [originally 1744] translated by T.G. Bergin and M.H. Fisch (Ithaca: Cornell University Press, 1970) paragraph 161. Vico's 'new science' is based on the idea that all civilisations have had to confront similar problems and have found diverse ways of articulating the practices with which they responded to these problems. Different languages thus have similar material bases and this should make it possible to find equivalences among civilisations which are not based upon the imposition of one civilisation's meanings upon others.
2. I have suggested that the concept of *asabiya* in Ibn Khaldun has such a similarity with Machiavelli's *virtù* and thus points to a potentially universal political hypothesis. See Cox (1992).

Bibliography

ABRAHAM, D. (1981) *The Collapse of the Weimar Republic. Political Economy and Crisis* (Princeton University Press).

ADAMS, P. (1992) 'The World Bank and the IMF in sub-Saharan Africa', *Journal of International Affairs*, Vol. 46, No. 1, pp. 97–117.

AGANBEGJAN, A. (1989) *De Toekomst van de Perestrojka. Revolutie in de Sovjet-economie* (Baarn, Anthos).

AHLÉN, K. (1989) 'Swedish Collective Bargaining under Pressure', *British Journal of Industrial Relations*, Vol. 27, No. 3.

AKGUNDUZ, A. (1993) 'Labour migration from Turkey to Western Europe (1960–1974). An analytical review', *Capital & Class*, Vol. 51, Autumn, pp. 153–94.

ALBERT, M. (1992) *Kapitalisme contra kapitalisme* (Amsterdam and Antwerp: Contact).

ALTVATER, E. (1993) *The Future of the Market. An Essay on the Regulation of Money and Nature after the Collapse of 'Actually Existing Socialism'.* Translated by Patrick Camiler (New York: Verso).

AMIN, S. (1989) *Eurocentrism* (New York: Monthly Review Press).

AMSDEN, A. (1989) *Asia's Next Giant: South Korea and Late Industrialization* (New York: Oxford University Press).

ANDERSON, B. (1983) *Imagined Communities. Reflections on the Origin and Spread of Nationalism* (London: Verso).

ANDERSON, P. (1979) *Lineages of the Absolute State* (London: Verso).

ANDERSSON, J-O. & L. MJØSET (1987) 'The Transformation of the Nordic Models' *Cooperation and Conflict*, Vol. XXII, pp. 227–43.

ANDERSSON, J-O. (1989) 'Controlled Restructuring in Finland?' *Scandinavian Political Studies*, Vol. 14, No. 4, pp. 373–87.

ARRIGHI, G. (1994) *The Long Twentieth Century* (London: Verso).

ÅSARD, E. (1978) *LO och löntagarfondsfrågan* (Stockholm, Rabén & Sjögren).

ÅSARD, E. (1985) *Kampen om löntagarfonderna* (Stockholm, Norstedts).

BAKKER, I., ed. (1994) *The Strategic Silence: Gender and Economic Policy* (London: Zed Press).

BDI (1984) *Bundesverband der Deutschen Industrie, Jahresbericht 1983–84* (Bonn, BDI).

BECKMAN, B. (1992) 'Empowerment or Repression? The World Bank and the Politics of African Adjustment'. In P. Gibbon *et al.* (eds) *Authoritarianism, Democracy and Adjustment* (Uppsala: Proceedings of the Scandinavian Institute of African Studies) pp. 83–105.

BENERIA, L. (1992) 'The Mexican Debt Crisis: Restructuring the Economy and the Household', in Beneria and S. Feldman (eds) (1992). *Unequal*

Burden: Economic Crises, Persistent Poverty and Women's Work (Boulder: Westview) pp. 83–104.

BENERIA, L. & S. FELDMAN (eds) (1992) *Unequal Burden* (Boulder: Westview Press).

BENTHAM, Jeremy (1859) *The Works of Jeremy Bentham* (Edinburgh: William Tait).

BERGERON, S. (1993) The Nation as a Gendered Subject of Macroeconomics. Paper prepared for the conference 'Out of the Margin: Feminist Perspectives on Economic Theory', Amsterdam, 2–5 June, 1993.

BERGHOLM, F. & L. JAGRÉN (1985) 'Det utlandsinvesterande företaget: en empirisk studie' in Gunnar Eliasson *et al. De svenska storföretagen* (Stockholm, IUI) pp. 71–160.

BERGSTRÖM, V. (1993) 'Finansplanen och den ekonomiska politiken' in Villy Bergström (ed.) *Varför Överge den Svenska Modellen?* (Stockholm: Tiden) pp. 159–64.

BILDERBERG (1989) *Thirty-Seventh Bilderberg Meeting*, Official Documents (La Toja: Spain). 12–14 May.

BLISHCHENKO, I. & N. ZHDANOV (1984) *Terrorism and International Law* (Moscow: Progress).

BLOCK, F. (1977) *The Origins of International Economic Disorder* (Berkeley: University of California Press).

BLOOM, D.E. & A. BRENDER (1993) 'Labor and the emerging world economy', Special edition of *Population Bulletin*, Vol. 2, pp. 1–39.

BORKENAU, F. (1942) *Socialism: National or International* (London: Labour Books).

BOSSCHER, E. (1990) 'La libre circulation des travailleurs: situation et perspectives', *Problèmes Économiques*, No. 2202, 5 décembre, pp. 5–7.

BOUSSEMART, B. & J.C. RABIER (1983) 'Division internationale du travail, industrie de main-d'oeuvre et évolution de l'emploi', *Revue Française des Affaires Sociales*, Vol. 46, No. 2, avril–juin, pp. 105–28.

BOYER, R. (1987a) 'Flexibility: Many Forms, Uncertain Effects', *Labour and Society*, Vol. 12, No. 1, pp. 108–28.

BOYER, R. (1987b) 'What is the Next Socio Economic System Made of?' (BRIE: Berkeley), September 10–12.

BRADSHER, K. (1991) 'Rain Forest Project Stirs Debate at the World Bank', *New York Times*, 14 October 1991.

BRAUDEL, F. (1980) 'History and the Social Sciences. The *longue durée*', in *On History* (University of Chicago Press) pp. 25–54,

BRAUDEL, F. (1981) *The Structures of Everyday Life: the Limits of the Possible*. Vol. I of *Civilisation and Capitalism, 15th–18th Centuries*, translated by Siân Reynolds (New York: Harper & Row).

BRAUDEL, F. (1990) *The Identity of France*, Vol. II, 'People and Production', translated by Siân Reynolds (New York: HarperCollins).

BREMNER, S. (1989) *The GLOBUS Model: Computer Simulation of Worldwide Political and Economic Developments* (Boulder: Westview Press).

BRETON, G. & J. JENSON (1992) 'Globalisation et citoyenneté: quelques enjeux actuels', paper presented to the colloquium of the Canadian Political Science Association, Charlottetown, 31 May–2 June.

BRETT, E.A. (1993) 'Voluntary Agencies as Development Organisations: Theorising the Problem of Efficiency and Accountability', *Development and Change*, Vol. 24, pp. 269–303.

BROAD, R. & J. CAVANAGH, J. 'No More NIC"s" ', *Foreign Policy*, No. 72, Fall, pp. 81–103.

BRODIE, J. (1995) 'Canadian Women, Changing State Forms, and Public Policy' in Janine Brodie, ed. *Women in Canadian Public Policy* (Toronto: Harcourt Brace Javonovitch).

BRÖKER, G. (1988) 'Automation of securities markets: implications for their functioning and surveillance', *13th Annual Conference of International Organisation of Securities Commissions*, Melbourne, Australia, November 14–17.

BULL, H. (1977) *The Anarchical Society* (New York: Columbia University Press).

CAFRUNY, A. (1989) 'Economic Conflicts and the Transformation of the Atlantic Order' in S. Gill (ed.) *Atlantic Relations. Beyond the Reagan Era* (New York: St Martin's), pp. 111–38

CANNER, G. & C.A. LUCKETT (1992) 'Developments in the pricing of credit card services' *Federal Reserve Bulletin*, September 1992, pp. 652–67.

CARR, E.H. (1964) *The Twenty Years' Crisis, 1919–1939* (New York and Evanston: Harper & Row).

CARRÈRE D'ENCAUSSE, J. (1980) *Le pouvoir confisqué. Gouvernants et gouvernés en URSS* (Paris: Flammarion).

CASTLES, S. & G. KOSACK (1973) *Immigrant Workers and Class Structure in Western Europe* (London: Oxford University Press).

CASTLES, S. (1989) 'Global workforce, global economy, global culture? Migration and modernization', in S. Castles (ed.) *Migrant Workers and the Transformation of Western Societies*, Western Societies Papers, Occasional paper No. 22 (Center for International Studies: Cornell University).

CAVANAGH, J. & CHERU (1986) *From Debt to Development: Alternatives to the International Debt Crisis* (Washington DC: Institute for Policy Studies).

CERNY, P. (ed.) (1993) *The Political Economy of International Finance* (Gloucester: Elgar).

CHANARON, J.J. & E. DE BANVILLE (1985) 'Le système automobile français: De la sous-traitance au partenariat? Eléments d'une problématique', Etude No. 56, Ministère du Redéploiement industriel et du Commerce extérieur & Ministère de la Recherche et de la Technologie, Paris, mars.

CHERU, F. & S. GILL (1993) 'Democratization and globalization: the G7 "nexus" and the limits of Structural adjustment in Africa, Eastern Europe and Russia', paper presented to the International Symposium on 'Global Political Economy and a New Multilateralism', Oslo, 15–17 August.

CHERU, F. (1994) 'The Prospects for Expanded Trade and Investment Between Kenya and South Africa', *South African Journal of International Affairs*, Vol. 1, No. 1 (Autumn) pp. 19–31.

CHERU, F. (1989) *The Silent Revolution in Africa: Debt, Development and Democracy* (London: Zed Books).

CHERU, F. (1992) *The Not So Brave New World: Problems and Prospects of Regional Integration in post-Apartheid Southern Africa*, South African Institute of International Affairs, Bradlow Occasional Series, June.

CHESNOT, C. (1993) 'Les objectifs cachés du Grand Projet anatolien', *Le Monde Diplomatique*, octobre.
CHOSSUDOVSKY, M. (1993) 'Risques de famine aggravés dans le Sud', *Le Monde Diplomatique*, septembre.
CLARKE, S. (1987) 'Capitalist Crisis and the Rise of Monetarism' in R. Miliband & J. Saville (eds) *The Socialist Register 1987* (London: Merlin Press), pp. 393–427.
COHEN, R. (1987) *The New Helots: Migrants in the New International Division of Labour* (Brookfield: Gower).
COHEN, R. (1991) 'East–West and European migration in a global context', *New Community*, Vol. 18 No. 1, October, pp. 9–26.
COLLECTIVE (1988) 'Der soziale Fortschritt in der Welt von heute. Thesen zur Diskussion'. *Gesellschaftswissenschaftliche Beiträge*, No. 6.
CORNIA, G.A., R. JOLLY & F. STEWART (eds) (1987) *Adjustment with a Human Face. A Study by UNICEF* (Oxford University Press).
CORRIGAN, P. & D. SAYER (1985) *The Great Arch: English State Formation as Cultural Revolution* (London: Basil Blackwell).
COTTRELL, R. (1986) 'The Silent Empire of the Kuok Family.' *Far Eastern Economic Review*, 30 October, pp. 59–63.
COURAULT, B.A. (1990) 'Les étrangers catégorie du marché dual ou vecteur de la flexibilité du travail?', in G. Abou Sada *et al.*, *L'Immigration au Tournant* (Paris: Seuil) pp. 109–22.
COX, R.W. (1981) 'Social Forces, States and World Orders: Beyond International Relations Theory'. *Millennium* Vol. 10, No. 2, pp. 162–75.
COX, R.W. (1987) *Production, Power and World Order: Social Forces in the Making of History* (New York: Columbia University Press).
COX, R.W. (1991) 'Programme on Multilateralism and the United Nations System, 1990–1995' (Tokyo: United Nations University).
COX, R.W. (1992) 'Towards a post-hegemonic conceptualization of world order: reflections on the relevancy of Ibn Khaldun' in J. Rosenau & E.-O. Czempiel (eds) *Governance Without Government* (Cambridge: Cambridge University Press).
CZICHON, E. (1989) *Wer verhalf Hitler zur Macht? Zum Anteil der deutschen Industrie an der Zerstörung der Weimarer Republik* (Köln: Pahl-Rugenstein).
DALY, H. & J.B. COBB, Jr. (1989) *For the Common Good* (London: Merlin/ Green Print).
DAVIS, K. (1974) 'The migrations of human populations', *Scientific American*, Vol. 231, No. 3, September, pp. 92–107.
DAVIS, M. (1984) 'The Political Economy of Late Imperial America', *New Left Review*, No. 143, pp. 6–38.
DAVIS, M. (1990) *City of Quartz* (New York: Vintage).
DE GEER, H. (1989) *I vänstervind och högervåg* (Stockholm: Allmäna förlaget).
DELAMAIDE, D. (1993) 'The Coming of Age of G7' *Euromoney*, September, pp. 73–8.
DICKEN, P. (1992) *Global Shift: The Internationalization of Economic Activity* (New York. Guildford Press).
DIXON, C. (1991) *South East Asia in the World-Economy* (Cambridge University Press).

DONER, R.F. (1991) *Driving a Bargain: Automobile Industrialisation and Japanese Firms in Southeast Asia* (Berkeley: University of California Press).

DRAPER, E. (1991) *Risky Business. Genetic Testing and Exclusionary Practices in the Hazardous Workplace* (Cambridge: Cambridge University Press).

ECONOMIST (1994) 'Aid and the Environment', 25 December 1993–7 January 1994.

ECONOMOU, P. *et al.*, (1993) 'Europe 1992 and foreign direct investment in Africa', in I.W. Zartman (ed.) *Europe and Africa. The New Phase* (Boulder: Rienner), pp. 95–119.

EDIN, P-O (1993) 'Den svenska räntans bestämningsvillkor', Mimeo (Stockholm: LO).

EL MELLOUKI RIFFI, B. (1989) *La Politique de Coopération avec les États du Maghreb* (Paris: Publisud).

ELSON, D. (1992) 'Gender Analysis and Development Economics', Paper for the ESRC Development Economics Group, Annual Conference, Manchester, UK.

ELSON, D. (1994) 'Micro, Meso and Macro: Gender and Economic Analysis in the Context of Policy Reform.' in I. Bakker (ed.) *The Strategic Silence*, pp. 33–45.

EMMERIJ, L. (1992) 'Globalization, Regionalization and World Trade', *Columbia Journal of World Business*, Vol. 27, No. 2, pp. 6–13.

ERINGER, R. (1980) *The Global Manipulators* (Bristol: Pentacle).

ERIXON, L. & N. FRAZER (1984) 'Tränger den offentliga sektorn undan den privata?' *Häften för kritiska studier*, Vol. 17, pp. 71–90.

ERIXON, L. (1984) 'Den svenska modellen i motgång', *Nordisk tidsskrift för politisk ekonomi*, Nos. 15/16, pp. 109–57

ERIXON, L. (1989) 'Den tredje vägen: inlåsning eller förnyelse?' *Ekonomisk debatt* Vol. 3, pp. 181–95.

ESCOBAR, A. (1995) *Encountering Development: The Making and Unmaking of the Third World* (Princeton, NJ: Princeton University Press).

ESPING-ANDERSEN, G. (1985a) *Politics Against Markets* (Princeton, NJ: Princeton University Press).

ESPING-ANDERSEN, G. (1985b) 'Power and Distributional Regimes', *Politics and Society*, Vol. 14, No. 2, pp. 223–56.

ESPING-ANDERSEN, G. (1990) 'De-commodification and Social Policy' in Esping-Andersen, *The Three Worlds of Welfare Capitalism* (Cambridge: Polity Press), pp. 35–54.

FAGERBERG, J. (1991) 'The Process of Economic Integration in Europe: Consequences for EFTA Countries and Firms', *Cooperation and Conflict*, Vol. XXVI, pp. 199–215.

FAGERBERG, J. *et al.* (1990) 'The Decline of Social Democratic State Capitalism in Norway' *New Left Review*, No. 181, pp. 60–94.

FALLOUX, F. and T. TALBOT (1993) *Crisis and Opportunity, Environment and Development in Africa* (London: Earthscan).

FEINBERG, R.E. (1989) 'Defunding Latin America: reverse transfers by multilateral lending agencies' *This World Quarterly*, Vol. 11, pp. 71–84.

FELDT, K-O. (1991) *Alla dessa dagar* (Stockholm: Norstedts).

FENNEMA, M. (1982) *International Networks of Banks and Industry* (The Hague: Nijhoff).

FERNÁNDEZ, K. & M. PATRICIA (1989) 'International Development and Industrial Restructuring: The Case of Garment and Electronics Industries in Southern California', in A. MacEwan and W. Tabb (eds) *Instability and Change in the World Economy*, pp. 147–65 (New York: Monthly Review Press).

FINANCIAL TIMES (1994) 'Donors back environmental fund accord', 17 March 1994.

FISCHER, F. (1984) *Griff nach der Weltmacht. Die Kriegszielpolitik des kaiserlichen Deutschland* (Düsseldorf: Droste).

FLAHERTY, P. (1988) 'Perestroika Radicals: The Origins and Ideology of the Soviet New Left', *Monthly Review*, Vol. 40, No. 4, pp. 19–33.

FLORA, P. (ed.) (1986) *Growth to Limits. Vol. 1* (Berlin: de Greuyter).

FOLBRE, N. (1994) *Who Pays for the Kids? Gender and the Structures of Constraint* (London and New York: Routledge).

FOLBRE, N. (1986) 'Cleaning House: New Perspectives on Households and Economic Development', *Journal of Development Economics*, Vol. 22, No. 1, pp. 5–40.

FONG, P.E. (1993) 'Labour Migration to the Newly-Industrialising Economies of South Korea, Taiwan, Hong Kong and Singapore', *International Migration*, Vol. 31, Nos 2/3, special issue 'Japan and International Migration', pp. 300–13.

FOUCAULT, M. (1979) *Discipline and Punish: The Birth of the Prison*, translated by Alan Sheridan (New York: Vintage Books).

FOUCAULT, M. (1980) *Power/Knowledge: Selected Interviews and Other Writings*, edited by Colin Gordon, translated by Colin Gordon *et al.* (New York: Pantheon Books).

FRASER, N. & L. GORDON (1994). 'A Geneology of Dependency: Tracing a Keyword of the U.S. Welfare State', *Signs*, Vol. 19, No. 2, pp. 309–36.

FRIEDMAN, M. (1962) *Capitalism and Freedom* (University of Chicago Press).

FRÖBEL, F. *et al.* (eds) (1980) *The New International Division of Labour: Structural Unemployment in Industrialised Countries and Industrialisation in Developing Countries*, trans. by P. Burgess (Cambridge University Press).

FUKUYAMA, F. (1989) 'The End of History', *The National Interest*, Vol. 16, pp. 3–18.

FUKUYAMA, F. (1992) *The End of History and the Last Man* (Harmondsworth: Penguin).

GALBRAITH, J.K. (1992) *The Culture of Contentment* (Boston: Houghton Mifflin).

GANDY, O.H. Jr (1993) *The Panoptic Sort: A Political Economy of Personal Information* (Boulder: Westview Press).

GARSON, J.P. (1992) 'International migration, Facts, figures, policies', *OECD Observer*, No. 176, June–July, pp. 18–24.

GARTON ASH, T. (1993) *In Europe's Name. Germany and the Divided Continent* (New York: Random House).

GEORGE, S. (1992) *The Debt Boomerang: How Third World Debt Harms Us All* (Boulder: Westview Press).

GERBIER, B. (1987) 'La course aux armements: l'impérialisme face au nouvel ordre international', *Cahiers de la Faculté des Sciences Economiques de Grenoble*, No. 6.

GEREFFI, G. & S. FONDA (1992) 'Regional Paths of Development.' *Annual Review of Sociology*, Vol. 18, pp. 419–48.

GEREFFI, G. & M. KORZENIEWICZ (eds) (1994) *Commodity-Chains and Global Capitalism* (Westport, CT: Greenwood Press).

GEREFFI, G. (1990) 'Paths of Industrialization: An Overview' in G. Gereffi and D.L. Wyman (eds) *Manufacturing Miracles: Paths of Industrialization in Latin America and East Asia* (Princeton University Press), pp. 3–31.

GERMAIN, R. (1992) 'From Money to Finance: the International Organization of Credit', Paper to Annual Meeting of the Canadian Political Science Association, Charlottetown, PEI, 2 June.

GIDDENS, A. (1990) *The Consequences of Modernity* (Stanford, CA: Stanford University Press).

GILL, S. (1990) *American Hegemony and the Trilateral Commission* (Cambridge: Cambridge University Press).

GILL, S. (1991a) 'Historical Materialism, Gramsci, and International Political Economy', in C. Murphy & R. Tooze (eds) *The New International Political Economy* (Boulder: Lynne Rienner) pp. 51–75.

GILL, S. (1991b) 'Reflections on Global Order and Socio-Political Time', *Alternatives*, Vol. 16, No. 3, pp. 275–314.

GILL, S. (1992a) 'The emerging world order and European change: the political economy of European economic union', in R. Miliband & L. Panitch (eds) *New World Order? Socialist Register 1992* (London: Merlin) pp. 157–96.

GILL, S. (1992b) 'Economic Globalization and the Internationalisation of Authority: limits and contradictions' *Geoforum*, Vol. 23, No. 3, pp. 269–3.

GILL S. (ed.) (1993a) *Gramsci, Historical Materialism and International Relations* (Cambridge: Cambridge University Press).

GILL, S. (1993b) 'Global finance, monetary policy and cooperation among the Group of Seven, 1944–92', in P.G. Cerny (ed.) *Finance and World Politics* (Aldershot, UK: Elgar), pp. 86–113.

GILL, S. (1994a) 'Structural change and global political economy: globalising élites in the emerging world order', in Y. Sakamoto (ed.) *Global Transformation. Challenges to the State System* (Tokyo: United Nations University Press) pp. 169–99.

GILL, S. (1994b) 'Knowledge, Politics and Neo-Liberal Political Economy', in R. Stubbs & G. Underhill (eds) *Political Economy and the Changing Global Order* (Toronto: McClelland and Stewart) pp. 75–88.

GILL, S. (1994c) ' "Globalization" and the Emerging World Order', paper presented to *International Studies Association Conference on Globalization*, American University, Washington DC, March 1994.

GILL, S. (1995a) 'Globalisation, Market Civilisation and Disciplinary Neoliberalism', *Millennium*, Vol. 24, No. 3, pp. 399–422.

GILL, S. (1995b) 'Theorizing the Interregnum: The Double Movement and Global Politics in the 1990s', in B. Hettne (ed.) *International Political Economy: Understanding Global Disorder* (London: Zed Books) pp. 65–99.

GILL, S. (1996) 'Globalization, Democratization and the Politics of Indifference', in J.H. Mittelman (ed.) *Globalization: Critical Reflections*, International Political Economy Yearbook, Vol. 9 (Boulder: Lynne Rienner) pp. 205–28.

GILL, S. & D. LAW (1989) 'Global hegemony and the structural power of capital' *International Studies Quarterly*, Vol. 36, pp. 475–99, edited and reprinted in S. Gill (ed.) *Gramsci, Historical Materialism and International Relations*, pp. 93–124.

GOODWIN-GILL, G. (1989) 'International Law and Human Rights: Trends concerning international migrants and refugees', *International Migration Review*, Vol. 23, No. 3, Fall, pp. 526–6.

GORDON, D. (1988) 'The Global Economy: New Edifice or Crumbling Foundations?' *New Left Review*, No. 168, pp. 24–64.

GORDON, R. *et al.* (1982) *Segmented Work, Divided Workers: The Historical Transformation of Labor in the U.S.* (Cambridge: Cambridge University Press).

GOSS, J. & B. LINDQUIST (1995) 'Conceptualizing international labor migration: A structuration perspective', *International Migration Review*, Vol. 29, Summer, pp. 317–51.

GOSSWEILER, K. (1975) *Grossbanken, Industriemonopole, Staat. Ökonomie und Politik des staatsmonopolistischen Kapitalismus in Deutschland, 1914–1932* (Berlin, DEB).

GOULD, S.J. (1981) *The Mismeasure of Man* (New York: W. W. Norton).

GRAHL, J. & P. TEAGUE (1989) 'The Cost of Neo-Liberal Europe', *New Left Review*, No. 174, pp. 33–50.

GRAMSCI, A. (1971) *Selections from the Prison Notebooks of Antonio Gramsci* translated by Q. Hoare and G. Nowell Smith (New York: International Publishers; London: Lawrence & Wishart).

GRAMSCI, A. (1977) *Selections from Political Writings 1910–1920* Q. Hoare (ed.) (New York: International Publishers).

GRAMSCI, A. (1978) *Selections from Political Writings 1921–1926*, Q. Hoare (ed.) (New York: International Publishers).

GROSZ, E. (1990) 'Philosophy.' in S. Gunew (ed.) *Feminist Knowledge* (New York: Routledge).

GUNEW, S. & A. YEATMAN (eds) (1993) *Feminism and the Politics of Difference* (Halifax, NS: Fernwood).

HALL, S. & M. JACQUES (1983) *The Politics of Thatcherism* (London: Lawrence and Wishart).

HALL, S. & B. SCHWARTZ (1988) 'State and Society 1880–1930' in S. Hall (ed.) *The Hard Road to Renewal* (London: Verso) pp. 95–122.

HANSSON, S.O. (1984) *SAF i politiken* (Stockholm: Tiden).

HARAWAY, D. (1991) *Simeans, Cyborgs and Women: The Reinvention of Nature* (New York: Routledge).

HARDING, S. (1986) *The Science Question in Feminism* (Ithaca and London: Cornell University Press).

HARVEY, D. (1989) *The Condition of Postmodernity* (Oxford: Blackwell).

HAYTER, T. & C. WATSON (1985) *Aid, Rhetoric and Reality* (London: Pluto Press).

HELD, D. (1991) 'Democracy, the Nation-state and the Global System', *Economy and Society*, Vol. 20, No. 2, pp. 138–72.

HELLEINER, E. (1992) 'States and the Future of Global Finance' *Review of International Studies*, Vol. 18, No. 1, 31–49.

HELLEINER, E. (1994) *States and the Reemergence of Global Finance* (Ithaca: Cornell University Press).

HENDERSON, J. (1989) *The Globalisation of High Technology Production: Society, Space and Semiconductors in the Restructuring of the Modern World* (London: Routledge).
HENG, P.K. (1992) 'The Chinese Business Elite of Malaysia' in R. McVey (ed.) *Southeast Asian Capitalists* Ithaca, NY; Cornell University Southeast Asia Program, pp. 127–44.
HERBST, J. (1993) *The Politics of Reform in Ghana, 1982–1991* (Berkeley: University of California Press).
HERMANSSON, C.H. (1989) *Ägande och makt* (Stockholm: Arbetarkultur).
HERSH, S.M. (1994) 'The Wild East', *The Atlantic Monthly*, Vol. 273, pp. 61–86
HETTNE, B. (ed.) (1995) *International Political Economy: Understanding Global Disorder* (London: Zed Books).
HEWITT, D. (1991) 'Military Expenditures in the Developing World', *Finance and Development*, Vol. 28, No. 3, pp. 22–5.
HILL, C. (1961) *The Century of Revolution, 1603–1714* (New York: W.W. Norton).
HOLLOWAY, D. (1984) *De Sovjet-Unie en de bewapeningswedloop* (Amsterdam: Mets).
HOLMAN, O. (1992) 'Transnational Class Strategy and the New Europe', *International Journal of Political Economy*, Vol. 22, No. 1, 3–22.
HOPKINS, T.K. & I. WALLERSTEIN (1986) 'Commodity Chains in the World Economy Prior to 1800', *Review*, Vol. 10, No. 1, pp. 157–70.
HÖRNGREN, L. (1993) 'Normer eller diskretion': Om möjliga och omöjliga val i stabiliseringspolitiken' in Villy Bergström (ed.) *Varför överge den svenska modellen?* (Stockholm: Tiden) pp. 185–201.
HUGON, P. (1991) 'Secteur informel au Nord et au Sud: convergence des créations endogènes d'emploi ou divergences structurelles des modes de régulation?' in J. Lemmers, *et al.*, *Emploi et Interdépendance Nord-Sud* (Paris: Publisud) pp. 225–47.
HUGON, P. (1993) *L'Économie de l'Afrique* (Paris: La Découverte).
HYMAN, R. & W. STREECK (eds) (1988) *New Technology and Industrial Relations* (Oxford: Basil Blackwell).
IMBER, M. (1993) 'Too Many Cooks? The post-Rio reform of the United Nations', *International Affairs*, Vol. 69, No. 1, pp. 55–70.
IMF (1990) *Balance of Payments Yearbook* (Washington DC: IMF).
IMF, *World Economic Outlook*, various years (Washington DC: IMF).
INTERNATIONAL INSTITUTE FOR LABOUR STUDIES (1994) *Women Workers in a Changing Global Environment: Framework for Discussion*. For the International Forum 'Equality for Women in the World of Work: Challenges for the Future', Geneva, 1–3 June 1994.
INTERNATIONAL LABOUR ORGANISATION (1989) *Yearbook of Labour Statistics* (Geneva: ILO).
INTERNATIONAL LABOUR ORGANISATION (1993) *The Impact of Recession and Structural Adjustment on Women's Work in Developing and Developed Countries. Equality for Women in Employment: An Interdepartmental Project*, IDP Women/WP-19, December.
ISLAM, S. (1993) 'Russia's Rough Road to Capitalism', *Foreign Affairs*, Vol. 72, pp. 57–66.

JANES (1971) *Jane's Major Companies of Europe 1971* (New York: McGraw-Hill).

JENSON, J. & G. ROSS (1986) 'Post-War Class Struggle and the Crisis of Left Politics' in R. Miliband and J. Saville (eds) *The Socialist Register 1985/1986* (London: Merlin Press) pp. 23–49.

JESSOP, B. (1993) 'Reflections on the Financial Crisis of the Postsocialist State', *International Journal of Political Economy*, Vol. 23, pp. 9–35.

JOFFE, A. *et al.* (1993) 'South Africa's Industrialisation: The Challenge Facing Labor', presented to the University of the Witwatersrand's History Workshop and Sociology of Work Unit Symposium on 'Work, Class and Culture' Johannesburg, South Africa, June.

JOHNSON, S.P. (1993) *The Earth Summit: the UN Conference on Environment and Development* (London: Trotman and Martinus Nijhoff).

JORGENSEN, J. (1986) *Money Shock: Ten Ways the Financial Marketplace is Transforming Our Lives* (New York: American Management Association).

KABEER, N. & J. HUMPHREY (1990) 'Neo-liberalism, Gender, and the Limits of the Market', in C. Coclough and J. Manor (eds) *States or Markets? Neo-liberalism and the Development Policy Debate* (Oxford: Clarendon Press).

KABEER, N. (1989) 'Cultural Dopes or Rational Fools? Women and Labour Supply in the Bangladesh Garment Industry', *European Journal of Development Research*, November.

KAIMOWITZ, D (1993) 'The Role of Nongovernmental Organisations in Agricultural Research and Technology Transfer in Latin America', *World Development*, Vol. 21, No. 7, pp. 1139–50.

KAMM, H. (1993) 'In Europe's Upheaval, Doors Close to Foreigners', *New York Times*. February 10.

KAPLINSKY, R. (1984) *Automation: New Technology and Society* (Geneva: ILO).

KARDAM, N. (1994) 'Development Approaches and the Role of Policy Advocacy: The Case of the Bank', *World Development*, Vol. 21, No. 11, pp. 1773–86

KARVONEN, L. (1981) *Med vårt västra grannland som förebild* (Turkku: Åbo Akademi Foundation).

KATZENSTEIN, P. (1983) 'The Small European States in the International Economy: Economic Dependence and Corporatist Politics' in John G. Ruggie (ed.) *The Antinomies of Interdependence* (New York: Columbia University Press) pp. 91–130.

KATZENSTEIN, P. (1985) *Small States in World Markets* (Ithaca: Cornell University Press).

KAWAI, S. (1993) 'Japan and International Migration: Situation and Issues', *International Migration*, Vol. 31, Nos 2–3, pp. 276–84.

KELLER, B. (1993) 'South Africa's Wealth is Luring Black Talent', *New York Times*, 12 February.

KEOHANE, R.O. (1990) 'Multilateralism: An Agenda for Research', *International Journal*, Vol. 45, No. 4, pp. 731–64.

KORNAI, J. (1986) *Contradictions and Dilemmas* (London: MIT Press).

KORPI, W. (1983) *The Democratic Class Struggle* (London: Routledge & Kegan Paul).

KRASNER, S.D. (1985) *Structural Conflict. The Third World Against Global Liberalism* (Berkeley and London: University of California Press).

KUMAR, S. & T.Y. LEE (1991) 'A Singapore Perspective', in *Growth Triangle: The Johor–Singapore–Riau Experience* (ed.) Lee Tsao Yuan, pp. 1–36 (Singapore: Institute of Southeast Asian Studies).

LAIRD, R.D. & B.A. LAIRD (1970) *Soviet Communism and Agrarian Revolution* (Harmondsworth: Pelican).

LAMBERT, R. (1992) 'Constructing the New Internationalism: Australian Trade Unions and the Indian Ocean Regional Initiative', *South African Labour Bulletin*, Vol. 16, No. 5, pp. 66–73.

LARSON, B.A. (1994) 'Changing the Economics of Environmental Degradation in Madagascar: Lessons from the National Environmental Action Plan Process', *World Development*, Vol. 22, No. 5, pp. 671–89.

LASH, S. & J. URRY (1987) *The End of Organized Capitalism* (Cambridge: Polity Press).

LEBORGNE, D. & A. LIPIETZ (1988) 'New Technologies, New Modes of Regulation: Some Spatial Implications', *Society and Space*, Vol. 6, pp. 263–80.

LECLER, Y. & C. MERCIER (1990) 'La transformation des systèmes d'emploi et de rémunération', in E.de Banville and J.-J. Chanaron (eds) *Du Fordisme au Toyotisme? Les Voies de la Modernisation du Système Automobile en France et au Japon* (Paris: La documentation française).

LENIN, V.I. (various years) *Collected Works* (Moscow: Progress).

LEVER-TRACY, C. (1983) 'Immigrant Workers and Postwar Capitalism: In Reserve or Core Troops in the Front Line?', *Politics and Society*, Vol. 12, No. 2, pp. 127–57.

LEWIN, L. (1992) *Ideologi och strategi, 4th edn.* (Stockholm: Norstedts).

LEWIN, M. (1985) *The Making of the Soviet System. Essays in the Social History of Interwar Russia* (London: Methuen).

LEYSENS, A. & L. THOMPSON (1994) 'A Paper Tiger? Political Implications of an Export-led Growth Strategy for South Africa', *South African Journal of International Affairs*, Vol. 1, No. 2, pp. 47–78.

LIM, L.A. (1983) 'Chinese Economic Activity in Southeast Asia: an Introductory Review', in Lim L.A. & P. Gosling (eds) *The Chinese in Southeast Asia: Ethnicity and Economic Activity*, Vol. 1 (Singapore: Maruzen Asia) pp. 1–29.

LIM, L.A. (1992) 'International Labour Movements: A Perspective on Economic Exchanges and Flows', in M.M. Kritz *et al.* (eds) *International Migration Systems. A Global Approach* (Oxford: Clarendon Press) pp. 133–44.

LIM, L.A. (1995) 'The New International Context of Development: Southeast Asia', in B. Stallings (ed.) *Global Change, Regional Response. The New International Context of Development* (New York: Cambridge University Press).

LINDBECK, A. (1984) 'Tre grundproblem i svensk ekonomi', *Ekonomisk debatt*, Vol. 3, pp. 157–66.

LIPIETZ, A. (1985) *Mirages and Miracles: The Crisis of Global Fordism*, translated by D. Macey (London: Verso).

LIPIETZ, A. (1987) 'The Globalization of the General Crisis of Fordism' in J. Holmes and C. Leys (eds) *Frontyard/Backyard* (Toronto: Between the Lines) pp. 23–55.

LIPIETZ, A. (1989) *Towards a New Economic Order. Postfordism, Ecology and Democracy.* (New York: Oxford University Press).

LO (1986) *Ekonomiska utsikter* (Stockhom: LO).

MA MUNG, E. (1992) 'L'expansion du commerce ethnique: Asiatiques et Maghrébins dans la région parisienne', *Revue Européenne des Migrations Internationales*, Vol. 8, No. 1, pp. 39–58.

MACDONALD, M. (1994). 'Economic Restructuring and Gender in Canada: Feminist Policy Initiatives', paper prepared for the Gender and Macroeconomics Workshop, University of Utah, June.

MADEUF, B. & C.-A. MICHALET (1978) 'A new approach to international economics', *International Social Science Journal*, Vol. 30, No. 2, pp. 253–83.

MAHON, R. (1991) 'From Solidaristic Wages to Solidaristic Work: a Post-Fordist Historic Compromise for Sweden?' *Economic and Industrial Democracy*, Vol. 12, No. 3, pp. 295–325.

MAKHIJANI, A. (1992) *From Global Capitalism to Economic Justice: An Inquiry into the Elimination of Systemic Poverty, Violence and Environmental Destruction in the World Economy* (New York: Apex Press).

MANDELA, N. (1994) *Long Walk to Freedom* (Boston: Little, Brown).

MARIE, C.V. (1988) *La Lutte contre les Trafics de Main-d'Oeuvre en 1986–1987: Élargissement du Dispositif et Nouvelles Formes Illégales d'Emploi*, Rapport au ministère du Travail, de l'Emploi et de la Formation Professionnelle, Septembre.

MARKANDYA, A. (ed.) (1992) *The Earthscan Reader in Environmental Economics* (London: Earthscan).

MARKLUND, S. (1988) 'Welfare State Policies in the Tripolar Class Model of Scandinavia' *Politics and Society*, Vol. 16, No. 4, pp. 469–85.

MARTIN, A. (1984) 'Trade Unions in Sweden: Strategic Responses to Change and Crisis' in Peter Gourevitch *et al.*, *Unions and Economic Crisis* (London: Allen & Unwin) pp. 190–259.

MARTIN, P.L. (1993) 'Conference Report. Migration and Trade: The Case of the Philippines', *International Migration Review*, Vol. 27, No. 3, Fall, pp. 639–45.

MARTIN, P.L. *et al.* (1990) 'Europe 1992: effects on labor migration', *International Migration Review* Vol. 24, No. 3, Fall, pp. 591–603.

MARTIN, W.G. (1991) 'The Future of Southern Africa: What Prospects After Majority Rule?', *Review of African Political Economy*, No. 50, pp. 115–34.

MARX, K. (1967) *Capital, Vol. I: A Critical Analysis of Capitalist Production*, edited by F. Engels, translated from Third German Edition by S. Moore and E. Aveling (New York: International Publishers).

MATTERA, P. (1992) *World Class Business. A Guide to the 100 Most Powerful Global Corporations* (New York: Henry Holt & Co).

MAUCO, G. (1933) 'Immigration in France', *International Labour Review*, Vol. 27 No. 6, June, pp. 765–88.

McCANN, M. (1986) *Taking Reform Seriously: Perspectives on Public Interest Liberalism* (Ithaca: Cornell University Press).

McCARTHY, C.L. (1988) 'Structural Development of South African Manufacturing Industry', *South African Journal of Economics*, Vol. 56, No. 1, pp. 1–19.

McCARTHY, C.L. (1991) *Stagnation in the South African Economy: Where did things go wrong?* Economic Papers 1, Centre for Contextual Hermeneutics (University of Stellenbosch).

McLEAN PETRAS, E. (1992) 'The shirt on your back: Immigrant workers and the reorganization of the garment industry', *Social Justice*, Vol. 19 No. 1, pp. 76–114.

McNAMARA R.S. (1991) 'Reducing Military Expenditures in the Third World'. *Finance and Development*, Vol. 28, No. 3, pp. 26–8.

MEADOWS, D. (1991) *The Global Citizen* (Washington DC: Island Press).

MEADOWS, D. *et al.* (1972) *The Limits to Growth* (New York: Universal Books).

MEILLASSOUX, C. (1991) 'La leçon de Malthus', in C. Gendreau *et al. Les Spectres de Malthus (Paris: EDI).*

MEISSNER, D.M. *et al.* (1993) *International Migration Challenges in a New Era* (New York: Trilateral Commission).

MENSHIKOV, S. (1973) *Millionaires and Managers* (Moscow: Progress).

MERCHANT, C. (1992) *Radical Ecology* (London: Routledge).

MEW [*Marx-Engels Werke*] various years Collected works of Marx and Engels (Berlin: Dietz).

MILLER, M. (1995) 'Where is global interdependence taking us?' *Futures*, Vol. 27, No. 2, pp. 125–44.

MISHRA, R. (1984) *The Welfare State in Crisis* (Brighton: Wheatsheaf).

MITTELMAN, J.H. (1994a) 'Global Restructuring of Production and Migration' in Y. Sakamoto (ed.) *Global Transformation* (Tokyo: United Nations University Press) pp. 276–98.

MITTELMAN, J.H. (1994b) 'The Globalization of Social Conflict', in *World Society Studies*, Vol. 3. *Conflict and Its Solution in World Society* (eds) V. Bornschier and P. Lengyel, pp. 317–37 (New Brunswick, NJ: Transaction Publishers).

MITTELMAN, J.H. (1996) 'The Dynamics of Globalization' in Mittelman (ed.) *Globalization: Critical Reflections*, International Political Economy Yearbook, Vol. 9 (Boulder: Rienner) pp. 1–20.

MITTER, S. (1986) *Common Fate, Common Bond* (London: Pluto Press).

MJØSET, L. (1987) 'Nordic Economic Policies in the 1970s and the 1980s', *International Organization*, Vol. 41, No. 3, pp. 403–56.

MJØSET, L. (ed.) (1986) *Norden dagen derpå (Oslo: Universitetsforlaget).*

MOHANTY, C.T. (1988) 'Under Western Eyes: Feminist Scholarship and Colonial Discourses' in C.T. Mohanty *et al.* (eds) *Third World Women and the Politics of Feminism* (Bloomington, Indiana: Indiana University Press) pp. 51–80.

MONTAGNE-VILLETTE, S. (1990) *Le Sentier. Un Espace Ambigü* (Paris: Masson).

MOORE, B. Jr (1977) *Social Origins of Democracy and Dictatorship* (Harmondsworth: Pelican).

MOREAU DEFARGES, P. (1993) *La Mondialisation. Vers la Fin des Frontières?* (Paris: IFRI).

MOROKVASIC, M. (1991) 'Roads to independence. Self-employed immigrants and minority women in five European states', *International Migration*, Vol. 29, No. 3, pp. 407–17.

MORRIS, M. (1991) 'State, capital and growth: the political economy of the national question', in S. Gelb (ed.) *South Africa's Economic Crisis* (Zed Books: London) pp. 33–58.

MOSELY, P. (ed.) (1992) *Development Finance and Policy Reform* (London: Macmillan/St Martin's Press).

MOSELY, P. *et al.* (1991) *Aid and Power: The World Bank and Policy-based Lending* (London and New York: Routledge).

MOULIER-BOUTANG, Y. *et al.* (1986) *Économie Politique des Migrations Clandestines de Main-d'Oeuvre* (Paris: Publisud).

MOULIER-BOUTANG, Y. (1991) Personal interview, Paris, November.

MUNCK, R. (1988) *The New International Labour Studies: An Introduction* (London: Zed Books).

MYTELKA, L.K. (1991) 'Technological change and the global relocation of production in textiles and clothing', *Studies in Political Economy*, Vol. 36, Fall, pp. 109–43.

NATTRASS, N. (1989) 'Post-war Profitability in South Africa: A Critique of Regulation Analysis in South Africa', *Transformation*, No. 9, pp. 66–80.

NELSON, J. (1993) 'The Study of Choice or the Study of Provisioning? Gender and the Definition of Economics' in M. Ferber and J. Nelson (eds) *Beyond Economic Man: Feminist Theory and Economics* (University of Chicago Press).

NIELSEN, K. & O. PEDERSEN (1989) 'Is Small Still Flexible? An Evaluation of Recent Trends in Danish Politics' *Scandinavian Political Studies*, Vol. 12, No. 4, pp. 343–71.

NOVE, A. (1978) *An Economic History of the U.S.S.R.* (Harmondsworth: Pelican).

O'BRIEN, R. (1992) *Global Financial Integration: The End of Geography* (New York: Council on Foreign Relations Press).

OECD (1992a) *Industrial Policy in OECD Countries, Annual Review 1992* (Paris: OECD).

OECD (1992b) *International Direct Investment. Policies and Trends in the 1980s* (Paris: OECD).

OECD (1994) *Migration and Development. New Partnerships for Co-operation* (Paris: OECD).

OECD (1994) *Women and Structural Change* (Paris: OECD).

OHMAE, K. (1993) 'The Rise of the Region State.' *Foreign Affairs*, Vol. 72, No. 2, pp. 78–87.

OMGUS (1985) Office of the Military Government of Germany, United States, *Ermittlungen gegen die Deutsche Bank* (Nördlingen: Greno).

OMGUS (1986) *Ermittlungen gegen die Dresdner Bank* (Nördlingen: Greno).

ORLOFF, A. (1994) 'Restructuring Welfare: Gender, Work, and Inequality in Australia, Canada, the United Kingdom and the United States', paper for conference 'Crossing Borders: an International Dialogue on Gender, Social Politics and Citizenship', Stockholm, Sweden, 27–9 May.

OSBORNE, D. & T. GAEBLER (1992) *Reinventing Government. How the Enterprise Spirit is Transforming the Public Sector* (Reading, Massachusetts: Addison-Wesley).

OVERBEEK, H.W. (1990) *Global Capitalism and National Decline. The Thatcher Decade in Perspective* (London: Unwin Hyman).

OVERBEEK, H.W. (ed.) (1993) *Restructuring Hegemony in the Global Political Economy. The Rise of Transnational Neo-Liberalism in the 1980s* (London: Routledge).

OVERBEEK, H.W. & K. VAN DER PIJL (1993) 'Restructuring Capital and Restructuring Hegemony. Neo-Liberalism and the Unmaking of the Post-War Order', in Overbeek (ed.) *Restructuring Hegemony in the Global Political Economy*, pp. 1–27.

PALIDDA, S. (1992) 'Le développement des activités indépendantes des immigrés en Europe et en France', *Revue Européenne des Migrations Internationales*, Vol. 8, No. 1, pp. 83–95.

PASTOR, M. Jr (1989) 'The effects of IMF Programs in the Third World: debate and evidence from Latin America' *World Development*, Vol. 15, pp. 244–62.

PAYER, C. (1982) *The World Bank: A Critical Analysis* (New York: Monthly Review Press).

PEARCE, D. *et al.* (eds) (1991) *Blueprint 2: Greening the World Economy* (London: Earthscan).

PEKKARINEN, J. (1989) 'Keynesianism and the Scandinavian Models of Economic Policy' in P. Hall (ed.) *The Political Power of Economic Ideas* (Princeton, NJ: Princeton University Press).

PELLERIN, H. (1993) 'Global restructuring in the world economy and migration: the globalization of migration dynamics', *International Journal*, Vol. 48, pp. 240–54.

PETRELLA, R. (1989) 'La mondialisation de la technologie et de l'économie. Une (hypo)thèse prospective', *Futuribles*, 135, Septembre.

PFEIFFER, H. (1993) *Die Macht der Banken. Die personellen Verflechtungen der Commerzbank, der Deutschen Bank und der Dresdner Bank mit Unternehmen* (Frankfurt and New York: Campus).

PHIZACKLEA, A & R. MILES (1990) *Unpacking the Fashion Industry* (London: Routledge & Kegan Paul).

PIORE, M. & C. SABEL, (1984) *The Second Industrial Divide* (New York: Basic Books).

PIORE, M.J. (1979) *Birds of Passage. Migrant Labor and Industrial Societies* (Cambridge: Cambridge University Press).

PÖHL, G. & D. MIHALJEK (1989) 'Project Evaluation in Practice: A Statistical Analysis of Rate of Return Divergence of 1,015 World Bank Projects', Economic Advisory Staff, World Bank. December.

POLANYI, K. (1945) 'Universal Capitalism or Regional Planning?' *London Quarterly of World Affairs*, Vol. 10, No. 3, pp. 86–91.

POLANYI, K. (1957) *The Great Transformation: The Political and Economic Origins of Our Time* (Boston: Beacon).

PONTUSSON, J. (1992) *The Limits of Social Democracy* (Ithaca: Cornell University Press).

PONTUSSON, J. & P. SWENSON (1993) 'Varför har arbetsgivarna överivit den svenska modellen?' *Arkiv för studier i arbetarrörelsens historia*, Vol. 50, pp. 37–66.

PONTUSSON, J. (1987) 'Radicalization and Retreat of Swedish Social Democracy', *New Left Review*, No. 165, pp. 5–32.

PONTUSSON, J. (1988) *Swedish Social Democracy and British Labour: Essays on the Nature and Conditions of Social Democratic Hegemony* (Ithaca: Cornell Studies in International Affairs).

PRENDERGAST, R. & F. STEWART (1994) *Market Forces and World Development* (London: Macmillan).

PRETOT, X. (1990) *Le Droit Social Européen* (Paris. PUF).

PROWSE, M. (1994) 'Towards a leaner, greener bank' *Financial Times*, 20 July 1994.

PRUGL, E. (1994) 'Homework and the ILO: Constructions of Gender in International Discourse'. Paper to International Studies Association, 28 March–1 April, 1994, Washington, DC.

PUJOL, M. (1992) *Feminism and Antifeminism in Early Economic Thought* (New York: Gower Press).

REED, D. (ed.) (1992) *Structural Adjustment and the Environment* (London: Earthscan).

REGAN, D.T. (1988) *For the Record. From Wall Street to Washington* (San Diego: Harcourt Brace Jovanovich).

REGAN, P. (1993) 'Surveillance and New Technologies: Changing Nature of Workplace Surveillance', paper presented at Strategic Research Workshop, 'New Technology, Surveillance and Social Control', Queen's University, Kingston, Ontario Canada, 14–16 May.

REPUBLIC OF SOUTH AFRICA (1994) *White Paper on Reconstruction and Development: Government's Strategy for Fundamental Transformation*, Pretoria, 21 September, 1994.

RHODES, M. (1991) 'The Social Dimension of the Single European Market: National vs. Transnational Regulation', *European Journal of Political Research*, Vol. 12, pp. 147–69.

RICARDO, D. (1932) *Principles of Political Economy* (ed.) E.C.K. Gonner (London: G. Bell & Sons).

RICH, B. (1994) 'The Cuckoo in the Nest. Fifty years of Meddling by the World Bank', *The Ecologist*, Vol. 24, No. 1, pp. 8–13.

RICH, B. (1994) *Mortgaging The Earth. The World Bank, Environmental Impoverishment and the Crisis of Development* (London: Earthscan).

ROBISON, R. (1986) *Indonesia: The Rise of Capital* (Sydney: Allen & Unwin).

ROSS, G. (1992) 'Confronting the New Europe', *New Left Review*, No. 191, pp. 49–68.

ROSS, R.J.S. & K.C. TRACHTE (1990) *Global Capitalism. The New Leviathan* (Albany: State University of New York Press).

ROWBOTHAM, S. (1993) *Homeworkers Worldwide* (London: Merlin Press).

RUBERY, J. (1988) *Women and Recession* (London: Routledge & Kegan Paul).

RUGGIE, J.G. (1983) 'International Regimes, Transaction and Change: Embedded Liberalism in the Postwar Economic Order' in S. Krasner (ed.) *International Regimes* (Ithaca: Cornell University Press) pp. 195–232.

RUGGIE, J.G. (1992) 'Multilateralism: The Anatomy of an Institution', *International Organization*, Vol. 46, No. 3, pp. 561–98.

RUGGIE, J.G. (1993) 'Territoriality and Beyond: Problematizing Modernity in International Relations', *International Organization*, Vol. 47, No. 1, pp. 139–74.

RUIGROK, W. & R. VAN TULDER (1993) 'The elusive concept of globalisation and rival internationalisation strategies', paper presented at the seminar 'The Emerging World Order', Amsterdam, 21–2 October.

RYNER, M. (1993) 'The Economic "Success" and Political "Failure" of Swedish Social Democracy in the 1980s', *Swedish Centre for Working Life. Research Report* (Stockholm: SCWL).

SABEL, C.F. (1991) 'Moebius-strip organizations and open labor markets: Some consequences of the reintegration of conception and execution in a volatile economy', in P. Bourdieu & J.S. Coleman (eds) *Social Theory for a Changing Society* (New York: Westview Press), pp. 23–54.

SACHS, W. (1993) *Global Ecology, Conflicts and Contradictions* (London: Zed Books).

SADLER, D. (1992) *The Global Region: Production, State Policies and Uneven Development* (Oxford: Pergamon Press).

SAINSBURY, D. (1980) *Swedish Social Democratic Ideology and Electoral Politics 1944–1948* (Stockholm: Almqvist & Wicksell International).

SAKOLSKY, R. (1992) ' "Disciplinary power," the labor process, and the constitution of the laboring subject', *Rethinking Marxism*, Vol. 5, No. 4, pp. 115–26.

SAMPSON, A. (1978) *The Arms Bazaar* (London: Coronet).

SANDS, P. (1993) 'Enforcing Environmental Security', *Journal of International Affairs*, Vol. 46, No. 2, pp. 367–90.

SAP (1981) *Framtid för Sverige* (Stockholm: SAP).

SASSEN, S. (1991) *The Global City: New York, London, Tokyo* (Princeton, NJ: Princeton University Press).

SASSEN, S. (1993) 'Economic Internationalization: The New Migration in Japan and the United States', *International Migration*, Vol. 31, No. 1, pp. 73–99.

SASSEN, S. (1988) *The Mobility of Labor and Capital: A Study in International Investment and Labor Flow* (New York: Cambridge University Press).

SCHILLER, B. (1987) *'Det förödande 70-talet'* (Stockholm: Allmäna förlaget).

SCHILLER, B. (1989) 'En skandinavisk demokratimodell inför framtiden' in *Saltsjöbadsavtalet 50 år* (Stockholm: Arbetslivscentrum) pp. 218–34.

SCHROYER, T. (1992) 'Paths Beyond Economism', *Dialectical Anthropology*, Vol. 17, No. 4., pp. 355–90.

SCHWARTZMAN, S. (1986) *Bankrolling Disasters* (Washington: Sierra Club).

SCOTT, J.C. (1985) *Weapons of the Weak* (New Haven: Yale University Press).

SCOTT, J.C. (1993) 'Everyday forms of resistance', PRIME Meigaku Working Paper, Meiji Gakuin University, Yokohama, Japan.

SEN, A. (1984) *Resources, Value and Development* (Cambridge: Cambridge University Press).

SENDER, H. (1991) 'Inside the Overseas Chinese Network', *Institutional Investor*, September, pp. 37–42.

SENGHAAS, D. (1982) *Von Europa Lernen. Entwicklungsgeschichtliche Betrachtungen* (Frankfurt: Suhrkamp).

SHAH, N.M. (1994) 'An overview of present and future emigration dynamics in South Asia', *International Migration*, Vol. 32, No. 2, pp. 217–67.

SHIVA, V. (1993) *Monocultures of the Mind* (London: Zed Books).

SHOUP, L.H. & W. MINTER (1977) *Imperial Brain Trust. The Council on Foreign Relations and United States Foreign Policy* (New York: Monthly Review Press).

SKRAN, J. (1992) 'The international refugee regime: The historical and contemporary context of international responses to asylum problems', in G. Loescher (ed.) *Refugees and the Asylum Dilemma in the West* (University Park: Pennsylvania State University Press).

SMITH, A. (1976) *The Theory of Moral Sentiments*, D.D. Raphael & A.L. Macfie (eds) (London: Oxford University Press).

SMITH, A. (1967) *The Wealth of Nations*, A. Skinner (ed.) (Harmondsworth: Penguin).

SÖDERSTRÖM, H.T. (1989) *One Global Market* (Stockholm: SNS).

SOHN-RETHEL, A. (1975) *Grootkapitaal en fascisme. De Duitse Industrie Achter Hitler* (Amsterdam: Van Gennep).

SÖRGEL, A. (1985) 'Ermittlungen gegen die Deutsche Bank', *Blätter für Deutsche und Internationale Politik*, Vol. 30, No. 10, pp. 1225–37.

STANDING, G. (1988) *Unemployment and Labour Market Flexibility: Sweden* (Geneva: ILO).

STANDING, G. (1989) 'Global Feminization Through Flexible Labour' *World Development*, Vol. 17, No. 7, pp. 1077–95.

STEGMANN, D. (1976) 'Kapitalismus und Faschismus in Deutschland 1929–1934. Thesen und Materialien zur Restituierung des Primats der Gross-industrie zwischen Weltwirtschaftskrise und beginnender Rüstungskonjunktur', *Gesellschaft. Beiträge zur Marxschen Theorie*, No. 6. (Frankfurt: Suhrkamp).

STEINMO, S. (1994) The End of Redistribution? International Pressures and Domestic Tax Policy Choices', *Challenge*, Vol. 37, No. 6, pp. 9–17.

STOPFORD, J.M. & S. STRANGE (1991) *Rival States, Rival Firms. Competition for World Market Shares* (Cambridge University Press).

STRANGE, S. (1986) *Casino Capitalism* (Oxford: Basil Blackwell).

STRANGE, S. (1987) 'The Persistent Myth of Lost Hegemony', *International Organization*, Vol. 41, No. 4, pp. 551–74.

SUHRKE, A. (1993) 'A crisis diminished: refugees in the developing world', *International Journal*, Vol. 48, No. 2, Spring, pp. 215–39.

SUN, L.H. (1992) 'South China Drives Boom Region', *Washington Post*, 2 December.

SVALLFORS, S. (1989) *Vem älskar välfärdsstaten?* (Lund: Arkiv).

SWENSON, P. (1989) *Fair Shares: Unions, Pay and Politics in Sweden and West Germany* (Ithaca: Cornell University Press).

SZÜCS, J. (1988) 'Three Historical Regions of Europe' in John Keane (ed.) *Civil Society and the State* (London: Verso), pp. 291–332.

TAYLOR, L. (1993) 'The World Bank and the Environment: The World Development Report 1992, *World Development*, Vol. 21, No. 5, pp. 869–81.

TEACHER, D. (1993) 'The Pinay Circle Complex 1969–1989', *Lobster* No. 26, pp. 9–16.

THERBORN, G. (1989) *Borgarklass och byråkrati i Sverige* (Lund: Arkiv).

TILTON, T. (1974) 'The Social Origins of Liberal Democracy: The Swedish Case', *American Political Science Review*, Vol. 68, pp. 561–71.

TITMUSS, R. (1974) *Social Policy* (London: Allen and Unwin).

TJONNELAND, E.N. (1992) *Southern Africa After Apartheid* (Bergen, Norway: Michelsen Institute).

TOLCHIN, M. & S. TOLCHIN (1989) *Buying Into America. How Foreign Money is Changing the Face of Our Nation* (New York: Berkeley).

TURNER, R.K. (ed.) (1993) *Sustainable Environmental Economics and Management: Principles and Practice* (Boston: Belhaven Press).

US COMMITTEE FOR REFUGEES (1991) *World Refugee Survey* (Washington DC: The Committee).

UN (1992a) *Population Movements Associated with the Search for Asylum and Refuge*, Secretariat, internal document, 2 April.

UN, (1992b) *World Population Monitoring 1991*, Department of International Economic and Social Affairs (New York: United Nations Population Studies) No. 126.

UN (1993) *The State of World Population 1993* (New York: United Nations Population Fund).

UN DEVELOPMENT PROGRAMME (1994) *Human Development Report, 1994* (New York: Oxford University Press).

UN DEVELOPMENT PROGRAMME (1995) *Human Development Report: The Revolution for Gender Equality* (New York: Oxford University Press).

UN RESEARCH INSTITUTE FOR SOCIAL DEVELOPMENT (1995) *States of Disarray. The Social Effects of Globalization* (Geneva: UNRISD).

UPHOFF, N. (1993) 'Grassroots Organisations and NGOs in Rural Development: Opportunities with Diminishing States and Expanding Markets', *World Development*, Vol. 21, No. 4, pp. 607–22.

UUSITALO, P. (1984) 'Monetarism, Keynesianism and the Institutional Status of Central Banks', *Acta Sociologica*, Vol. 27, No. 1, pp. 31–51.

VAN DER PIJL, K. (1984) *The Making of an Atlantic Ruling Class* (London: Verso).

VAN DER PIJL, K. (1987) 'Neoliberalism versus Planned Interdependence. Concepts of Control and the Struggle for Hegemony', in J.N. Rosenau & H. Tromp (eds) *Interdependence and Conflict in World Politics* (Aldershot: Avebury), pp. 147–73.

VAN DER PIJL, K. (1989a) 'Ruling Classes, Hegemony and the State System', *International Journal of Political Economy*, Vol. 19, No. 3, pp. 7–35.

VAN DER PIJL, K. (1989b) 'Restructuring the Atlantic Ruling Class', in S. Gill (ed.) *Atlantic Relations: Beyond the Reagan Era*, pp. 62–87.

VAN DER PIJL, K. (1994) 'The Reich Resurrected? Continuity and Discontinuity in German Expansion', in R.P. Palan and B.K. Gills (eds) *Transcending the State/Global Divide. A Neostructuralist Agenda in International Relations* (Boulder: Lynne Rienner) pp. 169–88.

VAN TULDER, R. & JUNNE, G. (1988) *European Multinationals in Core Technologies* (Chichester: Wiley).

VATIKIOTIS, M. *et al.* (1991) 'Building Blocs', *Far Eastern Economic Review*, 31 January, pp. 32–3.

VERHAEREN, R. (1990) *Partir? Pour une Théorie Économique des Migrations Internationales* (Grenoble: Presses Universitaires de Grenoble).

VERNON, R. (1971) *Sovereignty at Bay* (New York: Basic Books).

VIEILLE, P. (1988) 'The World's Chaos and the New Paradigms of the Social Movement', Lelio Basso Foundation (eds) *Theory and Practice of Liberation at the End of the Twentieth Century* (Bruxelles: Bruylant) pp. 219–56.

VIVIAN, J. (1994) 'NGOs and Sustainable Development in Zimbabwe: No Magic Bullets'. *Development and Change*, Vol. 25, 167–193.

VON HAYEK, F.A. (1976) *The Road to Serfdom* (London: Routledge and Kegan Paul).

VON HAYEK, F.A. (1985) *De weg naar slavernij* [*The Road to Serfdom*] trans. H.L. and M.J. Swart (Amsterdam: Omega).

WALKER, R.B.J. (1993) *Inside/outside; International Relations as Political Theory* (Cambridge University Press).

WALKER, T. (1993) 'Beijing Fears Grow over Runaway Economy', *Financial Times* (London) 25 June.

WARING, M. (1988) *If Women Counted: A New Feminist Economics* (San Francisco: Harper & Row).

WATKINS, K. (1992) 'Rio Monitor', *The Guardian*, 16 October 1992.

WEBER, M. (1947) *The Theory of Social and Economic Organization* (ed.) T. Parsons (New York: Free Press).

WETTERN, J. (1993) 'The Place of Guestworkers in the German Political Economy: Continuation of a Failed Immigration Policy', Presented to the International Studies Association Annual Meeting, Acapulco, Mexico, March.

WIHTOL DE WENDEN, C. (1990) 'L'Islam en France', *Regards sur l'Actualité*, No. 158, février.

WILLIAMS, D. & T. YOUNG (1994) 'Governance, the World Bank and Liberal Theory,' *Political Studies*, Vol. XLII, pp. 84–100.

WILSON, F. & M. RAMPHELE (1989) *Uprooting Apartheid: The South African Challenge* (New York: W.W. Norton).

WISNEWSKI, G. *et al.* (1993) *Das RAF-Phantom. Wozu Politik und Wirtschaft Terroristen Brauchen* (München: Knaur).

WONG, L.L. (1993) 'Immigration as capital accumulation: The impact of business immigration to Canada', *International Migration*, Vol. 31, No. 1, pp. 171–87.

WOODWARD, B. (1994) *The Agenda. Inside the Clinton White House* (New York: Pocket Books).

WOON, Y.-F. (1993) 'Circulatory Mobility in Post-Mao China: Temporary Migrants in Kaiping County, Pearl River Delta Region', *International Migration Review*, Vol. 27, No. 3, pp. 578–603.

WORLD BANK (1991) *World Development Report. The Challenge of Development* (New York: Oxford University Press).

WORLD BANK (1992) *World Development Report 1992, Development and the Environment* (New York: Oxford University Press).

WORLD BANK (1993) *Economic Prospects and the Developing World* (New York: Oxford University Press).

WORLD BANK (1990–95) *World Debt Tables*, various years (Washington DC: World Bank).

WORLD BANK (1995) *Toward Gender Equality: The Role of Public Policy* (Washington DC: World Bank).

WORLD COMMISSION ON ENVIRONMENT & DEVELOPMENT ['Bruntland Commission'] (1987) *Our Common Future* (Oxford and New York: Oxford University Press).

WU, Y. and WU, C. (1980) *Economic Development in Southeast Asia: The Chinese Dimension* (Stanford: Hoover Institution Press).

YEATMAN, A. (1990) *Bureaucrats, Technocrats, Femocrats: Essays on the Contemporary Australian State* (Sydney: Allen & Unwin).

ZARENDA, H. (1989) 'The rationale underlying the policy of inward industrialisation in South Africa', *Development South Africa*, Vol. 6, No. 4, pp. 409–20.

ZIEGLER, R. *et al.* (1985) 'Industry and Banking in the German Corporate Network', in F.N. Stokman *et al.* (eds) *Networks of Corporate Power* (Cambridge: Polity), pp. 91–111.

ZINNIKER, L. (1993) 'The Presence of Arab Migrants and the Politics of French "Nationalism"' presented to the International Studies Association Annual Meeting, Acapulco, Mexico, March.

ZOLBERG, A. (1981) 'International migrations in political perspective', in M.M. Kritz *et al.* (eds) *Global Trends in Migration* (New York: Center for Migration Studies), pp. 3–27.

ZOLBERG, A. (1988) 'L'incidence des facteurs externes sur la condition des citoyens: approche comparative', in C. Wihtol de Wenden (ed.) *La Citoyenneté et les Changements de Structures Sociale et Nationale de la Population Française* (Paris: Edilig Fondation Diderot), pp. 203–19.

ZULU, J.B. & S.M. NSOULI (1985) *Adjustment Programs in Africa: The Recent Experience* (Washington, DC: IMF) Occasional Paper, No. 34.

Books and Articles Published (or to be Published) through MUNS

Robert W. Cox, 'Multilateralism and World Order', *Review of International Studies* 1992 (1) 161–180. Based on a 'concept paper' written at the launching of the MUNS programme.

Yoshikazu Sakamoto (ed.), *Global Transformation: Challenges to the State System* (Tokyo: United Nations University Press, 1994). Based on the symposium held in Yokohama in 1992.

Keith Krause and W. Andy Knight (eds), *State, Society and the UN System: Changing Perspectives on Multilateralism* (Tokyo: United Nations University Press, 1995). Based on the symposium held in Toronto in 1992.

Robert W. Cox (ed.), *The New Realism: Perspectives on Multilateralism and World Order* (London: Macmillan for the United Nations University Press, 1997). Based on the symposium held in Fiesole, Italy, in 1993.

Stephen Gill (ed.), *Globalization, Democratization, and Multilateralism* (London: Macmillan for the United Nations University Press, 1997). Based on the symposium held in Oslo in 1993.

Michael G. Schechter (ed.), *Innovation in Multilateralism* (London: Macmillan for the United Nations University Press, forthcoming). Based on the symposium held in Lausanne in 1994.

Michael G.Schechter (ed.), *Future Multilateralism: The Political and Social Framework* (London: Macmillan for the United Nations University Press, forthcoming). Based on the symposium held in San José, Costa Rica, in December 1995.

James P. Sewell (ed.), *Multilateralism in Multinational Perspective: Viewpoints from Different Languages and Literatures* (London: Macmillan for the United Nations University Press, forthcoming).

Robert W. Cox, *Multilateralism and the United Nations System: Final Report* (United Nations University Press, March 1996).

Sequel to the MUNS programme

Michael G. Schechter, Martin Hewson and W. Andy Knight, *Global Governance for the Twenty-First Century: The Realistic Potential* (London: Macmillan, forthcoming).

Tables of Contents of Titles in MUNS Subseries

Michael G. Schechter (ed.), *Innovation in Multilateralism* (London: Macmillan for the United Nations University Press, forthcoming).

Michael G. Schechter, Martin Hewson and W. Andy Knight, *Global Governance*
for the Twenty-First Century: The Realistic Potential **(London: Macmillan,**
forthcoming).

Index of Names

AEG (1929, GE), 203, 204, 206, 207, 208
African National Congress (ANC), 224, 225, 226, 228, 233
Albert, Michel, 200
Algeria, 151
Angola, 111, 222, 236
Arbitration Treaty, 1911 (US–UK), 198
Argentina, 85, 151
Association of South East Asian Nations (ASEAN), 86, 87, 88
Atlantik-Brücke ('Atlantic bridge'), 209, 214
Attali, Jacques, 155, 212, 216
Australia, 55

Baker Plan, 144
Bangladesh, 109, 116, 135, 181
Belgium, 84, 85
Bentham, Jeremy, 51, 52–3, 55, 82
Bernhard, Prince of the Netherlands, 208
Bilderberg Conferences, 208, 209, 210, 212, 213
Bismarck, Otto von, 6, 82
Blessing, Werner, 211
Boorstin, Daniel, 62
Botswana, 232
Brady Plan, 144
Brandt, Willy 196, 197, 199–200, 206, 207, 209
Brazil, 11, 85, 151, 232
Bretton Woods system, 6, 20, 21, 22, 198
Breuel, Birgit, 214, 215
Britain, *see Index of Subjects*
British Commonwealth, 152, 198
Brundtland Report, 172, 178, 182
Brunei, 116
Brzezinski, Zbigniew, 210
Bukharin, Nicolai, 197
Bull, Hedley, 8

Bush Administration, 217
Bush, George, 5, 172, 174, 217
Buthelezi, Mangosothu, 224

Cambodia, 88
Camdessus, Michel, 159
Canada, 62, 68, 150
Carr, Edward Hallet, 198
Carter Administration, 209
Castro, Fidel, 144, 211, 212
Central Intelligence Agency (CIA), 162, 210, 217, 218
Chicago, 67
China, 11, 54, 87, 88, 99, 181
China, Greater, 87, 95–100
Citicorp, 212, 213
Colby, William, 209
Coleman, Fred, 216
Committee on the Present Danger, 210, 211
Concert of Europe, 6
Congo, 111
Cox, Robert W., 1, 182

d'Estaing, Giscard, 212
de Klerk, F.W., 224–5, 229
Delors, Jacques, 25
Deutsche Bank, 203, 204, 205–7, 209, 211–12, 215–16
Disraeli, Benjamin, 6
Douglas Home, Alec (Lord Home), 208
Dresdner Bank, 203, 204, 206, 207, 209–10, 215–16
Dublin Accord, 119, 120
Dumas, Roland, 216
Durkheim, Émile, 81, 82

Egypt, 150, 151, 181
European Bank for Reconstruction and Development (EBRD), 9, 155, 212–3
European Round Table of Industrialists (ERT), 214

Index of Subjects